Historic Places

EXPLORE AMERICA

Historic Places

Reader's Digest

THE READER'S DIGEST ASSOCIATION, INC.
Pleasantville, New York / Montreal

HISTORIC PLACES was created and produced by ST. REMY MULTIMEDIA, INC.

PRESIDENT: Pierre Léveillé
PUBLISHER: Kenneth Winchester

STAFF FOR HISTORIC PLACES
Series Editor: Carolyn Jackson
Series Art Director: Diane Denoncourt
Senior Editor: Elizabeth Cameron
Art Director: Odette Sévigny
Picture Editor: Christopher Jackson
Assistant Editor: Alfred LeMaitre
Researcher: Rory Gilsenan
Contributing Researcher: Olga Dzatko
Designer: Hélène Dion
Cartographer: Maryo Proulx
Illustrator: Alain Longpré
Index: Christine Jacobs

Writers: Charles N. Barnard—Federal Philadelphia
Len R. Barnes—Straits of Mackinac
Ian Glass—Old St. Augustine
Kim Heacox—California Missions
Rick Marsi—Pilgrims of Plimoth
Sylvia McNair—Frontier Spirit
Jeremy Schmidt—Gold Rush Country
Bryce Walker—Confederate Charleston, Revolution in Boston
James S. Wamsley—Colonial Williamsburg

Contributing Writers: Margaret Caldbick,
Molly Collin, Joanna Ebbutt, Joe Fisher, Susan Purcell,
Stanley Whyte

Administrator: Natalie Watanabe
Production Manager: Michelle Turbide
Systems Coordinator: Jean-Luc Roy

READER'S DIGEST STAFF
Editor: Fred DuBose
Art Director: Evelyn Bauer
Art Associate: Martha Grossman

READER'S DIGEST GENERAL BOOKS
Editor in Chief: John A. Pope, Jr.
Managing Editor: Jane Polley
Executive Editor: Susan J. Wernert
Art Director: David Trooper
Group Editors: Will Bradbury, Sally French,
Norman B. Mack, Kaari Ward
Group Art Editors: Evelyn Bauer,
Robert M. Grant, Joel Musler
Research Director: Laurel A. Gilbride
Copy Chief: Edward W. Atkinson
Picture Editor: Richard Pasqual
Rights and Permissions: Pat Colomban
Head Librarian: Jo Manning

Opening photographs
Cover: Mount Vernon, Virginia
Back Cover: Barrel-making, New Salem, Illinois
Page 2: Governor's Palace,
    Colonial Williamsburg, Virginia
Page 5: Middleton Place, Charleston, South Carolina

The credits and acknowledgments that appear on page 144 are hereby made a part of this copyright page.

Library of Congress Cataloging in Publication Data

Historic Places.
        p.   cm.—(Explore America)
     Includes index.
     ISBN 0-89577-506-9
     1. Historic sites—United States—Guidebooks. 2. United States—
History, Local. 3. United States—Guidebooks.   I. Reader's Digest
Association. II. Series
     E159.H7138   1993
     917.304'928—dc20   93-21872

Printed in the United States of America
Third Printing, September 1996

CONTENTS

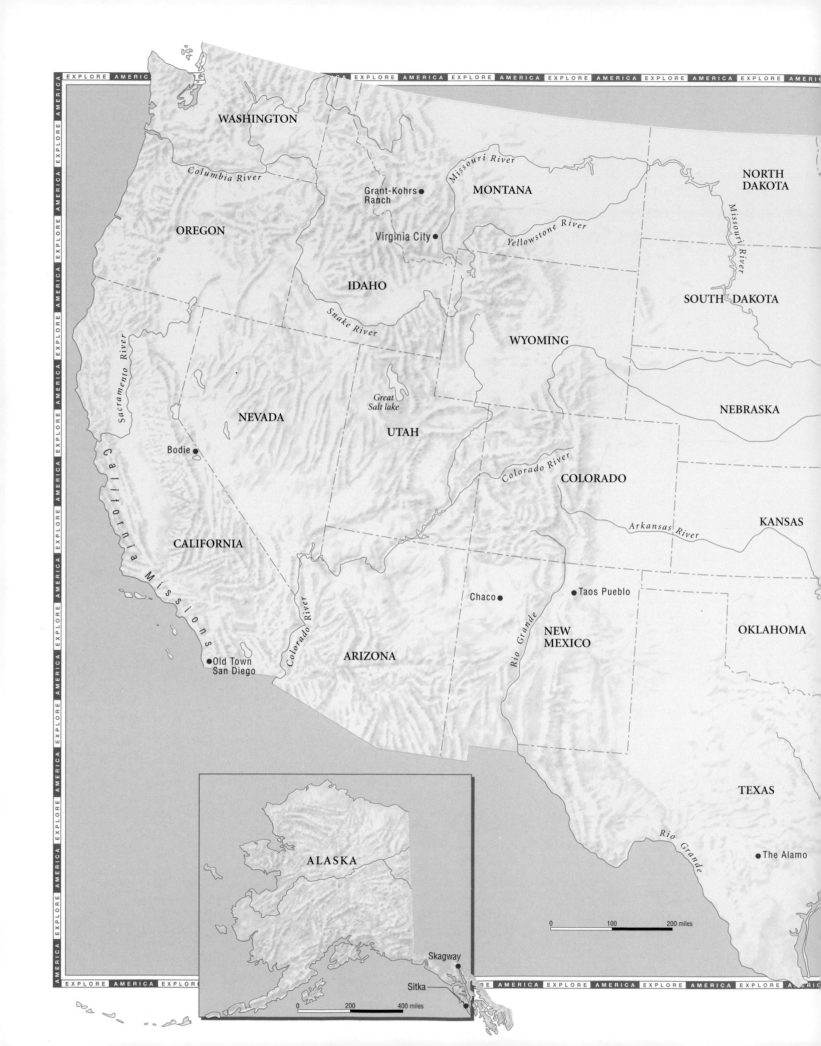

WASHINGTON

OREGON

Columbia River

Grant-Kohrs ● Ranch

MONTANA

Missouri River

Virginia City ●

IDAHO

Yellowstone River

Snake River

Missouri River

NORTH DAKOTA

SOUTH DAKOTA

WYOMING

Sacramento River

NEVADA

Great Salt lake

UTAH

Bodie ●

California Missions

CALIFORNIA

Colorado River

Colorado River

COLORADO

NEBRASKA

Arkansas River

KANSAS

Chaco ●

● Taos Pueblo

● Old Town San Diego

ARIZONA

Rio Grande

NEW MEXICO

OKLAHOMA

ALASKA

Skagway

Sitka

TEXAS

Rio Grande

● The Alamo

0   100   200 miles

0   200   400 miles

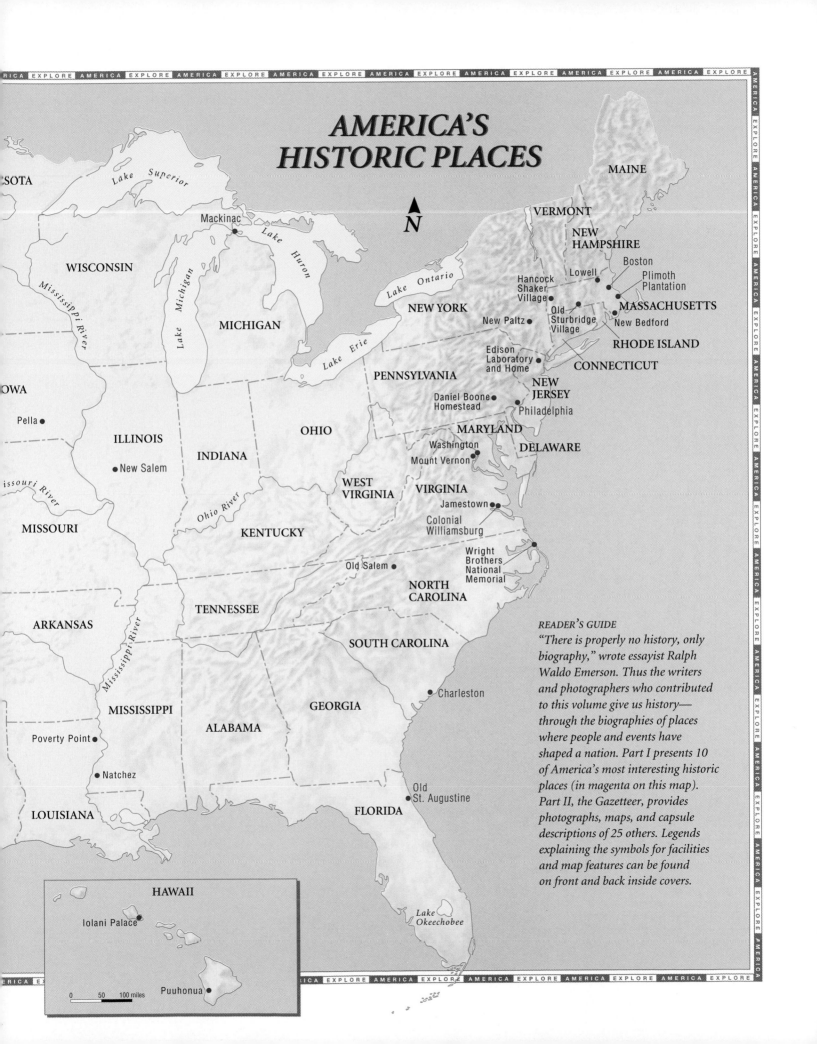

AMERICA'S HISTORIC PLACES

N

SOTA

Lake Superior

WISCONSIN

Lake Huron

Lake Michigan

Mackinac

MICHIGAN

Mississippi River

Lake Ontario

NEW YORK

Lake Erie

PENNSYLVANIA

MAINE

VERMONT

NEW HAMPSHIRE

Boston

Lowell

Plimoth Plantation

Hancock Shaker Village

MASSACHUSETTS

Old Sturbridge Village

New Paltz

New Bedford

RHODE ISLAND

CONNECTICUT

Edison Laboratory and Home

NEW JERSEY

Daniel Boone Homestead

Philadelphia

OWA

Pella

ILLINOIS

INDIANA

New Salem

OHIO

MARYLAND

DELAWARE

Washington

Mount Vernon

ssouri River

MISSOURI

KENTUCKY

Ohio River

WEST VIRGINIA

VIRGINIA

Jamestown

Colonial Williamsburg

Old Salem

NORTH CAROLINA

Wright Brothers National Memorial

ARKANSAS

TENNESSEE

SOUTH CAROLINA

Mississippi River

MISSISSIPPI

ALABAMA

GEORGIA

Charleston

Poverty Point

Natchez

Old St. Augustine

LOUISIANA

FLORIDA

Lake Okeechobee

HAWAII

Iolani Palace

Puuhonua

0   50   100 miles

READER'S GUIDE
"There is properly no history, only biography," wrote essayist Ralph Waldo Emerson. Thus the writers and photographers who contributed to this volume give us history— through the biographies of places where people and events have shaped a nation. Part I presents 10 of America's most interesting historic places (in magenta on this map). Part II, the Gazetteer, provides photographs, maps, and capsule descriptions of 25 others. Legends explaining the symbols for facilities and map features can be found on front and back inside covers.

OLD ST. AUGUSTINE

Florida's oldest city was built to guard Spain's treasure route in the days of galleons and buccaneers.

On a warm day in September 1565, the Spanish captain Pedro Menéndez de Avilés splashed ashore on a beach in northeastern Florida to the cheers of the 600 heavily armed soldiers under his command.

Menéndez had been named governor of Florida by the Spanish king, Philip II, who ordered him to explore and colonize the region in order to counter a growing French presence at the mouth of the St. Johns River, a few miles to the north. The Spanish landing took place on September 8, but Menéndez had first sighted land on August 28—the feast day of Saint Augustine. He accordingly named the new settlement San Augustin. Known today as St. Augustine, the town became the first permanent European settlement in what is now the United States, predating by 42 years the founding of the Jamestown colony and by 55 the landing of the Pilgrims at Plymouth.

Menéndez was not the first Spaniard to tread these shores. That distinction belongs to Juan Ponce de León, an explorer and adventurer who

COLONIAL DEFENDER
The bronze cannon that defended St. Augustine is today fired only on major holidays and weekends. The city protected the northern flank of Spain's Florida colony and the route of the treasure ships back to Spain.

LIMESTONE LEVIATHAN
Overleaf: The impregnable ramparts of Castillo de San Marcos were built of limestone quarried on nearby Anastasia Island, and proved strong enough to withstand five sieges. Construction of the fort began in 1672 and took more than 15 years to complete.

first set foot in the New World in 1513. King Ferdinand V had promised that Ponce de León would enjoy the rewards of any treasures he found. Legend has it that he was also beguiled by tales of a magical spring—the Fountain of Youth—whose waters flowed with youth-giving powers. Landing at Easter time on the northeast shore of the Florida peninsula, Ponce de León named the territory *La Florida*, after *Pascua florida*, the Spanish term for Easter.

Eight years after his landfall, Ponce de León died in battle against the Florida Indians. He never found a fortune, but instead discovered the Gulf Stream, the warm, fast-moving ocean current that flows the length of Florida, a few miles offshore, on its way to Europe. The stream provided an admirable shipping route for the Spanish galleons taking the plundered gold and silver of South America back home to Spain.

CATHOLIC AGAINST PROTESTANT

The settlement at St. Augustine was born out of conflict for control of the treasure route and the savage passions of Europe's wars of religion. In 1562, three years before Menéndez's landing, three French ships under the command of Jean Ribault, an ardent Protestant, had explored the mouth of the St. Johns River, near what is now Jacksonville. Ribault's second-in-command came back to the area in 1564 and built the triangular Fort Caroline to protect a small settlement of Huguenots (French Protestants). When Pedro Menéndez de Avilés arrived at St. Augustine, his first move was to attack the French settlement.

Menéndez captured Fort Caroline on September 20, 1565, killing some 140 Frenchmen, either by the sword or by the noose, and sparing only women and children. Menéndez then fell upon a shipwrecked French force led by Ribault himself, at a place 14 miles south of St. Augustine at the south end of the Matanzas River (*matanzas* is Spanish for "slaughter"). Nearly all the French soldiers, including Ribault, were beheaded. Ten Frenchmen who proved they were Catholic were spared. Menéndez justified the killings on the grounds that the victims were either pirates or heretics. He ordered a sign to be placed above the bodies of the executed that read, "I do this, not as to Frenchmen, but as to Lutherans."

In 1565, soon after the founding of St. Augustine, Father Francisco López de Mendoza Grajales established the Franciscan mission of Nombre de Dios on the site. The missionaries devoted themselves

ALCAZAR HOTEL
The former Alcazar Hotel, which today houses the Lightner Museum, was one of three hotels built by railroad baron Henry M. Flagler.

INFORMATION FOR VISITORS

To reach St. Augustine, take Hwy. 1 south from Jacksonville. The St. Augustine Visitor Information and Preview Center is located at 10 Castillo Drive; (800) OLD-CITY. The Spanish Quarter Museum, operated by the Historic St. Augustine Preservation Board, is open daily from 9:00-5:00. There is an admission charge. The rest of restored St. Augustine can be toured by carriage, trolley, boat or on foot. Castillo de San Marcos and Fort Matanzas National Monuments are open daily, except Christmas Day. Fort Matanzas is located 14 miles south of St. Augustine; take Hwy. A1A south to the park entrance, and then the free ferry to the fort itself.
For more information: Historic St. Augustine Preservation Board, P.O. Box 1987, St. Augustine, FL 32085. (904) 825-5033.

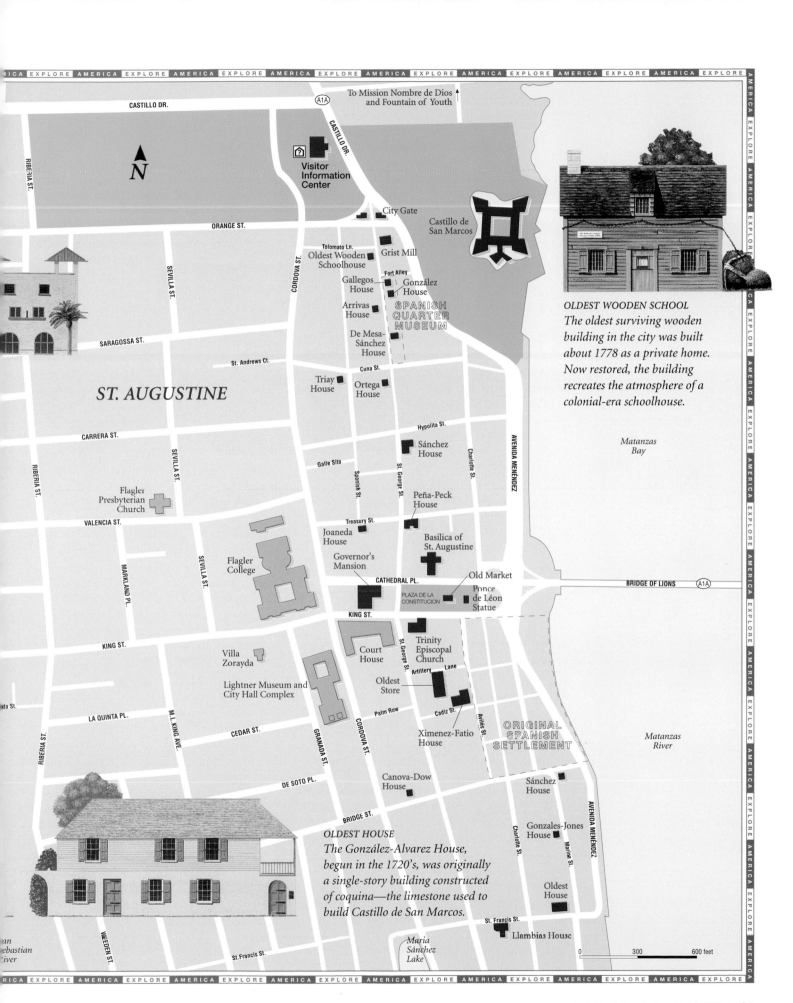

CASTILLO DR.

To Mission Nombre de Dios
and Fountain of Youth

A1A

CASTILLO DR.

N

Visitor
Information
Center

City Gate

Castillo de
San Marcos

ORANGE ST.

RIBERIA ST.

SEVILLA ST.

CORDOVA ST.

Tolomato Ln.
Oldest Wooden
Schoolhouse

Grist Mill

Fort Alley

Gallegos
House

González
House

SPANISH
QUARTER
MUSEUM

Arrivas
House

De Mesa-
Sánchez
House

SARAGOSSA ST.

St. Andrews Ct.

Cuna St.

Triay
House

Ortega
House

ST. AUGUSTINE

Hypolita St.

Sánchez
House

Charlotte St.

CARRERA ST.

SEVILLA ST.

Galle Sita

Spanish St.

St. George St.

AVENIDA MENÉNDEZ

RIBERIA ST.

Flagler
Presbyterian
Church

Peña-Peck
House

Treasury St.

VALENCIA ST.

Joaneda
House

Governor's
Mansion

Basilica of
St. Augustine

Flagler
College

Old Market

CATHEDRAL PL.

Ponce
de Léon
Statue

BRIDGE OF LIONS

A1A

MARKLAND PL.

SEVILLA ST.

PLAZA DE LA
CONSTITUCION

KING ST.

KING ST.

Villa
Zorayda

St. George St.

Trinity
Episcopal
Church

Court
House

Artillery
Lane

Lightner Museum and
City Hall Complex

Oldest
Store

LA QUINTA PL.

M.L. KING AVE.

CEDAR ST.

GRANADA ST.

CORDOVA ST.

Palm Row

Cadiz St.

Aviles St.

Ximenez-Fatio
House

ORIGINAL
SPANISH
SETTLEMENT

Matanzas
River

DE SOTO PL.

Canova-Dow
House

Sánchez
House

Charlotte St.

Marine St.

AVENIDA MENÉNDEZ

BRIDGE ST.

Gonzales-Jones
House

an
ebastian
iver

WEEDEN ST.

OLDEST HOUSE
*The González-Alvarez House,
begun in the 1720's, was originally
a single-story building constructed
of coquina—the limestone used to
build Castillo de San Marcos.*

Oldest
House

St. Francis St.

St.Francis St.

Maria
Sánchez
Lake

Llambias House

0   300   600 feet

*Matanzas
Bay*

OLDEST WOODEN SCHOOL
*The oldest surviving wooden
building in the city was built
about 1778 as a private home.
Now restored, the building
recreates the atmosphere of a
colonial-era schoolhouse.*

EXPLORE AMERICA EXPLORE AMERICA EXPLORE AMERICA EXPLORE AMERICA EXPLORE AMERICA EXPLORE AMERICA EXPLORE AMERICA EXPLORE AMERICA EXPLORE

OLD ST. AUGUSTINE 11

to converting the Timucuan, Appalachee and Creek Indians to Christianity. The Franciscans eventually established a chain of missions through northern Florida, Georgia and the Carolinas.

Today, a stainless steel cross more than 200 feet high marks the original site of the mission, where the first Roman Catholic mass to be celebrated in what is now the United States took place in 1565. The cross was erected in 1965 to celebrate the city's 400th birthday. St. Augustine enjoys the further distinction of having been home to America's first church, its first school, its first hospital—Our Lady of Solitude—and its first ordained priests.

As a garrison town on the edge of Spain's empire, St. Augustine depended on supplies from Mexico and Spain. Gradually a little town grew up on the site claimed by Menéndez, laid out in a grid pattern radiating out from the central Plaza de la Constitucion, and protected by a small garrison in a wooden fort. Despite the hopes of the early Spanish explorers, Florida held no hidden sources of gold, so St. Augustine was never the home of fortune-seekers. Its hardworking population consisted mainly of craftsmen, farmers, missionaries, soldiers and small traders. By 1648, St. Augustine's population numbered 2,000 souls, including Indians and slaves.

THE FORTRESS ON THE BAY

The tides of war swept over St. Augustine many times in its history. In 1586, the English corsair Sir Francis Drake arrived with a fleet of 42 ships and some 2,000 men, and laid siege to the town. St. Augustine's 300 colonists and soldiers managed to kill 20 of Drake's invaders. But one of these had been a close friend of the corsair, and in furious retaliation, Drake burned the town. English buccaneers again attacked St. Augustine in 1668, leaving in their wake 60 Spanish dead.

By the early 1670's, English settlements farther north, such as Charleston, posed a new threat to Spain's Florida colony. To bolster St. Augustine's defenses, the Spaniards started work in 1672 on a stone fortress to replace the vulnerable wooden palisade. It was to be called Castillo de San Marcos, and its star shape incorporated the most up-to-date ideas in European military architecture. The fort was built of coquina, a solidified mix of sand and shells of remarkable strength. Its walls are about 10 feet thick and stand between 20 and 30 feet above its moat. Although a mixture of financial and labor problems delayed its completion until 1695, the fort amply served its purpose. It successfully withstood two major British assaults, first in 1702, when Governor James Moore of Carolina led an unsuccessful two-month siege, and again in 1740, when General James Oglethorpe of Georgia fruitlessly bombarded the fort for 27 days. The fort remains the only major building to have survived intact—although with minor restoration—from the days when Florida was ruled by Spain, and is the oldest masonry fort in the continental United States.

It was following the siege of 1740 that the Spanish bolstered St. Augustine's defences by building Fort Matanzas, a strong stone blockhouse on Rattlesnake Island, off the southern tip of Anastasia Island at the entrance to Matanzas Bay. A wooden watchtower had stood here since the days of St. Augustine's founding, warning its defenders of the approach of hostile forces, and it was here in 1565 that the victorious Spanish had put their Huguenot captives to the sword.

England eventually won at the negotiating table what it had previously failed to gain in battle. In 1763, a defeated Spain gave control of Florida to England, in exchange for Havana, which Spain had conquered the year before. British rule lasted only two decades. In the Treaty of Paris, signed in 1783, England ceded Florida back to a by now impoverished Spain, which, 38 years later, traded it to the United States. On July 10, 1821, the Spanish flag was hauled down for the last time at St. Augustine, and Castillo de San Marcos became a United States military post. It was used to hold rebellious Seminole Indians during the 1830's, and during the Civil War a small Union force held the fort from its capture in March 1862 until the war's end.

For many northerners, St. Augustine was not an attractive addition to the United States. New York politician Alexander Hamilton, Jr., sent to the town in 1822 as Attorney for East Florida, wrote that he found the city "dirty, ruinous and crumbling," though much of this degeneration might be attributed to a yellow fever epidemic the year before.

An anonymous writer published an open letter to St. Augustine not long after, predicting that the city would one day become "the retreat of the opulent, the gay, and the fashionable, a destiny which bountiful Nature seems to have intended."

FAN FAIR

The Lightner Museum's extensive collection of 19th-century decorative art ranges from fans and printed matter to antique mechanical musical instruments, stained glass and fine china. The museum's collection was donated to St. Augustine by Chicago magazine publisher Otto C. Lightner, who opened the building in 1948.

WARRIOR FOUNDER

A statue honoring Pedro Menéndez de Avilés, the Spanish soldier who founded St. Augustine in 1565, is outlined against the former Alcazar Hotel, right. Menéndez was sent by the Spanish government to counter the threat posed by Fort Caroline, a French Protestant settlement set up at the mouth of the nearby St. Johns River.

ers, which he named after Ponce de León. It was opened to the public in 1888. In the same year he built the opulent Alcazar Hotel, facing the Ponce de León. Flagler helped to improve the appearance of the town by paving the streets, and by building churches, a courthouse and a waterworks. He even brought the railroad to St. Augustine.

There are several ways to take in the sights of Old St. Augustine. There are walking tours; open-air trolleys that wind for more than seven miles through the cobbled streets as guides point out the various landmarks; romantic horse-drawn carriages; and even 75-minute scenic cruises along the waterfront and Matanzas Bay.

Perhaps the most appropriate place to start is the northernmost site, the Fountain of Youth—a memorial park of trees and rusted cannons where

POWDER AND SHOT
Volunteer soldiers don the blue and red uniforms of the Spanish imperial army to reenact an 18th-century musket drill. In June and December of each year, St. Augustine's Grand Illuminations provide the occasion for candlelit processions of local residents dressed in period costume.

For the people of St. Augustine, that prophecy took some time to be fulfilled. The population was mostly Roman Catholic, Spanish-speaking and of Minorcan descent, subsisting on a mixture of fishing, picking oranges and gathering oysters. St. Augustine's isolation meant that for many years large-scale development passed the town by. As a result, many of its colonial-era buildings survived, as did the easy-going lifestyle of its people.

LURED FROM THE NORTH

However, lured by the sunshine and prospects of development, hard-working settlers from the North, mostly Protestant, began to migrate southward during the 19th century. The city's balmy winter climate slowly made it a popular winter resort, a spot where invalids could recuperate from the North's ravaging winters. One of these was a young tubercular Ralph Waldo Emerson. Another visitor, in 1831, was John James Audubon, the naturalist and painter. He, however, thought St. Augustine to be "the poorest hole in creation." His departure, he recorded, was "a happy event."

However, St. Augustine was, indeed, to become "the retreat of the opulent." It attained this position through the efforts of Henry Morrison Flagler, cofounder of Standard Oil Company of New Jersey. He arrived in St. Augustine in late 1883, hoping that the climate would improve his health. It did not take him long to envision the possibilities of enticing well-heeled visitors from the North for the winter to this "Southern Newport."

Flagler started to buy up land and built a 450-room, Spanish-style hotel with twin 165-foot tow-

Ponce de León is thought to have set foot. Just south is the Mission de Nombre de Dios, the spot where Menéndez landed and where Father López de Mendoza Grajales first said mass. On the bay, the majestic Castillo de San Marcos with its jutting bastions and moat is the city's most significant historic site. Volunteers dressed in period uniform carry out musket and cannon drill, meticulously following 18th-century Spanish drills. Fort Matanzas is situated 14 miles to the south, in a 298-acre park reached by ferry.

As befits a town of 16th-century vintage, St. Augustine abounds with places of interest that boast the appellation "oldest." There is, on St. Francis Street, the Oldest House (González-Alvarez House). Built of coquina in the early 18th century, it has been restored by the St. Augustine Historical Society. In the restored Old Spanish Quarter, craftsmen recreate early colonial life in a general store, a working blacksmith shop, a weaver's and spinner's, and a carpenter's shop. The Oldest Wooden Schoolhouse, on St. George Street, was constructed more than 200 years ago of cedar and cypress joined by wooden pegs; the schoolmaster and his wife lived upstairs. The Oldest Store Museum on Artillery Lane exhibits 100,000 pieces of memorabilia going back to the days of high-wheeled bicycles and lace-up corsets. Fifty colonial-era buildings have been preserved, restored or reconstructed.

In the more than 400 years since Spain claimed these shores, St. Augustine has remained a living community. Today, the town is more than just a museum of the colonial period. It is a place where history reaches into the present.

THE OLDEST MISSION
Near this chapel of the Mission de Nombre de Dios is a 208-foot cross marking the spot where the first mass to be said in the New World was celebrated. By the late 16th century, a chain of Franciscan missions like this one had been established along the Atlantic coast to convert the Indians to Christianity.

MUSEUM PIECES
A sparsely furnished room in St. Augustine's Oldest House is typical of the elegant simplicity of Spanish colonial style. The house has been designated a National Historic Landmark and is a museum of the city's history. Displays include furnishings from the British and American periods as well.

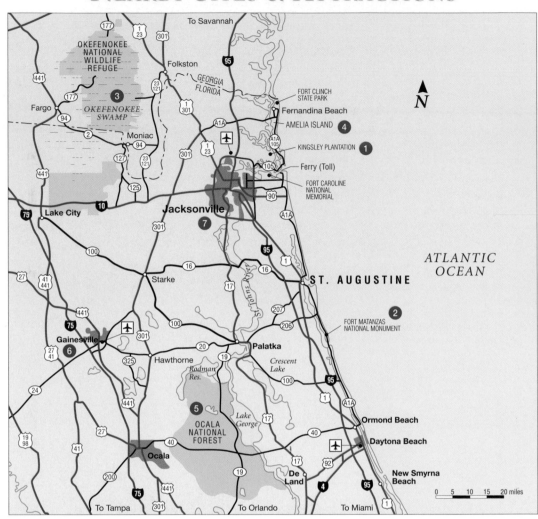

The wood-frame Kingsley Plantation house was built in the 1790's by slaves owned by John McQueen, who was granted Fort George Island by the King of Spain.

① KINGSLEY PLANTATION

This 40-acre estate, located on Fort George Island, was originally a plantation, whose owners employed African slaves to farm sea island cotton and other cash crops. The site preserves two of the oldest houses in Florida. One, a nine-room frame house, was built by John McQueen when he was granted Fort George Island by the King of Spain in 1791. The other, the kitchen house, is made of tabby—a simple but strong concrete composed of oyster shell, sand and water. In 1817, the plantation passed to Zephaniah Kingsley, a politician and slave trader. Visitors can tour the restored Kingsley home and view historical artifacts and exhibits. Located east of Jacksonville just off Hwy. 105.

② FORT MATANZAS NATIONAL MONUMENT

Located on Rattlesnake Island, 14 miles south of St. Augustine, Fort Matanzas stands on the site of a succession of wooden watchtowers built by the Spanish. The fort proved its worth during the British blockade of 1740 when it provided protection for food shipments. The present stone structure was completed in 1742 and consists of a platform for six cannons and a two-story sentry tower. The 298-acre park also covers the southern section of Anastasia Island; a free ferry runs between the islands. On Anastasia, the park's visitor center contains exhibits about the massacre of Huguenots that took place here in 1565. From St. Augustine, take Hwy. A1A south to the park entrance.

③ OKEFENOKEE SWAMP

Located in southeastern Georgia and northern Florida, this 684-square-mile swamp is a watery wilderness shaded in parts by towering cypress trees. A web of channels threads between sandy islands covered with longleaf and slash pine. Marsh plants and water lilies grow in profusion, while floating islands—actually thick mats of decaying vegetation—and sandy islands that support oak, laurel oak, gum trees and magnolias abound. Okefenokee is home to a rich variety of animal life, including alligators, black bears and otters, as well as such bird species as sandhill cranes, ospreys, egrets, wood ducks, woodpeckers and owls. The Okefenokee National Wildlife Refuge covers most of the swamp. Visitors can take canoe trips through the swamp and camp on specially constructed platforms. Facilities at the northern entrance include a nature trail on a raised boardwalk, an interpretive center, a serpentarium and Pioneer Island Homestead. Located north of Jacksonville off Hwy.1 or Hwy. 441.

4 AMELIA ISLAND

White quartz eroded into powdery white sand has created Amelia Island's 200 acres of pristine beach. The island's undeveloped southern tip has been set aside as a park. Here, beachcombers can enjoy solitary walks along shell-strewn beaches, and hikers can trek through groves of spiky wild palmettos and ancient twisted scrub oaks draped with Spanish moss. For birdwatchers, the island's scenic inlets, marshes and lagoons are a staging area for many migratory waterfowl and shorebirds. Take Hwy. 95 north from Jacksonville, and Hwy. A1A across the Intracoastal Waterway onto Amelia Island. Follow Hwy. A1A south to the recreation area. To the north, and 12 miles away, is 1121-acre Fort Clinch State Park with a beach and its Civil War-era fort and 1864 living history program. The park's 1,500-foot-long fishing pier is the perfect place to cast a line for saltwater fish. Follow Hwy. A1A north.

5 OCALA NATIONAL FOREST

Referred to locally as "The Big Scrub," this temperate to sub-tropical forest of more than 300,000 acres contains the world's largest stand of sand pines. The sand pine is unique because it is the only tree that grows large enough in dry, sandy soil to be commercially logged. The forest also abounds with freshwater lakes and natural springs, and its lush vegetation includes scrub oak, hickory, slash and longleaf pine, tall palms and other sub-tropical plants. Miles of hiking trails snake through the forest and along meandering streams. The region has a large herd of deer among its plentiful wildlife, and a remarkable variety of birds that includes the mockingbird, Florida's official state bird. Located east of Ocala; Hwy. 40 and Hwy. 19 run through the forest.

6 FLORIDA MUSEUM OF NATURAL HISTORY, GAINESVILLE

The largest of its kind in the southeast United States, this impressive museum interprets the anthropological and biological history of Florida and the Caribbean. Visitors can explore a full-scale North Florida cave, stroll through typical natural Florida habitats and investigate an archeological dig. The museum's extensive fossil holdings demonstrate that the Florida peninsula was once covered by a sea. Other artifacts, dating back 10,000 years, trace the first human forays into this region. Interactive computer technology accompanies many permanent exhibits. Located on the campus of the University of Florida in Gainesville.

7 FORT CAROLINE NATIONAL MEMORIAL, JACKSONVILLE

This historic site is a reminder of the struggle waged between France and Spain for control of northern Florida during the 16th century. French Huguenots (Protestants) established a settlement near the mouth of the St. Johns River in 1564-65. They erected earthworks and a triangular log palisade that was named *fort de la Caroline* (fort in the land of Charles). In 1565, the fort was captured by a Spanish force from St. Augustine. The French returned in 1568. They seized and burned the fort. A smaller version of Fort Caroline occupies one acre on a 119-acre site near the original location. Located 13 miles east of downtown Jacksonville.

Waterlilies carpet the surface of Georgia's Okefenokee Swamp, and conceal an underwater world teeming with life. Animals as diverse as alligators, catfish and fishing spiders thrive in these waters.

Fort Matanzas was built in 1742 as an outpost of Castillo de San Marcos. The fort is situated on Rattlesnake Island.

PILGRIMS OF PLIMOTH

New England's colonial history began at Plymouth with the landing of the Mayflower.

Mistress Bradford, a Pilgrim, has just asked you into her thatch-roofed cottage to gripe about New England weather. "It's like to boil your blood in summer and freeze it in winter," says the wife of Governor William Bradford, looking out her low doorway at a chilly sunny morning in Plymouth, Massachusetts.

Alice Bradford is not the only one grumbling about Plymouth's climate. Across a dirt street, on which chickens peck, roosters crow and men return home after musketry practice, her neighbor, Goodman Peter Browne, chews on a sorrel leaf plucked from his herb garden and has observations of his own about the weather he's encountered since arriving in the New World on a ship called *Mayflower* seven years ago: "This climate," says Browne, "is begging for some order to be put to it." In a seeming time warp, modern visitors to Plymouth, alive more than 300 years after these people existed, stand among them and learn how they lived. But it's not science fiction; the setting is Plimoth Plantation, an outdoor

THE ROCK
Plymouth Rock, now sheltered in its own small temple at the base of Cole's Hill, is honored as a symbol of the spirit of those first settlers who stepped ashore to face life in a new land.

WINTER WHITE
Overleaf: Though this pastoral scene at today's Plimoth Plantation has a serene air, the Pilgrims who spent their first winters in such crudely constructed shelters suffered badly and fell ill in the New England cold.

museum depicting Pilgrim life in 1627, seven years after the three-masted merchant ship, *Mayflower*, slipped inside Plymouth Harbor on Dec. 16, 1620. Upon its arrival, the fit among *Mayflower*'s 102 passengers set about constructing the crude dwellings that they hoped would help them survive a bone-chilling winter. With their efforts the very first page of New England's colonial history was written.

Spelled with an "i," one of the ways the colony's chronicler and second governor, William Bradford, spelled Plymouth, Plimoth Plantation isn't located on the exact spot where the Pilgrims established their colony. That spot is occupied today by the modern town of Plymouth, three miles north of the plantation along the scenic Massachusetts coast. There, amid the traffic and bustle one would expect in a town just 40 miles south of Boston, visitors seeking historical insight find it mixed with the real world, in a working-class town where revering the past sometimes plays second fiddle to finding a permanent job.

Not so at Plimoth Plantation. Here, on a gentle hillside overlooking Cape Cod Bay, the past rules, yet lives in the present. In this conversational museum, skilled interpreters become living artifacts, assuming the identities of Plymouth's earliest residents. Carrying out daily chores in a humble alignment of primitive wooden houses, they bring Pilgrims to life with an ease that belies the painstaking research behind each convincing portrayal.

Their clothing, the food they cook, the accents in which they encourage over 450,000 visitors a year to join them in conversation—every aspect of the lives they depict is anchored in fact.

What better place to find out the Pilgrims did not eat pumpkin pie and cranberry sauce at the three-day harvest feast now called Thanksgiving; that they really had roast goose, corn meal, cod and sea bass, and venison brought by the Indians? What better venue in which to savor these delicious ironies: that clams and mussels were considered "hard rations" by the early inhabitants of Plymouth and that some Pilgrim farmers deemed lobsters fit only for pigs?

Goodman Browne will admit he'd prefer a fat cockerel. As you stroll past his house, you may notice a few telltale feathers swirling aimlessly by the front door. A cockerel tastes good when it's flavored with sorrel, he'll tell you.

Browne's is but one of some 15 dwellings in the village. In the streets, gardens and fields surrounding them, villagers plant and harvest crops, shear sheep, bake bread in clay ovens, make clapboards, salt fish and build fences. Inside each house, Pilgrims cook, sew, clean muskets and talk of their New World adventure.

EXPLORE AMERICA EXPLORE AMERICA EXPLORE AME

INFORMATION FOR VISITORS

Plimoth Plantation is located south of Plymouth on Hwy. 3A. From Boston, take Hwy. 3, Exit 4 for Plymouth. The site is open daily from 9:00-5:00 from April to November. Admission tickets are available at the Visitor Center, which offers a brief orientation, slide show and exhibits on Plimoth Plantation, the adjoining Wampanoag Indian Homesite and Mayflower II. Costumed interpreters provide commentary throughout the Plantation site. Mayflower II, a full-size reproduction of the original Pilgrim ship, is moored at State Pier on Water Street on Plymouth's waterfront, 3 miles north of Plimoth Plantation on Hwy. 3A. There is an admission charge for both Plimoth Plantation and Mayflower II (combination tickets are available). Plymouth Rock also is located on Water Street in downtown Plymouth. The town's Visitor Information Center, located on the waterfront on Park Avenue, has information on accommodations and other local attractions. For more Information: Plimoth Plantation, P.O. Box 1620, Plymouth, MA 02362. (508) 746-1622.

HISTORY COMES ALIVE
Plimoth's interpreters carry out everyday 17th-century activities in period dress and even use the dialects of their characters' home regions in order to immerse visitors in history. Idle hands were unheard of in those first hard years of adapting to a new world.

EXPLORE AMERICA EXPLORE AMERICA EXPLORE AME

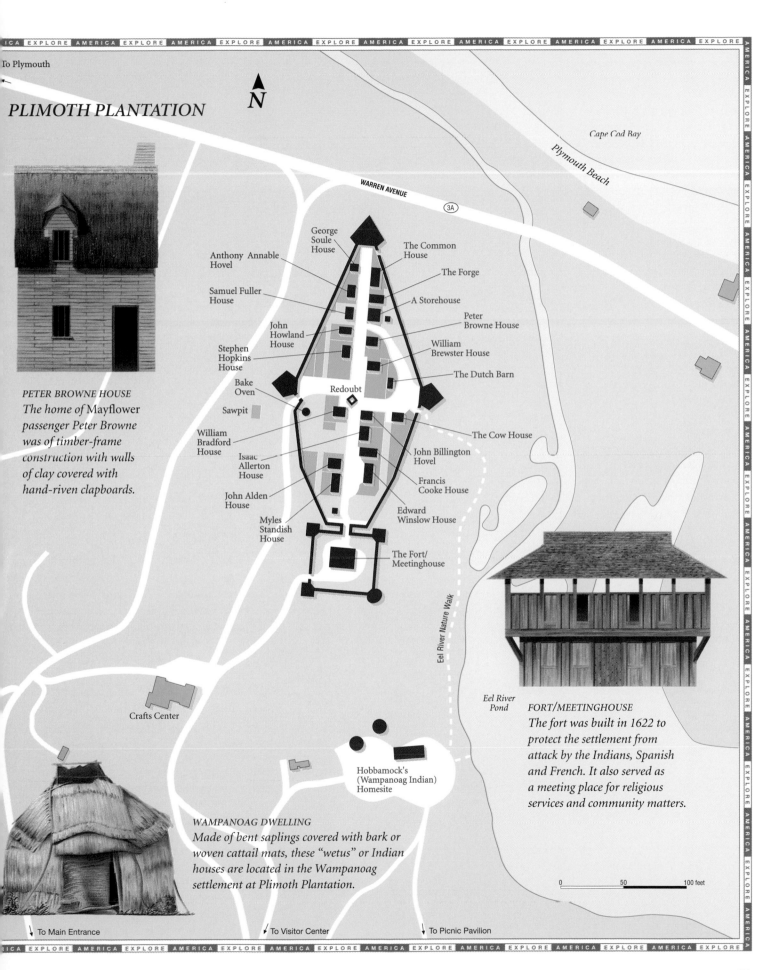

To Plymouth

PLIMOTH PLANTATION

N

Cape Cod Bay

Plymouth Beach

WARREN AVENUE

3A

George Soule House

The Common House

Anthony Annable Hovel

The Forge

Samuel Fuller House

A Storehouse

John Howland House

Peter Browne House

William Brewster House

Stephen Hopkins House

Bake Oven

Redoubt

The Dutch Barn

Sawpit

William Bradford House

The Cow House

Isaac Allerton House

John Billington Hovel

John Alden House

Francis Cooke House

Myles Standish House

Edward Winslow House

The Fort/Meetinghouse

Eel River Nature Walk

Crafts Center

Eel River Pond

Hobbamock's (Wampanoag Indian) Homesite

PETER BROWNE HOUSE
The home of Mayflower passenger Peter Browne was of timber-frame construction with walls of clay covered with hand-riven clapboards.

FORT/MEETINGHOUSE
The fort was built in 1622 to protect the settlement from attack by the Indians, Spanish and French. It also served as a meeting place for religious services and community matters.

WAMPANOAG DWELLING
Made of bent saplings covered with bark or woven cattail mats, these "wetus" or Indian houses are located in the Wampanoag settlement at Plimoth Plantation.

0   50   100 feet

↑ To Main Entrance   ↑ To Visitor Center   ↑ To Picnic Pavilion

ICA EXPLORE AMERICA EXPLORE AMERICA EXPLORE AMERICA EXPLORE AMERICA EXPLORE AMERICA EXPLORE AMERICA EXPLORE AMERICA EXPLORE AMERICA EXPLORE

PILGRIMS OF PLIMOTH 21

SAFE HARBOR
Massachusetts' mist softens the lines of Mayflower II *as she sits anchored at the State Pier in Plymouth. Interpreters play the roles of the sailors and passengers who sailed from the Old World to the New in 1620 in the original* Mayflower *and bring to life the hardships of a 66-day crossing in cramped quarters.*

LOCAL TRADE
The local Wampanoag Indians introduced the settlers to new crops and farming techniques. In fact, the Indian corn the Pilgrims learned to grow was providing a surplus by the mid-1620's and was traded to more northern native groups for pelts.

Goodman Browne will tell you they sometimes hear wolves at night—hungry wolves attracted by fish heads the Pilgrims buried as fertilizer in their cornfields. Across the street, Bridget Fuller may give you her recipe for a pie of roast duck resting on a bed of onions; or, better yet, a swan pie. Mistress Fuller's husband, Samuel, sits by her cleaning his musket. Ask and he'll tell you the reasons the Pilgrims came here.

A deacon in the Separatist church, he remembers the trials his sect suffered in England in the early 1600's; how their efforts to reform the Church of England were considered treasonous by the crown and led to Separatist persecution. He recounts how the Separatists fled to the Netherlands in 1608, where they practiced religious freedom for 12 years but were denied good employment and lived in poverty. He remembers hearing favorable accounts of the New World and thinking that perhaps they should set out for this land—where a family could practice its preferred religion, preserve its English heritage and work hard to gain economic security.

decks like human cordwood? Can it bring back the noises and smells of chickens and pigs penned in the bow? Is it too much to ask of a wooden reproduction to evoke centuries-old feelings of seasickness, loneliness and fear?

They did go, of course, setting sail from England on Sept. 6, 1620. And for that story visitors should leave the plantation and drive three miles north to Plymouth Harbor, in downtown Plymouth. There, at the State Pier, the *Mayflower*'s modern reincarnation, *Mayflower II*, lies at anchor. She is a full-scale reproduction of the type of ship that brought the Pilgrims to Plymouth in 1620. She is tiny by today's shipping standards—106½ feet long, with a 25½-foot beam and a 13-foot draft. Designed by U.S. naval architect William A. Baker, and built in England, she set sail for Plymouth from Devon on April 20, 1957. Steering a more southerly course than the original *Mayflower* to avoid heavy seas, she made the entire voyage under her own sail. Seas are calm for *Mayflower II* these days. She serves as a dockside museum, welcoming visitors intent on sensing what those first 102 Pilgrims and 26 crewmen experienced on their 66-day crossing.

But how can a latter-day vessel transport back in time those who walk its sloped decks today? Is it possible for a ship built in the 1950's to vividly convey the claustrophobia of being packed between

AUTHENTIC AND IMAGINATIVE

Mayflower II succeeds thanks to efforts on two different fronts. The first is the ship itself, meticulously constructed to resemble the type of merchant vessel that plied Atlantic waters in the early 17th century. Unfortunately, not one written or pictorial description of the original *Mayflower* exists. To compensate, *Mayflower II*'s designer researched other merchant ships of the time in exhaustive detail. No efforts were spared to lend this reproduction an air of authenticity—from its hand-sewn sails to the weathered casks stacked in its hold.

Authenticity is one thing, but can it breathe life into *Mayflower II* and her story? Enter the human component. Once again, as they do throughout Plimoth Plantation, interpreters bridge the time gap. When visitors board *Mayflower II*, they meet men and women portraying both crewmen and passengers who sailed on that first Pilgrim voyage.

Time on the ship stands still. It is March of 1621, and with the cold weather finally subsiding, crewmen are busily preparing the ship for its return voyage to England. Winter exacted a heavy toll on the settlers. Of the 102 passengers who arrived in Plymouth in December, nearly half have succumbed to disease and the cruel weather. The

VILLAGE THOROUGHFARE
By 1627, the village had one main road, called "the Street," that sloped up from the harbor. The early homes, made of hand-riven clapboard, lined both sides of the street and a white oak palisade surrounded the village. Outside the palisade were the fields whose crops sustained the settlers, though every home had its own raised kitchen garden and herb bed.

remaining Pilgrims—some of whom spent the winter on board the *Mayflower*—are preparing to disembark for the last time.

In the great cabin, behind steerage, the ship's master, Christopher Jones, recalls the *Mayflower*'s troublesome journey to the New World; the two deaths that took place; the two births that balanced the ledger. In the crowded chartroom, Jones and his mates had worked day and night to guide *Mayflower*'s course. And steady she was, considering the Pilgrims were hoping to land at the mouth of the Hudson River, in present-day New York Harbor. Where they did first touch land, at present-day Provincetown on the tip of Cape Cod, was not that far off their target.

The *Mayflower*'s passengers lived below steerage, in the 'tween decks area, during their long

voyage, suffering deprivation and sickness. Visitors to this cramped, dark world need not work very hard to imagine the life they endured.

A costumed interpreter, portraying a passenger, remembers how crowded the decks were with Pilgrims, their bedding and a number of small cannons called minions, which were carried on board to discourage pirates and privateers. She talks of the passengers' beds—wooden slabs built into tiny partitioned cubicles along the ship's sides. She remembers how lice infested their bedding; how they yearned for access to their personal belongings but realized all but the barest essentials had been stored in the hold below.

The hold—crammed with household goods, tools and supplies, stacked with food, canvas, cannon shot and powder—held nearly every tangible

object with which the Pilgrims would start to build their new world in the wilderness. Their ordeal continued after anchoring in Plymouth Harbor. Disease ran rampant on board that first winter, a time during which many *Mayflower* passengers remained on the ship while the colony's first dwellings were built.

Fearful that Indians would realize their numbers had been decimated, the Pilgrims buried these unfortunates at night, on nearby Cole's Hill. Modern-day visitors often walk its grassy slopes in conjunction with a visit to Plymouth Rock, which rests at the base of the hill.

Did the Pilgrims really use this world-famous boulder as a stepping stone when they came ashore? Some historians have cast doubt on the story, calling it no more than a charming legend. Believers continue to rely on the testimony of Thomas Faunce, an elder in the Plymouth Church, who identified Plymouth Rock in 1741 as the landing place of the *Mayflower* party. His information came from his father, who had come to Plymouth on the ship *Anne* in 1623. Faunce also knew several members of *Mayflower*'s landing party, who were still alive when he was a boy. Resting today under a canopy of granite—and receiving as many visitors as ever—the boulder continues to outlast its would-be detractors.

EVERYDAY ITEMS FROM THE PAST

No doubt exists about the authenticity of exhibits in the Pilgrim Hall Museum on Court Street in Plymouth. Here, at the oldest museum in continuous service in America, the nation's largest collection of Pilgrim artifacts is on display. These include the chair of Governor Bradford, the sword of famous Pilgrim Myles Standish, and the cradle of Peregrine White, born on the *Mayflower* in Provincetown Harbor.

Elsewhere in modern Plymouth, a number of early houses offer glimpses of life shortly after the Pilgrims arrived. The oldest wood frame house among them, the Richard Sparrow House, was built in 1640. Now a museum, it features huge open hearths, thick, hand-hewn beams and wide floorboards that creak as they may have 300 years ago.

High on Burial Hill, overlooking Sparrow House and Plymouth Harbor, gravestones date back to the 17th century. Chosen as the site of the Pilgrims' original fort and meetinghouse, this easily defended hilltop also became the final resting place for many of the colony's early inhabitants. The earliest graves in the cemetery are unmarked. Many of the first marked graves feature headstones so badly pitted and encrusted with lichens that their inscriptions have become illegible. However, visitors

who walk the winding paths beneath Burial Hill's leafy canopy of shade trees will find many headstones whose names and dates stand out clearly.

The earliest of six 17th-century headstones on the hill remembers Edward Gray, who arrived in Plymouth in 1643 and set about becoming a wealthy merchant. Gray died in 1681.

Plymouth Colony's second governor, William Bradford, is thought to be buried on the brow of a hill overlooking the harbor, near the gravesite of his son, Major William Bradford. Gazing out from this spot, over rooftops and down toward the State Pier and *Mayflower II*, one can only hope Bradford is there. No other place offers such a grand view of the harbor, the bay and beyond.

EVERYDAY CHORES
The colony's housewives were for the most part responsible for food—cooking at the hearth at home, baking at the communal oven, tending and harvesting the household garden and producing the butter and cheese. At the same time, they managed to take on the early education of their children.

NEARBY SITES & ATTRACTIONS

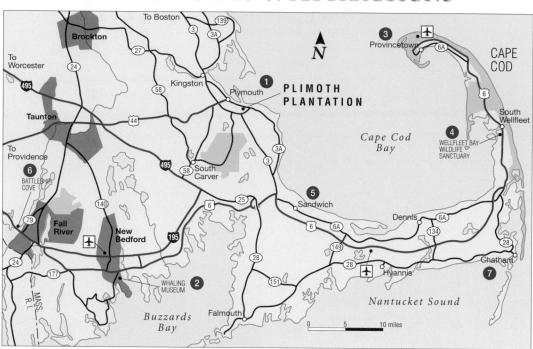

A box turtle suns itself on a fallen log at the Wellfleet Bay Wildlife Sanctuary.

1 PILGRIM HALL MUSEUM, PLYMOUTH

This Greek Revival building, designed in 1824 by Alexander Parris, is the country's oldest public museum in continuous operation and houses an admirable collection of Pilgrim artifacts and possessions, many of which belonged to passengers on the *Mayflower*. On display are Myles Standish's sword, a Bible and chair that belonged to Governor William Bradford, the cradle of Peregrine White (who was born on the *Mayflower*). The collection includes everyday household utensils, muskets, armor and furniture used by the Pilgrims in the New World. Also on exhibit is a 17th-century transatlantic vessel, named the *Sparrow Hawk*, which foundered off Cape Cod in 1626. Located in central Plymouth on Hwy. 3A, two blocks south of Hwy. 44.

2 NEW BEDFORD WHALING MUSEUM

Located within a harpoon's throw of the historic New Bedford waterfront, this repository of whaling history includes model sailing ships, scrimshaw, whittled whalebone carvings, harpoons and whaling tools, and figureheads. Visitors can board the *Lagoda*, an authentic half-scale replica of a square-rigged whaler that measures 89 feet in length—the largest ship model in the world. In 1850, New Bedford was the nation's greatest whaling port, and consequently one of its richest cities. On display are examples of the fine silver, china, art and pewter that were brought home from faraway exotic ports to decorate the great mansions of local sea captains and traders. Located at 18 Johnny Cake Hill, New Bedford.

3 PILGRIM MONUMENT AND PROVINCETOWN MUSEUM

On November 11, 1620, after a tumultuous 66-day voyage across the stormy Atlantic, the *Mayflower* set anchor in Provincetown Harbor at the tip of Cape Cod. An agreement signed aboard the ship, the Mayflower Compact, pledged the 41 signers to form a "civil Body Politick," creating the first instrument of self-government in the New World. The tallest all-granite monument in the United States, the 252-foot Pilgrim Monument and Provincetown Museum, commemorates the Pilgrims' first landing site. The observation deck, 352 feet above sea level, provides visitors with a spectacular view of Cape Cod and the Atlantic Ocean. Other excellent museums in Provincetown display Pilgrim and maritime artifacts, such as whaling equipment and a half-scale model of the famous fishing schooner *Rose Dorothea*. Located on Cape Cod, just off Hwy. 6

4 WELLFLEET BAY WILDLIFE SANCTUARY

This wildlife sanctuary, operated by the Massachusetts Audubon Society, protects 1,000 acres of moorlands, marshes and beaches inhabited by scores of migrating waterfowl and shorebirds. Five miles of easy walking trails wind through fields and pinewoods, and along the banks of ponds and streams. Birdwatchers who are alert may see herons, egrets, gulls, terns and shorebirds among the salt marshes and tidal flats, and sometimes hawks and peregrine falcons circling overhead. Boats take visitors to Monomoy National Wildlife Refuge, the principal feeding area of a great variety of migrating birds; during the winter, there are also seal-watching tours. Located on Hwy. 6, in South Wellfleet, Cape Cod.

5 SANDWICH GLASS MUSEUM

Sandwich, founded in 1639, is Cape Cod's oldest town. It is renowned for the beautiful glass that was manufactured in the town by the Boston and Sandwich Glass Company between 1825 and 1888. The Sandwich Historical Society's Glass Museum contains an internationally acclaimed collection of the subtly colored Sandwich Glass, which was emulated throughout Europe and America. Among the museum's collections are pressed lacy glass made before 1840 and rare examples of blown glass. A diorama, built in 1940 by students from the Massachusetts Institute of Technology, depicts the factory as it looked in 1850 when it was the source of the whole town's livelihood. A bitter labor dispute closed the glass factory in 1888 and Sandwich fell into decline. Happily, slow growth has helped preserve the town's historic district, which includes a number of impressive homes and public buildings that date back as far as the late 1600's. Located on Cape Cod on Hwy. 130.

6 BATTLESHIP COVE AND MARINE MUSEUM

The floating museum at Battleship Cove houses the world's largest exhibit of historic fighting ships. On display are two 20th-century U.S. Navy fighting ships, a submarine and two PT boats from World War II. Visitors can climb aboard *Big Mamie*, a 35,000-ton battleship, which is longer than two football fields. This enormous ship fought 35 battles in World War II and logged more than 225,000 miles without losing a single man in combat. Another ship, the destroyer *USS Joseph P. Kennedy*, saw action in both the Korean and Vietnam conflicts. It provides a realistic picture of life aboard this floating "tin can." Visitors can tour the conning tower and control room of the *USS Lionfish*, a preserved World War II submarine, and inspect the cramped living quarters that housed 75 men. On shore, the Marine Museum recalls the age of sail and steamship travel with photographs, memorabilia and more than 150 ship models, including a 28-foot model of the *Titanic* which was used in the 1953 Hollywood movie. Located in Battleship Cove in the city of Fall River.

Clapboard houses and historic sea captains' homes line the narrow streets of Provincetown, a lively fishing community.

7 CHATHAM

The earliest mention of the region near Chatham was in 1606, when French explorer Samuel de Champlain landed here while he was exploring the coastline. His arrival ignited a violent skirmish with the local Indians and created an aura of distrust that plagued future relationships between settlers and native Americans. A granite monument marks the spot of this ill-fated landing. Today, the quiet village of Chatham is home to a number of small but interesting museums. The Railroad Museum, housed in an 1887 railroad station, has many railroad models, a photograph collection and a restored 1910 caboose. The Old Atwood House, a 1752 structure, contains antiques dating from 1635. Chatham is also a departure point for excursions to Monomoy National Wildlife Refuge, an offshore sandbar that is a staging area for more than 250 species of migrating birds. Located on Cape Cod on Hwy. 28.

The exciting saga of whaling ships and the men who manned them comes to life at the New Bedford Whaling Museum.

STRAITS OF MACKINAC

*Forts, furs and fish chronicle
the varied history of this crossroads
in the upper Great Lakes.*

In the eastern Straits of Mackinac, at the entrance to Lake Michigan, the limestone hump of Mackinac Island rises above the deep blue waters of Lake Huron like a sentinel at one of history's crossroads. Of the many islands that dot the Great Lakes—the world's largest body of fresh water—Mackinac has the most varied history. The island has seen the passage of Indians, French explorers, missionaries and fur traders, and been the scene of epic struggles for control of the continental interior. In the 19th century, the island became the Midwest's favorite summer resort, and its elegant wooden cottages and hotels are still a byword for gracious living. In 1976, Pulitzer Prize-winning historian Bruce Catton described the island in this way: "More than any other place in Michigan, this is a refuge from the present." History is just one reason that more than 800,000 tourists a year come here each summer.

Amid Victorian splendor, they enjoy an unhurried resort atmosphere and the Great Lakes' cooling summer breezes.

But as early as A.D. 1000, Indians were summering on this island and nearby Bois Blanc Island. They came to fish, plant corn, worship and bury their dead. In hunting season they retreated by canoe to mainland Michigan. Some say they named the island Mishinnimakong (land of the great fault) because of a large crack visible from the water. Others say the name meant "land of the great turtle," after its shape. The French and the British preferred to call it Mackinac, pronounced "Mackinaw." The island, its fort, Fort Michilimackinac in Mackinaw City, Mackinac County and the famous Mackinac Straits suspension bridge—one of the longest in the world—are all pronounced the same way today.

The island's strategic importance was recognized early. The first European to pass

SAFE AND SOUND
A pair of geese enjoy their dinner within the palisaded grounds of the stockade at Fort Michilimackinac. It protected more than just its inhabitants. The fortified settlement was the great fur trade center of the Northwest.

ISLAND VIEW
Overleaf: Mackinac Island, dubbed the Island of the Big Turtle because of its humped shape, was first settled in 1780 during the American Revolution. A small, crescent-shaped harbor at the island's southern tip breaks its eight miles of shoreline. The white-washed walls of Fort Mackinac are visible in the background.

by the island was the French explorer Jean Nicolet in 1634, who was searching for a water route to China. To show their reverence for the place, and to please the island spirits, his Indian guides are said to have dropped into the water strands of tobacco given to them by Nicolet. One of the first descriptions of Mackinac Island came in 1669, from a French missionary, Father Claude Allouez, who was impressed by its high bluffs. Another priest, Jesuit Father Claude Dablon, wintered on the island in 1670, and erected a small bark chapel.

However, a French presence in the Straits area dates from 1671, when Father Jacques Marquette founded the mission of St. Ignace—named for the founder of the Jesuits—on the northern shore of the Straits of Mackinac. Marquette, who went on to discover the Mississippi in 1673, brought with him a group of Huron Indians, refugees fleeing from the warlike Iroquois. The mission, where Marquette was buried, was located on a site that had been used for some years by fur traders. The Mackinac area became a vital link in the great chain of forts, missions, trading posts and settlements by which explorers, missionaries and fur traders began to unlock the secrets of the vast continent.

In 1698, the small French garrison that had provided protection for the mission since 1680 was withdrawn to what is now Detroit. Although St. Ignace then went into decline, the soldiers returned in 1715 and constructed a strong, palisaded fort on the southern shore of the Straits, which they called Fort St. Philippe de Michilimackinac. For some 50 years, the guns of the fort commanded the strategic waterway, and the site served as a center of the fur trade. Possession of the Straits helped the French to cement alliances with the Ottawa and Ojibwa Indians and to keep the British, their imperial rivals, at bay.

Fort Michilimackinac passed into British possession in 1761, following the French defeat at Quebec. However, discontent among the Indians, who had been allied with the French, soon exploded into violence. On June 2, 1763, during a game of lacrosse held on King George III's birthday, a group of Ojibwa seized the fort and put many of its British garrison to death. The event was part of a rebellion led by the Ottawa chief, Pontiac. It would eventually convulse the entire region and force the British to change their settlement policy. When peace returned, the Straits once again became the scene of a thriving fur-trading business. A reconstruction of Michilimackinac now stands on the site of the original fort.

In 1780, the threat of attack from rebellious American colonists prompted the fort's Lieutenant Governor, Patrick Sinclair, to move Fort Michilimackinac, its garrison and fur traders to

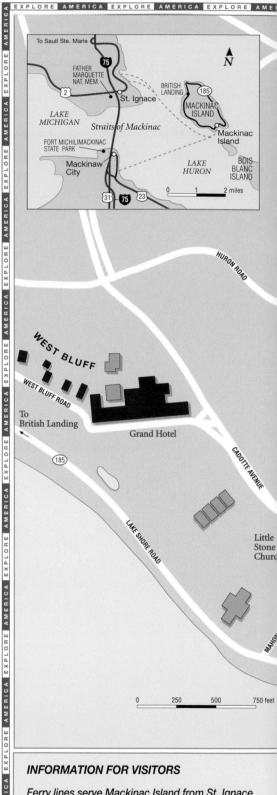

INFORMATION FOR VISITORS

Ferry lines serve Mackinac Island from St. Ignace and Mackinaw City, both of which are accessible by car via Hwy. 75 from Detroit or Sault Ste. Marie. The nearest airports are in Traverse City, Detroit, Chicago and Pellston. There is also air taxi service from Pellston to the island. No cars are allowed on Mackinac, but bicycles can be rented and visitors can take 90-minute horse-

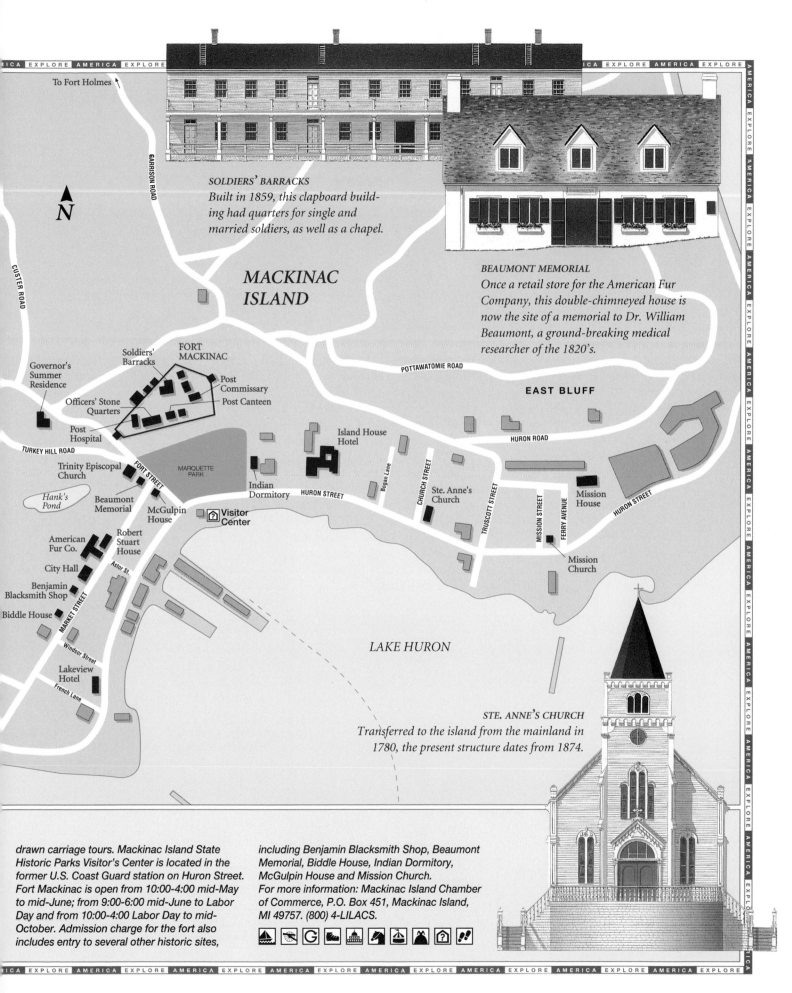

GARRISON ROAD

N

CUSTER ROAD

SOLDIERS' BARRACKS
*Built in 1859, this clapboard build-
ing had quarters for single and
married soldiers, as well as a chapel.*

**MACKINAC
ISLAND**

BEAUMONT MEMORIAL
*Once a retail store for the American Fur
Company, this double-chimneyed house is
now the site of a memorial to Dr. William
Beaumont, a ground-breaking medical
researcher of the 1820's.*

POTTAWATOMIE ROAD

EAST BLUFF

Governor's
Summer
Residence

Soldiers'
Barracks

FORT
MACKINAC

Post
Commissary

Post Canteen

HURON ROAD

Officers' Stone
Quarters

Post
Hospital

TURKEY HILL ROAD

FORT STREET

MARQUETTE
PARK

Island House
Hotel

Trinity Episcopal
Church

*Hank's
Pond*

Beaumont
Memorial

McGulpin
House

Indian
Dormitory

HURON STREET

Bogan Lane

CHURCH STREET

Ste. Anne's
Church

TRUSCOTT STREET

MISSION STREET

FERRY AVENUE

Mission
House

HURON STREET

Visitor
Center

American
Fur Co.

Astor St.

Robert
Stuart
House

City Hall

MARKET STREET

Benjamin
Blacksmith Shop

Biddle House

Mission
Church

Windsor Street

Lakeview
Hotel

French Lane

LAKE HURON

STE. ANNE'S CHURCH
*Transferred to the island from the mainland in
1780, the present structure dates from 1874.*

drawn carriage tours. Mackinac Island State
Historic Parks Visitor's Center is located in the
former U.S. Coast Guard station on Huron Street.
Fort Mackinac is open from 10:00-4:00 mid-May
to mid-June; from 9:00-6:00 mid-June to Labor
Day and from 10:00-4:00 Labor Day to mid-
October. Admission charge for the fort also
includes entry to several other historic sites,

including Benjamin Blacksmith Shop, Beaumont
Memorial, Biddle House, Indian Dormitory,
McGulpin House and Mission Church.
For more information: Mackinac Island Chamber
of Commerce, P.O. Box 451, Mackinac Island,
MI 49757. (800) 4-LILACS.

STRAITS OF MACKINAC 31

the more easily defended Mackinac Island. Sinclair chose a site atop the bluffs that rise 150 feet from the island's fine natural harbor. Deposits of limestone provided the raw material for the new fort—Fort Mackinac—while traders and merchants built a new town around the harbor.

The Treaty of Paris in 1783 awarded the island to the United States. But the British, mindful of the island's importance as the crossroads of the lucrative fur trading routes, maintained their garrison at Fort Mackinac until 1796. In that year the British withdrew their troops and a small U.S. force stood mounted guard over the Straits.

On July 17, 1812, the startled American garrison of 57 men awoke to find themselves surrounded by a powerful force of 1,000 British soldiers, French voyageurs and Indians who had landed on the island the previous night. No shots were fired in this, the opening engagement of the War of 1812, but blood stained Mackinac's soil two years later, when American forces tried unsuccessfully to recapture the island. The U.S. officer in charge of recapturing Mackinac was undoubtedly frustrated when he found that the cannons of his five-vessel fleet could not be raised high enough to shell the fort. Matters became worse when British troops ambushed an American landing force near Dousman's Farm, now the site of one of Mackinac's two golf courses. Thirteen Americans, including second-in-command Major Andrew Holmes, died in the ensuing battle. Mackinac was finally awarded to the U.S. under the Treaty of Ghent in 1815, and the fort was garrisoned until 1895.

Fort Mackinac is now the single most visited spot on the Island. All 14 of the fort's buildings are original. The handsome Officers' Stone Quarters, Michigan's oldest building, was built with four-foot-thick limestone walls to withstand attack. Artifacts housed in original buildings and museum personnel dressed as soldiers bring this bygone era to life, giving visitors a glimpse of American military life during the 1880's. Periodically, a cannon is fired from a platform overlooking the lake, and Taps, sounded by a bugler at 10 p.m., signals the end of the day. Fort Holmes, a bastion originally built in 1814 by the British (who called it Fort George), stands not far away on the island's highest point, but has not yet been restored.

FURS FOR THE STRAITS EXCHANGE

Since the 1600's, the Mackinac area had been a focus of the fur trade. Every fall, traders set out from Michilimackinac, and spent the winter buying furs from Indian trappers in the interior. In the spring, when the ice broke up, the traders returned to the Straits to exchange furs for supplies and trade goods brought from Montreal. After the fur trading community was moved to Mackinac Island in 1780, it thrived as never before. For John Jacob Astor, a 43-year old German immigrant, the end of the war of 1812 was good business. Congress had ruled that only American citizens could trade with Indians within U.S. territory, so Astor bought out the English traders of the Southwest Company to establish the American Fur Company. This grew into one of the largest businesses of its day. From the company's headquarters on Mackinac Island, Astor's clerks collected, graded, baled and shipped millions of otter, fox, beaver, mink and wolf pelts to markets in Europe.

By 1820, Astor was by far the largest trader in the Great Lakes, employing 3,000 boatmen and 400 clerks on Mackinac Island. Besides making Astor a rich man, the trading accelerated Indian cultural breakdown, as well as the disappearance of the fur-bearing animals. By the 1830's, the fur industry had died in the Great Lakes region. Astor then sold his Mackinac business, and moved his operations to the west coast. A short distance from where visitors today disembark the ferry, stands the Robert Stuart House, the original island headquarters of the American Fur Company and the home of company agent Robert Stuart. In summer, Stuart House was the island's social center as agents gathered to celebrate another successful season in the bush. The house displays records of the fur company and original furniture.

The encampments of the Indian bands who accompanied the agents sprouted on the shore near

HISTORIC THREESOME

A trio of buildings on Fort Street illustrate the history of Mackinac Island. On the left, McGulpin House—a restored Canadian log residence—is typical of the island's earliest architecture. Next is the Beaumont Memorial, scene of Dr. William Beaumont's pioneering observations of the human digestive system during the 1820's. On the right is Trinity Episcopal Church, built in 1882 at the foot of Fort Mackinac. Local lore has it that an officer donated a substantial amount of money to the church building fund on the condition that it be located near the garrison.

A sentinel tower, located along the west stockade wall at Fort Michilimackinac, left, overlooks the Straits of Mackinac. The Church of Ste. Anne de Michilimackinac, to the right of the tower, was the center of religious activities at the fort. Above, skeins of wool hang inside Priest's House at Fort Michilimackinac. The house was built in the 1740's for the fort's resident priest. The blacksmith's shop, built adjacent to the priest's house, was connected to it by a covered passageway. The blacksmith worked for the priest, who wanted to be able to supervise the smithy easily.

the little trading town. Here the Indians waited for their annual payments from the government Indian agent. The most famous of these officials was Henry R. Schoolcraft, who married a métis woman. Schoolcraft published Indian legends and lore that were later used by Henry Wadsworth Longfellow as inspiration for his poem *Hiawatha*.

For many years, fishing and lumbering filled the gap that the disappearance of the fur trade had left in the island's economy. But it was tourism that rescued Mackinac from decline. In 1875, the island became the second U.S. national park after Yellowstone. It was turned over to the State of Michigan in 1895, when Fort Mackinac ceased to be an active military post. More than 80 percent of the island's 2,200 acres now constitutes Michigan's first state park.

By the mid-1800's, steamboats were bringing thousands of visitors from as far away as St. Louis to enjoy the moderate climate, natural beauty and recreational opportunities of the island. Many families came with steamer trunks and servants to escape the oppressive summer heat of the Midwest and its hay-fever-causing pollen. When wealthy families discovered they could either buy land on the part of the island not in the national park, or lease park land, they began to build "cottages" of Michigan white pine. Some of these cottages con-

tained as many as 30 rooms, many with turrets and long, covered front porches filled with white wicker furniture. Some had stables, servant quarters and swimming pools. Most of Mackinac's cottages have been maintained and today present an unmistakable Victorian outline along the bluff.

Today the island is a 15-30 minute ferry ride from Mackinaw City or St. Ignace on the mainland. The island soon comes into view, its slopes forested with white pine, beech, white cedar and birch. Dominating the approach are two long white structures on the bluffs set back from the harbor: the imposing building on the left is Grand Hotel, while that on the right is Fort Mackinac. A marina crowded with yachts appears on the right.

The Grand was built of good Michigan white pine by a consortium of railroad and steamship companies, and when it opened in 1887 it was said to be the largest and finest summer hotel in all the world. Its original two-month season has been regularly lengthened and the hotel now opens from mid-May until November 1st. In recent years the Grand has been completely restored. Set amid 50

GARRISON LIFE
Surgical instruments and a humble checkerboard in Fort Mackinac's restored hospital ward, above, are testimony to both the dangers and the tedium of 19th-century military life. The fort was an active military post until the 1890's. British troops built the Officers' Stone Quarters, shown right, using the island's native limestone. Its walls were thick enough to withstand American bombardment in 1814.

acres of manicured and sculpted greenery, the hotel's 680-foot-long porch—twice the length of a football field—was proclaimed "World's Longest" by Robert Ripley's *Believe It or Not.* Its four-story portico is supported by 33 white wooden columns.

BACK TO THE HORSE AND BUGGY AGE

Visitors must explore the island on foot, by bicycle or in one of the many horse-drawn carriages; motorized vehicles have been banned since 1896, except for emergency vehicles. In summer, almost 600 horses are stabled on Mackinac. Girdling the island is the eight-mile Lake Shore Road, which may be the only state highway in the U.S. that has never recorded a traffic accident, although an occasional runaway horse has overturned a carriage.

The island's main street, Huron, is a natural first stop. The ferry dock, many small hotels and the park's visitor center are here. Nearby is the Indian Dormitory at the base of the fort, built in 1838 to accommodate Indians who came to see the agent. It houses a museum and a working 1840 kitchen.

On Market Street—the other main thoroughfare—the Beaumont Memorial is dedicated to army surgeon Dr. William Beaumont, who pioneered studies of the human digestive system through his observations of a voyageur who had received a gunshot wound in the stomach. Other notable sites include the Benjamin Blacksmith Shop and Biddle House, the restored home of a fur trader. Here interpreters demonstrate 19th-century crafts.

The best way to see Mackinac is to get on a bicycle and discover the many trails and footpaths that crisscross the island. Wildflowers flourish among the thick forests, including Indian paintbrush, wild rose, trillium and columbine. Halfway around Lake Shore Road lies British Landing, where the British landed and captured Fort Mackinac in 1812, and where American soldiers tried and failed to emulate their success in 1814. Visitors fortunate enough to arrive in June can enjoy the lilacs that adorn every corner of the island. Believed to have been introduced by French missionaries during the 1600's, Mackinac's lilacs are a visible reminder of the storied past of this jewel of the Great Lakes.

VICTORIAN GRANDEUR
An elegant row of turreted Victorian "cottages" overlooks the Straits of Mackinac from West Bluff Road. These massive 10- to 30-room homes were built in the late 19th century by well-to-do summer visitors. Horse-and-carriage transport is still one of the most popular ways to get around the island, which does not permit any motorized vehicles.

Nearby Sites & Attractions

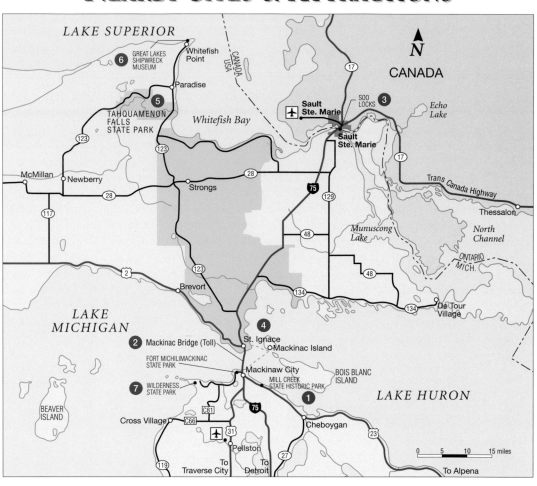

Every Labor Day, more than 60,000 people participate in the Annual Bridge Walk from St. Ignace to Mackinaw City across the imposing five-mile-long Mackinac Bridge.

① MILL CREEK STATE HISTORIC PARK

This reconstructed 18th-century settlement and water-powered mill lies nestled in a 625-acre nature park. A museum displays objects that were unearthed from the 1790's industrial settlement during ongoing archeological work. This was the mill that provided the finished lumber used to build Fort Mackinac. Today, costumed interpreters demonstrate their sawing skills for visitors, and park naturalists provide expert advice about the flora and fauna. The best place to sight wildlife is along the three miles of nature trails, the Lake Huron shoreline or the area near the beaver and mill ponds. There is a bird feeding station at the visitor center. The park is densely wooded and two forest trails lead to a hardwood and aspen tree farm. A reconstructed sugar shack is a popular venue. Located 3½ miles east of Mackinaw City on Hwy. 23.

② MACKINAC BRIDGE

Dubbed "Mighty Mac" by locals, this impressive feat of engineering connects Michigan's upper and lower peninsulas. The five-mile-long bridge is one of the world's longest suspension bridges. It took 3,500 men (350 of them engineers) four years to build. More than 42,000 miles of wire went into its construction. The steel structure is 19,243 feet long and has a mile and three-quarter span between anchorages. Its twin towers soar 552 feet above the straits. At midspan, the bridge is 200 feet above the water level. When it opened in 1957, the bridge eliminated the need for car-rail ferries between the two peninsulas as it spans the Straits of Mackinac between St. Ignace and Mackinaw City. More than 75 million motorists have crossed "Mighty Mac."

③ SOO LOCKS, SAULT STE. MARIE

Michigan's oldest town, Sault Ste. Marie, was first visited by French voyageur Étienne Brulé in 1620. Father Marquette and Claude Dablon established a mission here and named the town *Le Sault de Sainte Marie*—the falls of St. Mary—in honor of the Virgin Mary. The Indians portaged their canoes around St. Mary's rapids to reach Lake Superior. Today the Soo Locks, one of the largest in the world, raise and lower the water level 21 feet between Lake Superior and Lake Huron. A walkway, viewing platforms and a 22-story-high observation tower allow visitors to see thousand-foot freighters from all over the world going through the lock system. Visitors can also stroll along the historic canals linking Lake Superior with Lake Huron and visit the Steamer Valley Camp Maritime Museum. Located in a park area in Sault Ste. Marie.

4 ST. IGNACE

St. Ignace dates to 1671, when Father Jacques Marquette, a French missionary/explorer, and a group of Huron Indians built a mission on the site. The first settlement, now the Marquette Mission Park and Museum of Ojibwa Culture, includes a Huron longhouse and garden, interpretive plaques about Marquette's life and a statue of him. Important archeological artifacts found here date to the Huron, Ottawa and French settlements of the late 1600's and are housed in the museum, a 150-year-old church building. Located nearby is the Father Marquette National Memorial and Museum, an open-air memorial dedicated to the life and work of the French Jesuit. A monument marks the presumed location of Father Marquette's grave. There is more than a mile of boardwalk along Moran Bay. Located on the north side of the Mackinac Bridge.

The Upper Falls is one of the main attractions of Tahquamenon Falls State Park. The forests around the falls frame it with subtle autumn colors.

5 TAHQUAMENON FALLS STATE PARK

The highlights of this 36,000-acre park are its Upper and Lower Falls. The Upper Falls, made famous in Longfellow's *Song of Hiawatha*, drops 50 feet from a 200-foot-wide lip. It is the second-largest fall east of the Mississippi River (outdone only by Niagara Falls). An elaborate structure of stairs and observation platforms provides visitors with dramatic views of the waterfall—its copper-colored waters surge past at about 50,000 gallons per second. The Lower Falls is a series of three falls and rippling cascades that surrounds an island. Hiking trails offer close-up views of the Lower Falls. The Rivermouth area of the park has hiking trails that wind through the forest, and swimming facilities. Located on Hwy. 123, 60 miles northwest of Mackinac Bridge.

6 GREAT LAKES SHIPWRECK MUSEUM, WHITEFISH POINT

The museum chronicles more than a century of shipwrecks that took place off the stormy coast of Lake Superior. On display are artifacts and photographs from the wreck of the schooner *Invincible* in 1816 to the wreck of the *Edmund Fitzgerald* in 1975. A short film takes visitors beneath the waves to view

the remains of dozens of ships. The nearby Whitefish Point Lighthouse, which began operating in 1849, is the oldest working lighthouse on Lake Superior. Whitefish Point has a reputation as the "graveyard of the Great Lakes." Located on Whitefish Point on Hwy. 123.

7 WILDERNESS STATE PARK

The second-largest state park in the lower peninsula deserves its name: its 7,554 acres are a mixture of woodland and wetland. The park is situated on a peninsula of dense woodlands, marsh and sand-and-pebble beaches. A road encircles the park and several hiking trails lead to its interior. These trails lead past beaver dams and meadows of wildflowers. Deer, beaver and waterfowl may be sighted in the park. Alert and lucky visitors might spot a black bear, coyote or bobcat. One of the park's marshy areas, called Sturgeon Bay, is a good place to fish for smallmouth bass. The park also takes in an archipelago of islands just off the coast of Lake Michigan. Located 8 miles west of Mackinaw City off Hwy. 31.

The Soo Locks permit large freighters and small pleasure boats to travel between Lake Superior and lower-level Lake Huron. They also link Canada with the United States.

COLONIAL WILLIAMSBURG

*If ever there was a golden age,
it blazed across colonial Virginia
in the 18th century.*

For about 80 years, taking into account some inevitable ups and downs, the Old Dominion enjoyed an era of relative wealth, influence and fashionability. The future seemed grand, if perilous. England was still "home" to many citizens, yet—stirred by society-shaking ideas from Europe's Age of Reason—they debated heady notions of freedom in their taverns and council rooms. Nowhere in England's oldest and largest colony did the excitement and good times gleam brighter, and with more verve and beauty, than in the cosmopolitan royal capital of Williamsburg.

It was, said Thomas Jefferson, who was there and saw it for himself, "the finest school of manners and morals that ever existed in America." Jefferson still would feel quite at ease in today's town: it looks virtually as it did around 1770. An army of historians, archeologists, craftsmen and interpreters has spent more than 65 years turning back the hands of time, refashioning a town poised somewhere between reality and illusion. Along the majestic axis of mile-long Duke of

Gloucester Street and spreading across the historic area of 173 acres, the restoration of Colonial Williamsburg embraces more than 500 Queen Anne and Georgian period buildings, from the sumptuous Governor's Palace to the lowliest woodshed. Almost 90 are original 18th-century structures and 50 are major reconstructions; all important public buildings from the 18th-century town are now in place again. More than 100 gardens and greens, covering 90 acres, enhance the cityscape. Forty exhibition buildings tempt visitors into 225 authentically furnished period rooms. In shops, fields and yards, artisans of exquisite skill perform a score of different historic crafts and trades.

But the sum of these parts is life itself: 18th-century life. The sounds and smells of pre-Revolutionary Virginia greet the visitor on every hand, on each Tidewater breeze. The blacksmith's anvil chimes beside his smoky forge. To the squeal and rattle of fife and drum, the militia drills on Market Square, culminating in thunderous musket blasts and the drifting sulfur stench of black powder. Matched black horses come clip-clopping under centuries-old trees, drawing their regal carriage. The tinkle of a harpsichord, hum of violins and violas, and breathy, haunting toots of recorders waft from a chamber music concert, mingling with the delectable aromas from hot hearths and ovens. There is no need to speculate on how the 18th century looked, smelled and sounded. Along Duke of Gloucester Street, we know.

The town that would become the essence of the 18th century was launched in the last year of the 17th, forging a symbolic continuum with Virginia's ancient pioneering era, the swashbuckling days of Captain John Smith and Pocahontas. Only five miles down the road, at a mosquito-infested site called Jamestown, America's first permanent English settlement had endured almost a hundred years of devastating plagues, disastrous fires and endless worries about its indefensible position beside the broad and navigable James River. When in 1698 the Capitol burned for the fourth time, the colony's leaders decided to move the short distance inland to a more pleasant site known as Middle Plantation, on higher, healthier ground between the James and York rivers.

Already the site had been chosen for an important parish church and for the College of William and Mary, the New World's second institution of higher learning, chartered by its royal namesakes in

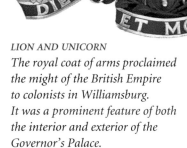

LION AND UNICORN
The royal coat of arms proclaimed the might of the British Empire to colonists in Williamsburg. It was a prominent feature of both the interior and exterior of the Governor's Palace.

STATELY GROUNDS
Overleaf: Three junior members of the Fife and Drum Corps take a break from practice in the elegant garden of the Benjamin Powell House. Tulips, American boxwood, dogwood and oak-leaf hydrangea grow in the symmetrically designed garden. Ninety of Colonial Williamsburg's 173 acres are gardens and greens.

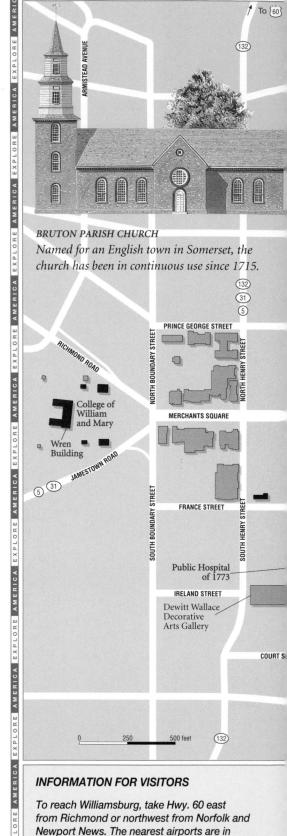

BRUTON PARISH CHURCH
Named for an English town in Somerset, the church has been in continuous use since 1715.

INFORMATION FOR VISITORS

To reach Williamsburg, take Hwy. 60 east from Richmond or northwest from Norfolk and Newport News. The nearest airports are in Newport News, Norfolk and Richmond. There is daily train service from Boston, Newport News, New York and Washington. Buses run regularly

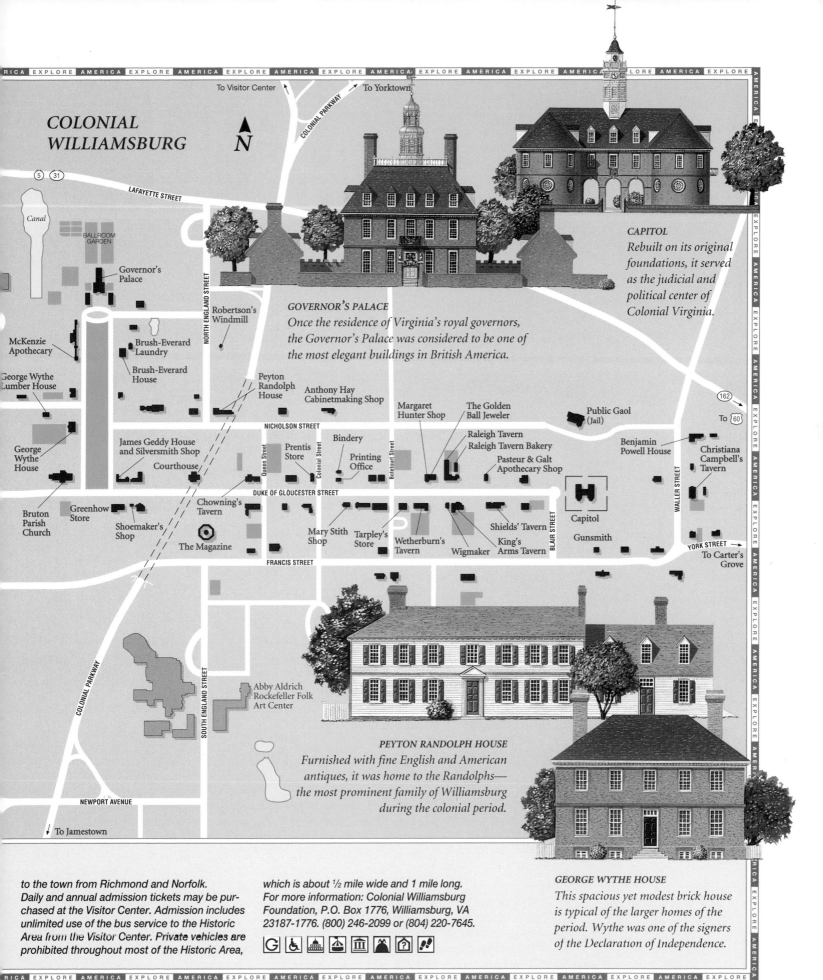

COLONIAL WILLIAMSBURG

N

To Visitor Center   To Yorktown

COLONIAL PARKWAY

(5) (31)

LAFAYETTE STREET

Canal

BALLROOM GARDEN

Governor's Palace

NORTH ENGLAND STREET

Robertson's Windmill

McKenzie Apothecary

Brush-Everard Laundry

Brush-Everard House

George Wythe Lumber House

Peyton Randolph House

Anthony Hay Cabinetmaking Shop

NICHOLSON STREET

George Wythe House

James Geddy House and Silversmith Shop

Courthouse

Queen Street

Prentis Store

Colonial Street

Bindery

Printing Office

Botetourt Street

Margaret Hunter Shop

The Golden Ball Jeweler

Raleigh Tavern

Raleigh Tavern Bakery

Pasteur & Galt Apothecary Shop

Public Gaol (Jail)

To (60)

(162)

Benjamin Powell House

Christiana Campbell's Tavern

WALLER STREET

Bruton Parish Church

Greenhow Store

Shoemaker's Shop

DUKE OF GLOUCESTER STREET

Chowning's Tavern

The Magazine

Mary Stith Shop

Tarpley's Store

Wetherburn's Tavern

Wigmaker

Shields' Tavern

King's Arms Tavern

BLAIR STREET

Capitol

Gunsmith

YORK STREET

To Carter's Grove

FRANCIS STREET

CAPITOL

Rebuilt on its original foundations, it served as the judicial and political center of Colonial Virginia.

GOVERNOR'S PALACE

Once the residence of Virginia's royal governors, the Governor's Palace was considered to be one of the most elegant buildings in British America.

COLONIAL PARKWAY

SOUTH ENGLAND STREET

Abby Aldrich Rockefeller Folk Art Center

PEYTON RANDOLPH HOUSE

Furnished with fine English and American antiques, it was home to the Randolphs— the most prominent family of Williamsburg during the colonial period.

NEWPORT AVENUE

To Jamestown

GEORGE WYTHE HOUSE

This spacious yet modest brick house is typical of the larger homes of the period. Wythe was one of the signers of the Declaration of Independence.

to the town from Richmond and Norfolk. Daily and annual admission tickets may be purchased at the Visitor Center. Admission includes unlimited use of the bus service to the Historic Area from the Visitor Center. Private vehicles are prohibited throughout most of the Historic Area,

which is about ½ mile wide and 1 mile long. For more information: Colonial Williamsburg Foundation, P.O. Box 1776, Williamsburg, VA 23187-1776. (800) 246-2099 or (804) 220-7645.

RICA EXPLORE AMERICA EXPLORE AMERICA EXPLORE AMERICA EXPLORE AMERICA EXPLORE AMERICA EXPLORE AMERICA EXPLORE AMERICA EXPLORE AMERICA EXPLORE

COLONIAL WILLIAMSBURG 41

FOIBLES OF FASHION
A dapper gentleman, dressed in the telltale wig, white stockings and breeches typical of men's fashion in the 18th century, stops to converse with a friend. Costumed historical interpreters stroll the streets of Williamsburg carrying on day-to-day life in the colonial city.

1693. In 1695, the foundations were laid for the college's Wren Building. Nearly one mile east of the new college, work on the new Capitol began in 1701; in between was Duke of Gloucester Street. Along the way were a spacious Market Square and a stately north-south boulevard soon capped by the magnificent Governor's Palace. The planner, Governor Francis Nicholson, specified the dimensions of streets, lots and building setbacks.

For all its creation as an artificial new town, a sort of colonial Brasilia, Williamsburg was an instant success. As the seat of a potent far-flung government it pulled in wealth via ambitious merchants, style-conscious tradesmen, and hospitable taverners. Lordly planters from outlying districts maintained townhouses in order to be present for legislative sessions and social activities. By the eve of the American Revolution, Williamsburg's population was about 2,000, equally divided between the white and black races.

FALLING INTO OBLIVION
Yet in 1780 came the comedown: time and events demanded another movement of the capital. It was not precisely a calamity, but the start of a long decline. The government moved to Richmond, and for almost 150 years Williamsburg would endure near-oblivion as a seedy, forgotten backwater. This torpor contributed to the sparing of many buildings, for there was no progress to disturb them. Much of the old town remained, decrepit but intact, when a local clergyman sparked the preservation era in 1926.

The Rev. W.A.R. Goodwin, rector of Bruton Parish Church, for years had dreamed of seeing the town restored. Now, he conveyed his obsession to one of the world's richest men, John D. Rockefeller, Jr. Quietly, the great financier/philanthropist began the incognito purchases of large chunks of the town. Colonial Williamsburg was established in 1928 as a non-profit organization, and soon began a historic restoration of a scope and scholarship never before attempted. Work continued in the teeth of the Great Depression. In quick succession, rising on their original foundations, the Raleigh Tavern, Capitol and Governor's Palace all returned to the streetscape by the early 1930's. Reunited with the still-standing Wren Building, by then also freshly restored, once again they composed the most important galaxy of Williamsburg buildings. No structures were moved in from other locations. It was a striking, auspicious start for the town's reincarnation.

Today, after some 55 years of additional restoration and fine-tuning, Williamsburg's architectural integrity may astound the first-time visitor, and

delight even the frequent guest with an inexhaustible source of new visual discoveries. Begun during the reign of William III, the buildings and their interior furnishings span the ages of Queen Anne and the first three Georges. Most are of the style known as Georgian, an enduring favorite reproduced across North America, roughly since World War I, in the path of the Colonial Revival Era. For most of us, raised among sometimes clumsy imitations, one of the pleasures of a visit to Williamsburg is the opportunity to study the real thing. We can examine the intricacies of masonry bond, the shape of ornamental bricks, the pitch of gambrel, hip or A-frame roof, and the way the wooden shakes are applied. The beauties of hand-planed molding and carved trim, the styles of black-

smith-forged hardware, and the subtleties of paint color all form an endless chain of cameo-like views.

Williamsburg's craftsmen create a fascination of their own, rooted in the admiration we feel for anyone who has mastered a complex and difficult trade. Crafts add the finishing textures of noise, work, smell and banter. Here, working before us, and patiently answering our questions, are silversmiths, printers, cabinetmakers, millers, engravers, shoemakers, blacksmiths, gunsmiths, harnessmakers, musical instrument makers, milliners, weavers, wheelwrights, coopers and carpenters.

Another collective delight is the look of backyards, with their myriad kitchens, smokehouses, privies and carriage houses. Such dependencies are so artfully arranged amid gardens, trees, picket fences and pathways as to create an unfolding picture of charm and interest on any walk through Williamsburg. Wherever a small sign on a white gate extends the message: "Welcome. Please visit garden," a visitor is well advised to accept, and stroll into a beguiling universe of blossoms and arbors, of paths and crosswalks of brick and oyster shell. Each 18th-century household had room for a vegetable garden, some fruit trees or bushes and a few domestic animals. It was a time of keen botanical interest, when gardeners experimented with native and imported plants of all kinds, from formal boxwood to humble cabbage, in often-intricate geometric designs.

Nowhere do landscaping, architecture, interior and historical interest come together with greater

18TH-CENTURY PHARMACOPOEIA
Dr. Kenneth McKenzie lived in this house with his family in the 1750's, and ran the McKenzie Apothecary from here. Today, the restored apothecary stocks mid-18th-century remedies such as medicinal herbs and elixirs, as well as spices, clay pipes and fragrant pomander balls.

The window of a milliner's shop, right, displays women's fashionable 18th-century hats. The word milliner stems from "Milaner"— a person who imported goods from Milan, Italy. Smartly dressed gentlemen such as the one below adorned their heads with wigs; the head pieces were somewhat of a status symbol: the style of a person's wig denoted his social standing in the community. Williamsburg kept eight wigmakers gainfully employed.

perfection than at the Governor's Palace. Today's guests see a building of beauty from every angle, a thing dreamlike in its exterior perfection of scale and harmony. Entering through a walnut paneled entrance hall bristling with hundreds of military flintlocks and swords, visitors pass through elegant parlors, reception rooms, bedrooms and ballrooms that, on the rim of a raw frontier in the early 1700's, must have been a dazzling expression indeed of the crown's authority.

It was an authority cut down by revolution, of course, and Virginia's royal governors may strike us as distant exotic creatures. The colonial era's other major governmental presence, the Capitol, somehow fits more familiarly into American history. It was in this elegant, H-shaped building with its graceful frontal curves that Patrick Henry delivered his "Caesar-Brutus" speech defying the Stamp Act. Here George Washington introduced the Virginia Resolves against the Townshend Acts, and Virginia's Resolution for Independence foreshadowed the Declaration of Independence. Here Thomas Jefferson presented the Statute for Religious Freedom. Many modern visitors, taking a bench seat in the hall of the House of Burgesses (oldest elected legislative body in America), are

moved deeply by thoughts of what occurred in this historic space. Standing as mute witness to the epic prerevolutionary drama is the room's most prominent piece of furniture, the massive walnut speaker's chair that has been present through it all.

ECHOES
OF
THE PAST

Dramatic events still seem to echo behind the pastel, Flemish-bonded brick walls of many Williamsburg buildings. The intriguing octagonal powder magazine, built in 1715, played a key role in the French and Indian War, and then, in 1775, was raided by British marines in a foray that hastened the onset of revolution. At the Raleigh Tavern, Williamsburg's most distinguished 18th-century inn, young Thomas Jefferson danced with his fair Belinda, Phi Beta Kappa was founded and patriots fomented revolutionary fervor. At the recently restored Courthouse, the evolution of American justice comes alive in a variety of living history reenactments. A grimmer view of the law takes shape at the Public Gaol, where punishment was frequently severe and often permanent, as when the imprisoned associates of Blackbeard the pirate were taken out of the building and hanged. Yet, in

other structures, such as the George Wythe House, all seems felicitous. As in all the literally hundreds of exhibition rooms open to Williamsburg visitors, this spacious residence of one of early America's most influential legal scholars is furnished entirely with appropriate antiques.

The last major public building to be reincarnated was the Public Hospital, originally built in 1773 as the first public institution in British North America for the mentally ill. In its willingness to restore and present such painful scenes, Colonial Williamsburg earns high marks for its own maturity and uncompromising scholarship.

All of the restored area is a museum, yet within it are two major institutions that differ significantly from their neighbors. The Abby Aldrich Rockefeller Folk Art Center, a noted fixture since 1957, reopened in 1992 in vastly enlarged quarters. The museum is the oldest in America devoted exclusively to folk art, and was founded on the collection of Mrs. John D. Rockefeller, Jr. One of the first to appreciate the beauty and importance of folk art, she began collecting in the 1920's and in 1939 presented more than 400 objects to Colonial Williamsburg. Building on that nucleus, the museum's collection has grown to almost 3,000 pieces.

MASTER PLAN
Governor Francis Nicholson was the town planner responsible for the design of the new capital city. The Wren Building of the College of William and Mary already stood at the western end of mile-long Duke of Gloucester Street. Nicholson flanked its eastern end with the new Capitol building. An elegant green, about halfway along Duke of Gloucester Street leads to the Governor's Palace. The rest of the land bordering the street was divided into orderly half-acre lots.

The galleries display folk paintings in every conceivable medium, as well as carvings, toys, weathervanes, shop signs, quilts, iron and tinware, and decorated furniture. Folk art is, according to one definition liked here, "the art of common people, done with uncommon style."

A few blocks away, the DeWitt Wallace Decorative Arts Gallery provides a stunning complement to the Folk Art Center. Named for its sponsor, the founder of *Reader's Digest*, the Wallace Gallery displays fine examples of American and British decorative arts from three centuries. Collections include furniture, silver, paintings, ceramics, prints, firearms, textiles and costumes. In the spacious gallery, visitors find a broader selection of antiques than in the town's period exhibition buildings and an opportunity to study them in more detail. The gallery is a contemporary structure, but so cleverly modeled on buildings of the period that it blends in with the landscape of the restored area. Partially underground, it is further screened by a brick wall that also encloses a formal, contemporary garden honoring Lila Acheson Wallace, co-founder with her husband of *Reader's Digest*. The reconstructed Public Hospital doubles as an entrance for the gallery.

Williamsburg is clearly up to its farthingales in adopting 21st-century techniques and attitudes to interpret the long ago. The most recent major examples are eight miles southeast of town at the 800-acre plantation called Carter's Grove, where a spectacular 1750's mansion overlooks the James River at one of its widest points. When the foundation acquired Carter's Grove in the 1960's, it was seen as an ideal supplement to the old capital, a rural arm that would demonstrate how plantation and town helped form an interlocking colonial culture. Yet when staff historians and archeologists went to work, they found a fascinating, centuries-long human pageant that defied typecasting as a vignette fixed in the 18th century.

ROYAL RESIDENCE

Completed in 1722, the elegant and imposing Governor's Palace was the residence of seven royal governors and the first two governors of the Commonwealth of Virginia—Patrick Henry and Thomas Jefferson. The Palace was furnished to impress colonial visitors with fine walnut and mahogany furniture, chandeliers, elegant damask upholstery, ornate wallpaper and priceless paintings. Now, historical interpreters in period dress show off these treasures to today's visitors.

First there was the mansion. Originally one of the great houses of the golden age, it had been altered significantly by former owners. Rather than try to roll back these changes, which were important in themselves as well as superb evocations of colonial renaissance, the house was left alone. Today's visitor gets the full perspective of almost 250 years of history, not of a single period frozen in time.

THE REALITY OF SLAVERY

Elsewhere at Carter's Grove, dramatic additions came in the 1980's and '90's. They included the slave quarter, a cluster of four rude structures of log, mud and rough boards. African-American interpreters, dressed in pale homespun, relate for visitors the social organization and work roles of their forebears, interpreted as if in the 1770's. Slavery is a reality that Colonial Williamsburg explores with increasing assurance, unblinkingly offering clear testimony that for at least half the population, the golden age was a tarnished illusion.

Long before the original slave quarter was built, and about 130 years before the great mansion of Carter's Grove rose on its majestic terrace, there was a riverside settlement on the same site known as Wolstenholme Towne. All of it was wiped out by an Indian massacre in 1622. Eventually other settlers returned, but Wolstenholme Towne was forgotten—until Colonial Williamsburg archeologists discovered it in the 1970's and '80's. Riveting finds from those digs are now displayed in the Winthrop Rockefeller Archaeology Museum just a few hundred feet from where they were found. This newest of Colonial Williamsburg's museums, a contemporary structure, is buried in a knoll overlooking the partially restored town of 1619.

A surprise awaits those visitors who would return to Williamsburg. The connection between plantation and town is delightfully literal: a private eight-mile country road. It goes only the one way, toward the town, winding through woods, fields and marshes virtually unchanged since the first settlers saw them. For the visitor with a mind full of images from Carter's Grove, the ride stirs personal thoughts on the past, the capriciousness of destiny, and time's treatment of mankind's proud ventures.

"History with its flickering lamp," Sir Winston Churchill said, "stumbles along the trail of the past, trying to reconstruct its scenes, to revive its echoes, and kindle with pale gleams the passion of former days." The past is gone indeed, but at Williamsburg the trail can be alluringly bright.

PROMINENT PARLOR
The parlor in the Peyton Randolph House is furnished with fine English and American antiques. The house, built between 1715 and 1750, belonged to one of Williamsburg's most esteemed citizens. Peyton Randolph was president of the first Continental Congress and his house was frequently the center of the town's social and political activities.

NEARBY SITES & ATTRACTIONS

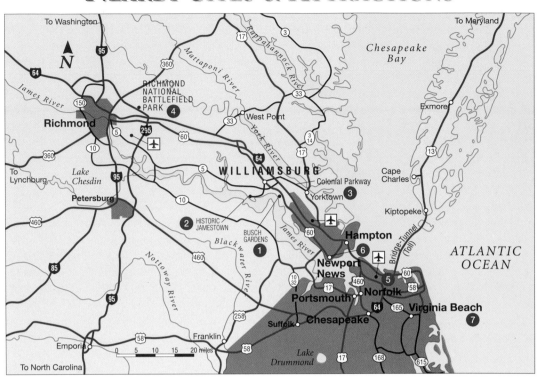

This carved wooden figurehead is just one example from the exclusive collection at the Mariners' Museum in Newport News.

① BUSCH GARDENS, WILLIAMSBURG

At this 360-acre European theme park visitors roam through 9 re-created 17th-century hamlets including Banbury Cross and Hastings (England), Heatherdowns (Scotland), Aquitaine (France), Rhinefeld and Oktoberfest (Germany), San Marco and Festa Italia (Italy) and New France (Canada). Among the electrifying rides is "Drachen Fire," one of the world's largest roller coasters, which turns passengers upside down six times through looping spirals and corkscrews. For a bird's-eye view of the panorama below, visitors can mount the Skyride; transportation on the ground is provided by an old-fashioned steam locomotive. Located 3 miles east of Williamsburg on Hwy. 60

② HISTORIC JAMESTOWN

In 1607, three small ships carrying 104 weary men and boys landed on Jamestown Island after an arduous crossing from England. Under the leadership of Captain John Smith, the newcomers founded the first permanent English settlement in the New World. Seventeen years later, Virginia became a royal colony with Jamestown as its capital. But in 1676, disgruntled citizens burned down much of town, calling it a stronghold of oppression; the settlement was abandoned after the seat of government moved to Williamsburg in 1699. A walking tour of the site traces the outline of the settlement and visits the foundations of many original structures. The only standing ruin is Old Church Tower with three-foot-thick walls of hand-made brick, believed to be part of one of the first brick churches in the country. The New Town area, where Jamestown expanded around 1620, has several homesites along its original

streets, including the Ambler House ruins, dating to the mid-18th century. The visitor center shelters one of the country's largest collections of 17th-century artifacts and shows a film about Jamestown; glassmaking and pottery demonstrations explain some of the first industries in America. Located on the Colonial Parkway, southwest of Williamsburg.

③ YORKTOWN BATTLEFIELD

On October 19, 1781, Britain's dream of an American Empire ended forever on Yorktown Battlefield when British General Cornwallis surrendered to American and French forces. Today, the site of the last major battle of the Revolutionary War surrounds and includes part of the town of Yorktown. From the observation deck of the visitor center, the entire field of action can be seen. Inside, visitors can inspect Washington's field tents and see special exhibits and a film about the siege. A self-guided battlefield tour takes in the headquarters sites of Lafayette, von Steuben and Washington. Other highlights include Moore House, where the Articles of Capitulation were drafted. Take the Colonial Parkway east from Williamsburg.

④ RICHMOND NATIONAL BATTLEFIELD PARK

Ten sites on 765 acres commemorate two of the major campaigns by Union troops to seize Richmond, the hotbed of secessionism and the capital of the Confederacy from 1861-65. At the visitor center, audiovisual programs and interpretive exhibits tell the story of the campaigns—the Seven Days Campaign in June and July, 1862, and the battle at

Cold Harbor in May and June, 1864. It was at Cold Harbor, on June 3, 1864, that Union General Ulysses S. Grant led an ill-fated charge against the dug-in Confederate army, losing 7,000 men in less than 30 minutes. Extensive remains of Union and Confederate earthworks are preserved at Cold Harbor and in several other park areas. The best way to gain a real understanding of the significance of the park is to pick up a map at the visitor center and tour the battlefields; the markers and recorded messages along the way bring to life the two unsuccessful Union offensives. The Chimborazo Visitor Center is located at 3215 East Broad St. in Richmond.

⑤ CHRYSLER MUSEUM, NORFOLK

A wide sampling of art from nearly every important culture and civilization of the last 4,000 years can be seen in this modern building located in the bustling seaport city of Norfolk. Formerly the Norfolk Museum of Arts and Sciences, the museum was renamed when it received Walter P. Chrysler's vast art collection in 1971. Its eclectic holdings include Oriental, Egyptian, pre-Columbian, European and modern American works. Of special note are Greek and Roman sculptures and celebrated works by Renaissance and Baroque artists. A broad range of American art covering the last two centuries includes paintings by Sargent, Cassatt, Benton, Pollock and Warhol. One of the finest collections of glassware in the world traces the history of glass-making from Roman times to the present. Located in the Ghent District, 245 West Olney Rd., Norfolk.

⑥ MARINERS' MUSEUM, NEWPORT NEWS

This 550-acre park and museum on the James River, entirely devoted to the romance and history of the sea, is considered one of the most complete maritime collections in the world. A tour of the museum begins with a short film that introduces the visitor to maritime culture around the world. The museum's impressive collection of hand-carved figureheads includes a massive gilded eagle with a wingspan of almost 20 feet. Twelve large galleries contain dioramas describing historical nautical events, detailed miniature ship models, scrimshaw, paintings, uniforms and navigational instruments. The museum's largest permanent exhibit looks back to the illustrious maritime history of the Chesapeake Bay. The Small Craft Building contains a collection of small boats from around the world, including a sampan, a gondola, fishing boats, yachts and dugouts. Located 3 miles off Hwy. I-64 Exit 258, in the city of Newport News.

⑦ VIRGINIA BEACH

One of America's great vacationlands offers 38 miles of wide, sandy beaches, bays and inlets. A 2-mile concrete boardwalk leads from town past shops and seafood restaurants that serve the famous Lynnhaven oyster. In summer, visitors can camp by the sea, surf, swim, take sightseeing cruises, water-ski, bicycle and play tennis. In winter, the long shoreline stretching from the Chesapeake along the

Atlantic makes for dramatic sightseeing. Piers jutting out into the Atlantic offer superb fishing and surf casting and the nearby inlets are famous for channel bass, speckled trout and flounder. Charter boats take visitors out to fish for sea bass, tuna and marlin. Among the town's historic homes is the Adam Thoroughgood House, built in 1636 and said to be the oldest brick house in America, and the Francis Land House, an 18th-century Dutch gambrel roof structure with period furnishings and gardens. Located on Hwy. 60, east of Norfolk.

The colonnaded arcade of Huber Court in the Chrysler Museum is Italianate in style. A glass dome more than three stories high protects this interior court.

The Jamestown Old Church Tower is the only standing structure left on the island, the site of the first permanent settlement in the New World. The church is believed to date from 1639 and to be one of the first brick churches in America.

REVOLUTION IN BOSTON

---

*Here, in the days of powdered wigs
and knee britches, ordinary citizens
began the march to freedom.*

There's no mistaking Boston. A briny tang gusts in from the harbor where the cod ships once landed. The streets dip and climb, and dogleg off, following their own brisk logic. The red brick sidewalks, trim housefronts with their odd angles and bays, the sensory explosion of turrets, towers, gables, domes and dormers: No other city seems quite so eccentric.

Yet there is an energy here, a sense of concentrated purpose. Not surprisingly, perhaps: Boston is, after all, the birthplace of the American Revolution and proudly conscious of that fact.

The story is hardly a secret—how, in the mid-18th century, the local citizens threw off the oppressions of British rule and embarked on a course that led, inexorably, to an independent United States. Their names sound a roll call of national patriotism: John Hancock, James Otis, Sam and John Adams, Paul Revere, among others. The landmark events—the Boston Massacre, the Boston Tea Party, the musket shots at nearby Concord and Lexington, the heroic stand on

FANEUIL HALL
The original, called the Cradle
of Liberty, was built in 1742. The
present structure, built in 1805,
encompasses the old structure.

Bunker Hill—still burn in the national consciousness. And in Boston, it all comes alive.

Much of the old colonial town has long since disappeared, to be sure. Not a house survives from the original settlement. The city's founder, John Winthrop, arrived in 1630 as governor of the newly chartered Massachusetts Bay Company and set up his headquarters on a fistlike bulge of land projecting into Boston Harbor. A rough meetinghouse, a marketplace, a dock for sailing ships and the barns and cabins of the first inhabitants—all have long since been covered over. Even Boston's shape has changed, with broad acres of landfill that have extended the shorefront.

Lodged between today's downtown high-rises, caught in a web of random streets and passageways that mark the patterns of early settlement, stand a number of 18th-century buildings, the living monuments of colonial Boston's revolutionary fervor. A red stripe on the sidewalk, the Freedom Trail, zigzags between them.

This pilgrimage route roughly chronicles the city's progress from colonial capital to revolutionary powder keg. Most visitors start at Boston's earliest surviving public building, the Old State House, which stands on the site of the first town hall. Built in 1713, the Old State House, originally the seat of Boston's colonial government, was gutted by fire in 1747 and immediately rebuilt. Now Boston's history museum, run by the Bostonian Society, it was originally the seat of Boston's colonial government.

The Royal Governor, appointed by the Crown, presided in the Council Chamber on the second floor of the Old State House. The Representatives' Hall, just across the stairwell, is where the popularly elected Massachusetts Assembly regularly met to debate and legislate. And while the governor could veto any measure he did not like, he seldom did so, for one simple reason: the Assembly controlled the budget. Too many vetoes, no more money. It was an arrangement the colonists held dear, for it allowed them to conduct their affairs as they liked. The system worked smoothly for generations—until, in 1763, it came to a screeching halt. The issue: taxes.

Throughout most of its history, the colony had paid no taxes to Britain other than a nominal tariff on imports. But even this it largely avoided. Shipowners would slip customs officials a few extra pennies to look the other way, and everyone profited. Everyone except Great Britain.

Then in 1763, Lord Grenville, Britain's Prime Minister, thought to study the account books. He discovered an astonishing fact: the colonial customs service was costing more than it brought in.

A NEW NATION'S SYMBOL
A gilded eagle, a symbol of
American independence, presides
over the west facade of the Old
State House, built in 1713.

OLD IRONSIDES
Overleaf: The U.S.S. Constitution, *the oldest commissioned warship afloat, got her nickname from the combat-proven strength of her stout oak sides, which repelled cannonballs. She was launched in 1797 and never lost a battle. Today the ship is a floating museum anchored at the Charlestown Navy Yard, but still seems ready to protect the city of Boston across the harbor.*

INFORMATION FOR VISITORS

To reach Boston, take Hwy. 95 north from New York or south from Portland, and Hwy. 93 to city center; Hwy 90 from Springfield and Albany. By air to Logan International Airport, located three miles from the city center; by train to South Station. Massachusetts Bay Transportation Authority (MBTA) buses run throughout the city; Rapid Transit System subway, known as the "T," runs on four color-coded lines (stations marked with a "T"). Sightseeing tours include bus and old-time trolley, water bus and walking.
Boston is compact and historic neighborhoods such as North End and Beacon Hill (site of the Black Heritage Trail) are located within easy walking distance of each other. The Boston Tea Party Ship and Museum are located at Congress Street Bridge (South Station subway station). U.S.S. Constitution (Old Ironsides) and Bunker Hill Monument are located in Charlestown, north of the Charles River.
Information Kiosk for the 16-stop Freedom Trail is on Boston Common (Park Street subway station). The Visitor Center for Boston National Historical Park is located at 15 State Street (State subway station). Greater Boston Convention and Visitors Bureau information centers located on Boston Common and at Prudential Plaza (Prudential subway station).
For more information: Greater Boston Convention and Visitors Bureau, Prudential Plaza, P.O. Box 990468, Boston MA 02199. (617) 536-4100.

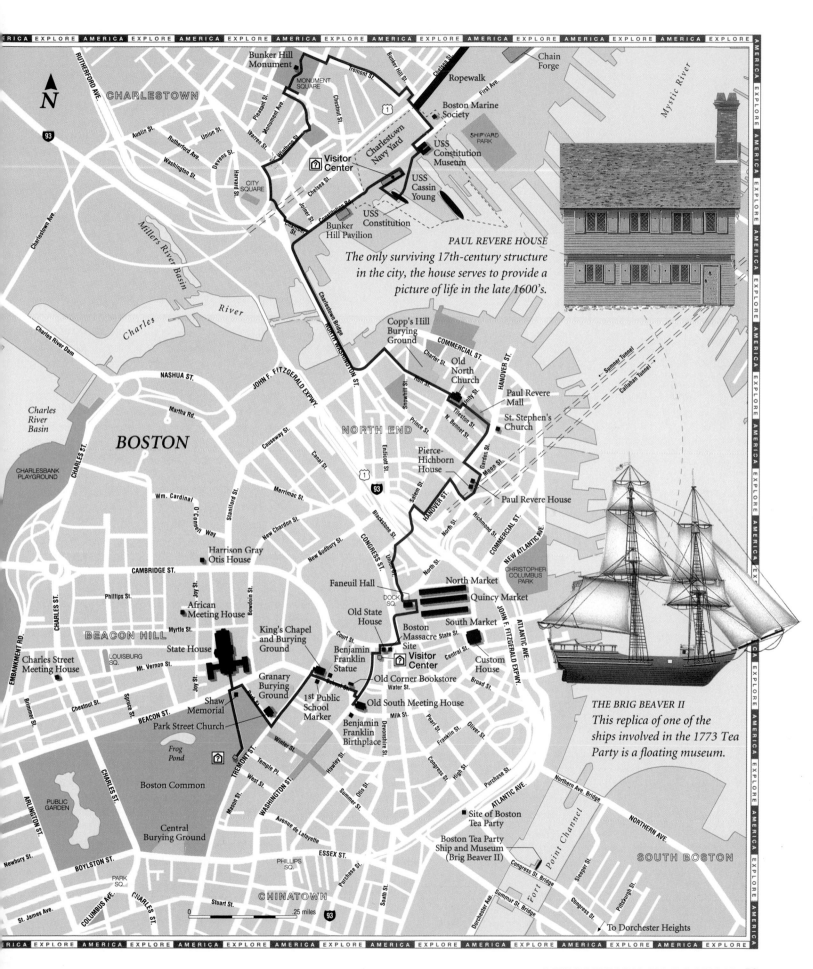

N

CHARLESTOWN

Bunker Hill
Monument

MONUMENT
SQUARE

Chain
Forge

Ropewalk

Boston Marine
Society

Charlestown
Navy Yard

USS Constitution
Museum

Visitor
Center

CITY
SQUARE

USS Cassin
Young

Bunker
Hill Pavilion

USS
Constitution

SHIPYARD
PARK

Mystic River

PAUL REVERE HOUSE
The only surviving 17th-century structure
in the city, the house serves to provide a
picture of life in the late 1600's.

Charles
River

Charles
River Dam

Charles
River
Basin

CHARLESBANK
PLAYGROUND

Millers River
Basin

BOSTON

Copp's Hill
Burying
Ground

COMMERCIAL ST.

Old
North
Church

Paul Revere
Mall

St. Stephen's
Church

NORTH END

Pierce-
Hichborn
House

Paul Revere House

Harrison Gray
Otis House

CAMBRIDGE ST.

African
Meeting House

BEACON HILL

Charles Street
Meeting House

State House

LOUISBURG
SQ.

Shaw
Memorial

Park Street Church

King's Chapel
and Burying
Ground

Granary
Burying
Ground

1st Public
School
Marker

Faneuil Hall

Old State
House

Boston
Massacre
Site

Benjamin
Franklin
Statue

Old Corner Bookstore

Old South Meeting House

Benjamin
Franklin
Birthplace

North Market

Quincy Market

South Market

Custom
House

Visitor
Center

CHRISTOPHER
COLUMBUS
PARK

THE BRIG BEAVER II
This replica of one of the
ships involved in the 1773 Tea
Party is a floating museum.

Frog
Pond

Boston Common

PUBLIC
GARDEN

Central
Burying Ground

CHINATOWN

PARK
SQ.

PHILLIPS
SQ.

Site of Boston
Tea Party

Boston Tea Party
Ship and Museum
(Brig Beaver II)

Fort Point Channel

SOUTH BOSTON

To Dorchester Heights

0   .25 miles

Then, a year later it enacted other taxes in the form of tariffs on just about everything. Again Boston protested, with proclamations, boycotts and street riots. Parliament dissolved the Massachusetts Assembly, and sent in two regiments of troops.

No move could have been more disastrous. British soldiers, outfitted in scarlet tunics, were roundly despised. Tensions came to a boil on March 5, 1770. A freak storm had dumped a foot of snow on Boston and the streets had turned to ice. A gang of youths began pelting snowballs and oyster shells at the shivering, redcoated sentries guarding the Customs House. A churchbell rang, summoning a crowd—"a motly rabble of saucy boys, negroes and mulatoes, Irish teagues and outlandish Jack tars," as John Adams, Sam's cousin, later described them. More soldiers arrived. Shots rang out. Three Bostonians lay dead on the pavement. Eight others had been wounded, two of them mortally. The victims of the Boston Massacre were carried with great ceremony to the Granary Burying Ground and placed in a common grave.

A visitor might begin at the site of the Massacre, shown by a circle of cobblestones in the traffic intersection in front of the Old State House. (The original Customs House has long since vanished.) Along the way are other venues of historic Boston.

Grenville needed funds to pay the bills from the French and Indian War, recently fought in defense of the North American Colonies. So he persuaded his Parliament to pass a Sugar Act, designed to force collection of a tariff on molasses.

The Colonies raised an indignant outcry, and started boycotting British goods. But Grenville was not finished. In 1765 he engineered the passage of a Stamp Act that levied a fee on all printed documents—land deeds and legal writs, diplomas and marriage licenses, newspaper advertisements, even playing cards. The outcry was deafening.

The flame of rebellion burned most brightly at Faneuil Hall, the next stop on the Freedom Trail. Here is where Boston held its town meetings and elected local delegates to the Massachusetts Assembly. The hall was brand new, having just been rebuilt after a fire destroyed the original structure, a dual-purpose auditorium and market arcade donated to the city in 1742 by shipowner Peter Faneuil. Inflamed by the outspoken rhetoric of Samuel Adams, Boston's citizens rallied against any measure by Great Britain that seemed to encroach upon their freedom. The logic was inescapable: Parliament had no right to tax the Colonies, because the Colonies sent no representatives to Parliament.

Faced with this strident opposition, Parliament waffled. First it repealed the Stamp Act in 1766.

FANNING THE TINDER OF REBELLION

First is Old South Meeting House, a Congregational church built in 1729 and now a non-profit museum. As the tinder of rebellion was fanned at Faneuil Hall, the preachers at Old South would ring down damnation on British rule in their Sunday sermons. ("Even the pulpits were converted into Gutters of Sedition," fumed a Royalist sympathizer.) Whenever the crowds jammed too tightly into Faneuil Hall, they would adjourn to Old South, the largest building in colonial Boston.

Turning a corner, the Trail moves on past the Old Corner Bookstore, built around 1712 as home and office by apothecary Thomas Crease and one of the city's few surviving examples of domestic colonial architecture. Its bookselling period began in the early 1800's, when it became a gathering place for such local literati as Emerson, Hawthorne, Longfellow and Harriet Beecher Stowe.

Farther up the street is the original site of the Boston Latin School, America's oldest institute of public education, founded in 1635 to teach the classics to young Puritans. In a nearby courtyard stands a bronze statue of the school's most famous dropout—Benjamin Franklin, who quit at the age of 10 to work in his brother's printing shop.

If Old South was a hotbed of sedition, the Trail's next place of worship, the 1749 edifice of King's

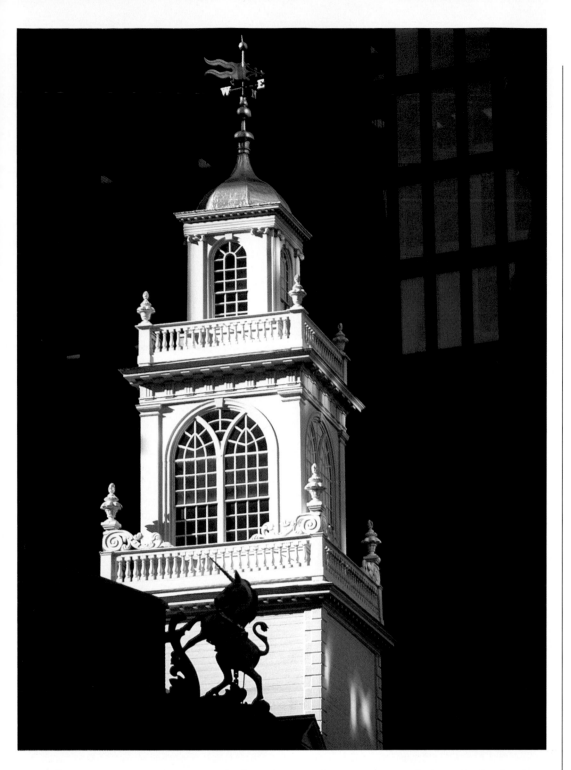

BRITISH SYMBOLS

When it was the seat of colonial government the Old State House supported statues of both the unicorn and lion, symbols of British rule. These were ripped from the roof and burned during the revolution. Today's figures are replicas. A circle of stones outside the Old State House, Boston's oldest public building, marks the spot where the Boston Massacre occurred. Below, the 191-foot-high steeple and original weathervane of Old North Church still stand as symbols of freedom. This is the tower from which hung the lanterns that warned the colonists in 1775 of the coming British attack. The church is the city's oldest standing place of worship.

Chapel, remained rock-solid Tory. The burial ground beside it is Boston's earliest and in it repose many a staunch Puritan. The Granary Burying Ground is just a few steps farther, in the shadow of the post-revolutionary Park Street Church.

Around the next corner, the city opens out onto the rolling green acres of Boston Common, the nation's oldest public park. The Common was used to graze cattle and drill the town militia—and to celebrate any victory against the British. The most lasting display of revolutionary triumph is architectural: the "new" State House, built by the great Boston architect Charles Bulfinch in 1795. It sur-

veys the Common in gilt-domed splendor from the hill at the park's northeast corner. The government of Massachusetts still meets here.

But before they won their freedom, the Colonies faced years of bloody strife. The next inflammatory crisis, in 1773, arrived at Boston Harbor in the form of three ships carrying tea. A tariff was due before the tea could be unloaded. Even worse, the tea's British supplier had received a government subsidy that, in effect, transformed it into a monopoly. Local merchants were outraged and refused to pay the tariff. The customs office would not allow the tea to land, and the governor would not

permit the ships to depart until the tea had been unloaded. Boston's citizens resolved to act. "The flame is kindled," wrote Abigail Adams, "and like lightning it catches from soul to soul."

A rally was held in Old South Meeting House on the night of December 16. A party led by Sam Adams and John Hancock—whose sloop *Liberty* had been seized in 1768 for nonpayment of customs duties—marched out of Old South and down to the wharfs, dressed as Indians. They then proceeded to dump more than a million dollars' worth of tea leaves (at today's prices) into Boston Harbor.

There was no backing down now. As punishment Parliament hit Boston with a series of painfully repressive Acts of Parliament. One banned further town meetings. Another closed the port to any type of commerce. And a full army of redcoats, under General Thomas Gage, took up bivouac in Boston Common.

Bloodshed was now certain. The rebellious Patriots began stocking arms at nearby Lexington and Concord. This General Gage could not allow. On the night of April 18, 1775, some 800 British troops crossed the Charles River basin in rowboats and started marching to Lexington. Their orders: to arrest Hancock and Sam Adams, known to be in Lexington, and then to seize the arms at Concord.

THE NIGHT OF PAUL REVERE'S RIDE

But the Patriots were a good step ahead. As the Redcoats set out, two horsemen galloped ahead to spread the news. William Dawes, a local craftsman, left Boston by the neck of land that connected it with the mainland. And Paul Revere—who also happened to be Boston's best silversmith—rowed across to Charlestown and lit out on a borrowed steed. Just in case he was caught before he could sound the alarm, Revere arranged for a signal to beam out from the steeple of Old North Church: a single lantern if the British marched out across Boston Neck and two if they should embark by water across the Charles River.

Old North Church and Paul Revere's house, in Boston's North End, are featured stops on the Freedom Trail. The house holds interest both as the Midnight Rider's workshop and dwelling—which he purchased in 1770 and lived in for 30 years, fathering 24 children—and also as Boston's only surviving building from the 17th century. Much altered over the years, it has been restored to a reasonable approximation of the 1680 original.

The next morning—April 19, 1775—Gage's Redcoats found a company of farmers armed with muskets assembled on Lexington Green. There was a hot, brief exchange of fire and eight Lexington Minutemen lay dead. The British marched on to Concord. As the vanguard British companies deployed at Concord bridge, the field opposite erupted in hot lead. The fusillade sent them reeling, ranks behind them broke and 800 soldiers of the world's most powerful empire trooped to Boston in disgrace. Massachusetts farmers had fired the shot heard around the world and had given the British a taste of things to come. For if Concord had been unpleasant, the next battle, for Bunker Hill, would be a bloodbath.

The Freedom Trail's last stop is the monument at Bunker Hill. A 220-foot granite obelisk, it rises not from Bunker Hill itself, but from adjacent Breed's Hill, site of the Patriots' earth-walled redoubt. After Concord, thousands of militiamen from the surrounding countryside and from as far afield as Connecticut and New Hampshire converged on Boston to drive out the British. The heights above Charlestown formed a strategic overlook. So here, on Breed's Hill, a large force of Americans—as many as 4,000—dug in.

The British, some 2,200 strong, landed at the Charlestown beach and then marched toward the American redoubt. An easy victory seemed in sight. They advanced to within 50 feet of the forward breastworks before a musket sounded. No one knows if the American commander truly issued his legendary order: "Don't fire till you see the whites of their eyes," but he might well have, for the discharge, at point-blank range, mowed down the British ranks like a scythe cutting hay.

The Redcoats regrouped and tried again—with the same dismal result. Only on the third attempt did they capture Breed's Hill and only because the Americans had run out of ammunition. General Gage pronounced the battle "a complete victory." But a London wit was closer to the mark: "If we have eight more such victories, there will be nobody left to bring the news."

During the next months the British hunkered down in Boston, while massive American reinforcements under George Washington prepared to smoke them out. The night of March 4, 1776, Washington's artillery occupied strategic Dorchester Heights. Two weeks later, the British left Boston for good. The celebration on Boston Common must have been mighty to behold.

NEARBY SITES & ATTRACTIONS

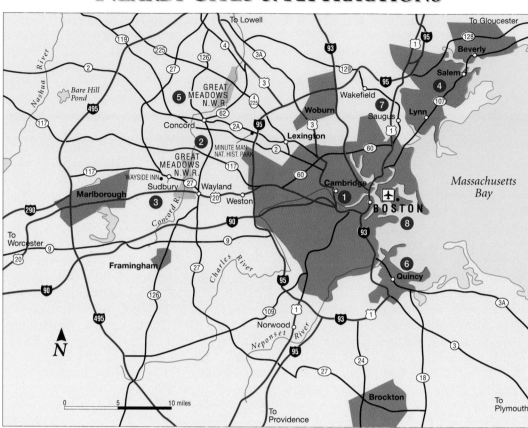

Harvard University, the oldest institute of higher learning in America, was originally founded to train ministers for the Massachusetts Bay colony. In 1640, the college established America's first printing press.

1 HARVARD UNIVERSITY, CAMBRIDGE

The oldest and one of the most esteemed institutes of learning in the country, Harvard University was founded in 1636. Its name honors John Harvard, an English clergyman who bequeathed land and his library to the fledgling college. Many of America's intellectual luminaries—William James, Oliver Wendell Holmes and Henry Wadsworth Longfellow among them—have passed through venerable Harvard Gate with its fitting inscription "Enter To Grow In Wisdom." Harvard Yard, just past the gate, contains Wadsworth House, built in 1726 and the university's second oldest structure. The university's network of museums and libraries includes the Widener Library, with more than 50 miles of shelves; the Museum of Comparative Zoology, the Botanical and the Mineralogical Museums, and the Peabody Museum of Archeology and Ethnology. It is the largest university library system in the world. Harvard's famed art collections are housed in the Fogg Art Museum, the Arthur M. Sackler Museum and the Busch-Reisinger Museum. Located in Cambridge on Hwy. 3.

2 MINUTE MAN NATIONAL HISTORICAL PARK, LEXINGTON AND CONCORD

The opening battles of the American Revolution took place at Lexington and Concord in April 1775. Minute Man National Historical Park celebrates the roles played by the two towns with numerous historic sites and museums. Visitor centers are located on Battle Road at the eastern end of the park—site of

the British victory on April 19—and at North Bridge in Concord, where the outnumbered colonial militiamen forced the British to retreat on April 19. Running battles took place between the British and the pursuing Minute Men along the four-mile Battle Road, which runs between the two towns. Henry Hudson Kitson's Minute Man statue stands on Lexington Green. Concord is also renowned for its place in American literature. Visitors can tour the restored homes of Ralph Waldo Emerson, Nathaniel Hawthorne, Louisa May Alcott and Henry David Thoreau. Located off Hwy. 2; Hwy. 2A connects the two towns.

The Robert Gould Shaw and 54th Regiment Memorial on the Black Heritage Trail is a stunning relief sculpture honoring the first black regiment to serve in the Civil War and its white commander.

③ LONGFELLOW'S WAYSIDE INN, SUDBURY

Wayside Inn has provided comfort to the traveler for close to 300 years, earning it the distinction of being the oldest operating inn in the country. The tavern got its present name from Henry Wadsworth Longfellow's *Tales of a Wayside Inn*. The building has been fully restored to its 18th-century appearance and furnished with period items and furniture. After a tour of the inn, visitors can stroll through the Longfellow Memorial Garden, an outdoor museum with an old gristmill and the red schoolhouse described in the classic children's poem *Mary Had a Little Lamb*. Located in Sudbury off Hwy. 20.

④ SALEM

Salem, one of the country's oldest settlements, was founded in 1626 by a group of fishermen from nearby Cape Ann. In the 1690's, the town was gripped by hysteria after a West Indian slave named Tituba frightened young women with tales of the supernatural. Witch House, the restored home of Magistrate Jonathan Corwin, contains the grim inquisition room where, local legend has it that, in 1692, some 200 witches were questioned. The Witch Museum dramatizes Salem's witch hunts using a multimedia sight-and-sound show. Salem is also famous as the birthplace of Nathaniel Hawthorne. The red-brick Custom House described in *The Scarlet Letter* contains the office and desk where the author worked; many of Hawthorne's family possessions can be viewed at the House of Seven Gables, made famous by the novel of the same name. Salem is located 15 miles northeast of Boston off Rte. 1.

⑤ GREAT MEADOWS NATIONAL WILDLIFE REFUGE

When the Sudbury and Concord rivers were harnessed to power a gristmill in the 19th century, the land flanking the rivers flooded and became a popular fishing and hunting region. Then, in 1989, all hunting ceased when the U.S. Fish and Wildlife Service set aside nearly 3,000 acres as a wildlife refuge. Today, thousands of waterfowl touch down during their migrations and a network of marshes and ponds supports a healthy ecosystem with foxes, deer, small mammals and indigenous bird species. Located west and north of Wayland off Hwy. 27.

⑥ ADAMS NATIONAL HISTORIC SITE, QUINCY

It is not surprising that Quincy bears the title "City of Presidents." Two American presidents were born here—John Adams and his son, John Quincy Adams. The Adams National Historic Site preserves the spacious clapboard family house where John Adams died on July 4, 1826—the 50th anniversary of the Declaration of Independence. The home is a rich repository of furnishings, furniture and paintings acquired by the Adams family over a period of 150 years. Located southeast of Boston off Hwy. 3A.

⑦ SAUGUS IRON WORKS NATIONAL HISTORIC SITE

In the early 1640's John Winthrop, son of the governor of Massachusetts Bay Colony, founded the first successful ironworks in America on the banks of the Saugus River. This carefully reconstructed national historic site helps interpret Massachusetts' important role as the cradle of American industry. The iron-making process is explained in the museum, and visitors can tour the site's buildings, which include the blast furnace, forge and blacksmith's shop. The only original building is the steep-gabled ironworks house, which dates from the mid-1600's. Located in Saugus, north of Boston on Hwy. 129.

⑧ BLACK HERITAGE TRAIL, BOSTON

After slavery was ruled illegal in Massachusetts in 1783, free blacks and abolitionists settled on the northern slopes of Beacon Hill in Boston. The neighborhood soon grew into one of the largest concentrations of freed slaves in the nation. African Meeting House, the oldest black church still standing in the United States, is the centerpiece for the Black Heritage Trail, a 14-stop walking tour that commemorates Beacon Hill's black community. The church earned the nickname the Black Faneuil Hall because of the heated antislavery meetings that took place there. Highlights of the Trail include the George Middleton House, the oldest home built by a black on Beacon Hill; the first black school (built in 1834), now the Museum of Afro-American History; the Lewis and Harriet Hayden House, an important stop on the Underground Railroad; and the Smith Court Residences, five homes owned by 19th-century black Bostonians. In Boston.

"The shot heard round the world" rang out at Concord's Old North Bridge on April 19, 1775, when colonial militiamen clashed with British regulars. The present bridge was erected in 1956.

A display of navigational instruments in Salem's Peabody Maritime Museum is a reminder of the town's links with the sea. The museum houses an impressive collection of nautical memorabilia, as well as treasures brought back by Massachusetts seafarers from the Pacific Islands and the Far East.

FEDERAL PHILADELPHIA

"Proclaim liberty throughout all the land unto all the inhabitants thereof."

On July 8, 1776, the sound of the bell in Philadelphia's State House steeple pealed out over the rooftops as the Declaration of Independence was read to a large, enthusiastic crowd in the courtyard below. That Liberty Bell, inscribed with the above proclamation of independence, is an enduring symbol of freedom and of the city of Philadelphia itself—the first capital of the United States.

Perched atop City Hall, a 37-foot-high statue of the Quaker William Penn surveys the metropolis whose name means "City of Brotherly Love." Penn established the city in 1682 as the capital of the new Pennsylvania colony. Its grid-pattern layout and wide streets created a model for future American cities. Renowned for its religious tolerance and political freedom, the city soon became home to a diverse population. As the largest and most prosperous city in British North America, Philadelphia naturally became the stage on which the drama of American freedom was enacted. Here, men like Benjamin Franklin—

A CRACKED ICON
The Liberty Bell got off to a bad start. Made by the Whitechapel Foundry of London, the bell, intended to announce important events and official town meetings, arrived intact in Philadelphia in 1752. But the first time it was rung, a crack appeared in the brim. The bell was recast and carried out its duties impeccably for 93 years. The bell, crack and all, remains a national symbol of freedom.

FRANKLIN'S NEIGHBORHOOD
Overleaf: In the 1780's, local resident Benjamin Franklin built three of the elegant row houses on Market Street, then a thriving commercial center. The houses were rented to small businessmen, one of them Franklin's grandson, Benjamin Franklin Bache, who leased 322 Market Street as an office for his newspaper, The Aurora. Benjamin Franklin, who lived nearby, divided his time between his house in Franklin Court and the State House, conveniently located just a few blocks away.

Philadelphia's greatest citizen, but an adopted son—took the momentous decisions that laid the foundations for a new nation. After visitors have spent a day or two in this lovely old city, they may well feel that Philly—as it is affectionately called—is still the historic capital of the nation.

Philadelphia's proud boast of being "the most historic square mile in America" is more than a catchy slogan; the 45 acres of land are home to 20 historic buildings and sites known as Independence National Historical Park. Designated as landmarks in 1948 and painstakingly restored over nearly three decades, the buildings and sites—all within an easy walk of each other—include Independence Hall and the Liberty Bell, two of the most popular historic attractions in the country.

Nor is all of Philadelphia's historic charm contained within the "square mile" itself. Apart from its birth-of-a-nation role, the city is rich in historical, scenic and cultural attractions. Some of these include the oldest hospital in the United States; Fairmount Park, the world's largest municipal park; the renowned Philadelphia Museum of Art; and wonderful old neighborhoods such as Germantown, Society Hill and picturesque Elfreth's Alley—the oldest continuously inhabited street in Philadelphia, dating back to 1702.

This small enclave casts its spell of the past as each year in June, the 30 lilliputian homes on the 25-foot-wide, cobblestoned alley hold open house for two days. Ladies in colonial dress and men wearing the uniforms of the Continental Army bring verisimilitude to the event. "Old soldiers" in tricorn hats, light blue tunics, knee stockings and buckle shoes carry muskets and post themselves in front of the houses to tell war stories to passersby. Some of Elfreth's tiny homes are "trinities," meaning they have only one room to a floor, three stories high. Taxation was based on frontage or width in Philadelphia in those days, so houses were built narrow and deep. Many front parlors seem no more than 10 or 12 feet wide; steep, narrow, curving stairs lead to the floors above.

But the emotional and geographic heart of Philadelphia's historic district is Independence Hall—the graceful brick structure at the heart of Independence Square. Designed in the Georgian style by amateur architect Andrew Hamilton and constructed from 1732-56, it was intended to house the Pennsylvania Assembly. Nearly two decades later, however, after the first shots of the Revolutionary War were fired at Lexington and Concord—Pennsylvania's State House was destined to play a much larger role in history.

In 1774, the American colonies were seething with discontent against England. Philadelphia became the site of the First Continental Congress,

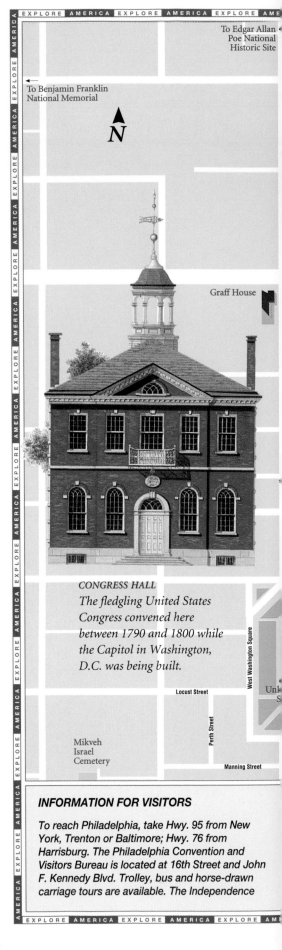

CONGRESS HALL
The fledgling United States Congress convened here between 1790 and 1800 while the Capitol in Washington, D.C. was being built.

INFORMATION FOR VISITORS

To reach Philadelphia, take Hwy. 95 from New York, Trenton or Baltimore; Hwy. 76 from Harrisburg. The Philadelphia Convention and Visitors Bureau is located at 16th Street and John F. Kennedy Blvd. Trolley, bus and horse-drawn carriage tours are available. The Independence

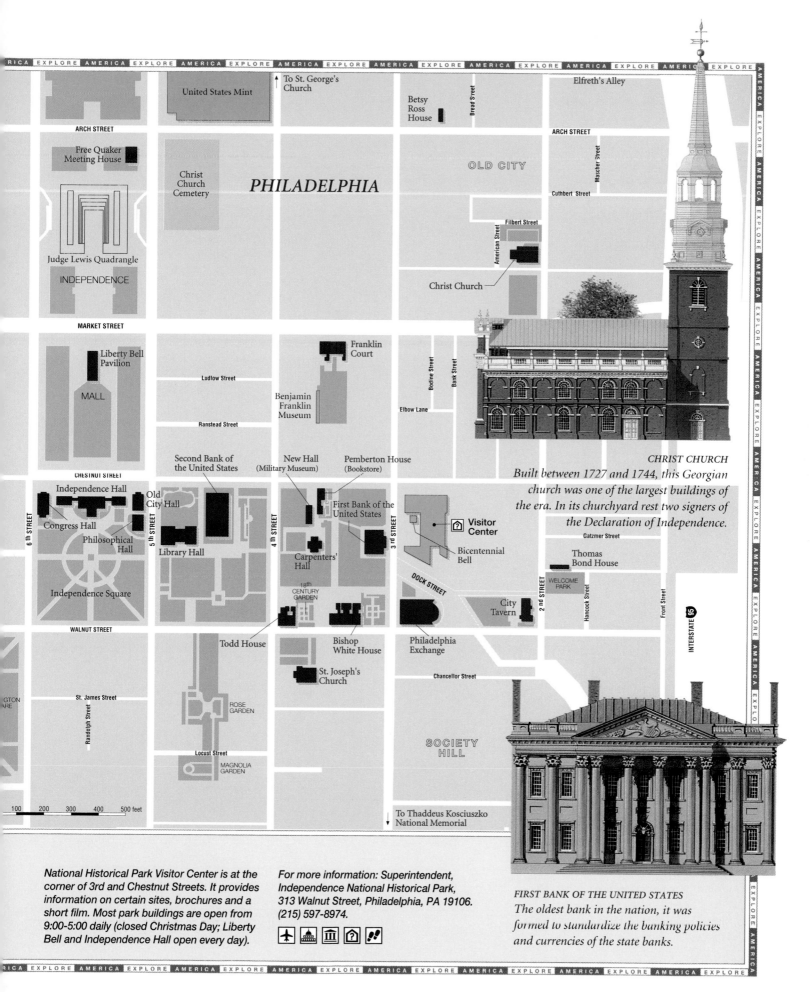

To St. George's Church

United States Mint

Betsy Ross House

Bread Street

Elfreth's Alley

ARCH STREET

Free Quaker Meeting House

OLD CITY

Mascher Street

Christ Church Cemetery

PHILADELPHIA

Cuthbert Street

Filbert Street

American Street

Judge Lewis Quadrangle

INDEPENDENCE

Christ Church

MARKET STREET

Liberty Bell Pavilion

Franklin Court

MALL

Ludlow Street

Benjamin Franklin Museum

Bodine Street

Bank Street

Elbow Lane

Ranstead Street

Second Bank of the United States

New Hall (Military Museum)

Pemberton House (Bookstore)

CHESTNUT STREET

CHRIST CHURCH
Built between 1727 and 1744, this Georgian church was one of the largest buildings of the era. In its churchyard rest two signers of the Declaration of Independence.

Independence Hall

Old City Hall

First Bank of the United States

6 th STREET

Congress Hall

5 th STREET

Library Hall

4 th STREET

Carpenters' Hall

3 rd STREET

Visitor Center

Gatzmer Street

Philosophical Hall

Bicentennial Bell

Thomas Bond House

Independence Square

18th CENTURY GARDEN

2 nd STREET

WELCOME PARK

Hancock Street

Front Street

WALNUT STREET

Todd House

Bishop White House

City Tavern

Philadelphia Exchange

DOCK STREET

INTERSTATE 95

St. James Street

Randolph Street

ROSE GARDEN

St. Joseph's Church

Chancellor Street

GTON ARE

SOCIETY HILL

Locust Street

MAGNOLIA GARDEN

100   200   300   400   500 feet

To Thaddeus Kosciuszko National Memorial

FIRST BANK OF THE UNITED STATES
The oldest bank in the nation, it was formed to standardize the banking policies and currencies of the state banks.

National Historical Park Visitor Center is at the corner of 3rd and Chestnut Streets. It provides information on certain sites, brochures and a short film. Most park buildings are open from 9:00-5:00 daily (closed Christmas Day; Liberty Bell and Independence Hall open every day).

For more information: Superintendent, Independence National Historical Park, 313 Walnut Street, Philadelphia, PA 19106. (215) 597-8974.

RICA EXPLORE AMERICA EXPLORE AMERICA EXPLORE AMERICA EXPLORE AMERICA EXPLORE AMERICA EXPLORE AMERICA EXPLORE AMERICA EXPLORE AMERICA EXPLORE

FEDERAL PHILADELPHIA 63

ELEGANT ALLEY

Eighteenth-century row houses line Elfreth's Alley, a 15-foot-wide passageway sandwiched between Front and 2nd Streets. These 33 humble yet charming colonial buildings are the oldest continuously inhabited homes in the city. The Alley houses were originally inhabited by artisans and tradesmen, and their families. Number 126, furnished with period pieces, is open to the public.

MODERN-DAY FRANKLIN

An actor, bearing a strong resemblance to Benjamin Franklin, portrays the man and his time. The 15th child of a modest Boston soapmaker, Franklin learned the printing trade from his older brother. An interest in politics made him one of the key players at the Constitutional Convention. Supporting approval of the final document, he said, "I consent to this Constitution because I expect no better and because I am not sure that it is not the best."

a gathering of representatives from the 13 colonies—Georgia excepted—convened to discuss common grievances against the British colonial regime. At first the delegates met at the City Tavern, one of the social and intellectual centers of 18th-century Philadelphia. Local radicals gathered under its streetfront awning or in one of its well-appointed club rooms to debate the issues of the day. John Adams, a delegate from Massachusetts, called the City Tavern "the most convenient and elegant structure of its kind in America." The present City Tavern, located near the park's visitor center, is a reconstruction of the original 1773 structure.

The Continental Congress soon moved from the City Tavern to the elegant Carpenters' Hall, at that time only recently completed. Of all Philadelphia's historic buildings, Carpenters' Hall must be one of the most agreeably proportioned. The three-story, cross-shaped building was opened in 1773 by the Carpenters' Company as a headquarters and meeting hall for its members. Exhibits today illustrate the tools, methods and materials that were used to build most of Philadelphia.

ROAD TO INDEPENDENCE HALL

Carpenters were the architects of the day, both well paid and well respected. They were also active in the movement for liberty and freedom from British rule. It was in Carpenters' Hall that the Congress drafted a petition asking King George III to restore their rights as Englishmen, agreed to boycott English goods and resolved to meet again the next year should their grievances not be addressed. The time for reconciliation was fast running out.

In May 1775, the Second Continental Congress convened not in Carpenters' Hall but in the State House, now Independence Hall. Fighting between the colonists and British forces had flared at Lexington and Concord in April of that year. Against this background of looming war, the delegates of the 13 angry colonies met in the Assembly Room on the ground floor. For a year, the members of the Congress, including Benjamin Franklin, John Adams, John Hancock, Sam Adams, the fiery Patrick Henry and a young lawyer from Virginia named Thomas Jefferson tried to find a way to avert full-scale war. It was not until the following summer that Congress finally voted to draft a resolution calling for complete independence.

Amid the serene red-brick surroundings of Independence Hall, America's quest for independence and freedom came of age. It was in Independence Hall that the Declaration of Independence was debated and eventually signed on July 4, 1776; where the design of the American flag was approved on June 14, 1777; where the Articles of Confederation were adopted in 1781; and where the Constitution would be forged six years later. Here the Virginia militia colonel George Washington was named leader of the Continental Army, and here Thomas Jefferson was chosen to put the Declaration of Independence into words.

The British destroyed almost all the original furniture in Independence Hall when they occupied Philadelphia during the winter of 1776-77. After careful restoration, 13 tables covered in green linen—one for each colony—are in their proper places once again. On a low platform at the front of the room is the original high-backed "rising sun" chair in which George Washington presided over

HISTORY IN THE MAKING
In 1770, construction began on Carpenters' Hall, a Georgian building constructed by the Carpenters' Company, an organization of master carpenters that still exists today. Delegates from the colonies voiced their grievances at the First Continental Congress, which met in Carpenters' Hall for seven weeks in 1774.

the drafting of the Constitution in 1787. On a table stands the original silver inkstand crafted by Philadelphia silversmith Philip Syng Jr., used in the signing of both the Declaration of Independence and the Constitution.

NOM DE PLUME
This silver inkstand was used by delegates to sign their names to the Federal Constitution. The inkstand, which survived the British occupation of Independence Hall in 1777, was designed by Philip Syng, Jr. in 1752 for the Pennsylvania Assembly.

THE GRAFF DRAFT

Just a short distance from Independence Hall is Graff House, where 33-year-old Thomas Jefferson rented two second-story rooms from a German bricklayer, Jacob Graff, during the hot, fateful summer of 1776. At that time the house stood some distance from the busy center of Philadelphia. Its seclusion suited the Virginian. For all his political genius, Jefferson had been handed a daunting writer's challenge: to put the colonies' case for independence into words.

Jefferson, hunched over a lap desk, wrote the Declaration of Independence between June 11 and June 28. Displayed in the house is a copy of his original longhand draft. In the Declaration, Jefferson wove together ideas from many sources, including English philosopher John Locke and George Mason of Virginia. After he had finished, Jefferson submitted the document for scrutiny by the Congress. Although they made remarkably few alterations, one of the most significant was the deletion of a clause renouncing slavery. On July 4, 1776, the Declaration was adopted by the Congress.

The two recreated upstairs rooms in Graff House are perfect replicas of the period. Jefferson's swivel chair and lap desk have been reproduced, and the shaving dish, watch holder, boot remover and copper foot basin in the bedroom are all objects that would have been used by him during his sojourn in the house. Piled up realistically are gift-wrapped packages sealed with sealing wax—perhaps presents bought for friends back home in Virginia.

From Independence Hall, the Independence Mall runs northward, forming the vertical bar of the park's L-shape. At the center of this sweeping panorama is the Liberty Bell, perhaps the most familiar feature of Independence National Historical Park.

The 2,080-pound bell was cast in England in 1752 in honor of the 50th anniversary of the Charter of Privileges granted to the colony of Pennsylvania in 1701 by William Penn. But when the bell was brought to the New World, it cracked. Local craftsmen John Pass and John Stow twice recast it, and the bell tolled for many years from the steeple atop State House. The name "Liberty Bell" actually dates from the 1830's, when the bell was adopted by the opponents of slavery as a symbol of freedom. But the Liberty Bell began to crack again—this time

irreparably—in the 1830's. In 1852, it was removed from the tower of Independence Hall and kept on display within the buildings. Then, in 1976, it was moved to the modern, glass-walled Liberty Bell Pavilion on the grassy mall. This low, rectangular structure displays the famous old bell and its trademark flaw in contemporary, air conditioned style—a striking contrast to the surrounding Georgian architecture.

Independence Hall and the Liberty Bell are firmly associated with revolutionary Philadelphia, but much of Independence National Historical Park belongs to the Federal period, when the newly independent colonies began to build a nation. Although the government first met in New York, from 1790 to 1800 it was Philadelphia that served as the capital of the United States. Even after the selection of the site on the Potomac River that is now Washington, D.C., many Philadelphians hoped that the offices of government would remain in their city.

Flanking Independence Hall are two distinguished brick buildings. On one side stands Old City Hall, built to be the seat of Philadelphia's city government, but taken over in 1791 by the U.S. Supreme Court when it moved from Independence Hall itself. On the opposite side is Congress Hall, where the U.S. Congress met from 1790-1800. The House of Representatives sat on the ground floor and the Senate upstairs. It is from this arrangement that the terms "upper house" and "lower house" were derived. Congress Hall was also the scene of the second inauguration of George Washington as well as the inauguration of John Adams, who was one of the moving spirits behind the Declaration of Independence.

The new nation now had a constitution, a government and a supreme court. With the construction of the First Bank of the United States in 1797, it also had a home for a national banking system. This handsome two-story structure is the oldest bank building in the U.S., and one of the first exam-

THE ORIGINAL JOHN HANCOCK
John Trumbull's painting depicts delegates of the 13 Colonies handing the unanimously signed Declaration of Independence to John Hancock, president of the Congress. Hancock had been the first person to step forward and sign the Declaration. Legend has it that he deliberately signed his name in large letters so that the King of England could read it without his spectacles.

ASSEMBLY OF IDEAS
The Assembly Room of the State House, described by one delegate as "neat but not elegant" was where the Declaration of Independence was hotly debated and finally signed on the morning of July 4, 1776. Representatives from each colony sat at one of the 13 tables, which were draped in green tablecloths.

ples of the classical style—featuring columns in the style of Greek or Roman temples—to be built in America. The exterior of the building has been restored, but the interior is closed to the public.

In 1816, the First Bank was replaced by the newly founded Second Bank of the United States. Until President Andrew Jackson vetoed its charter in 1832, the powerful Second Bank proclaimed Philadelphia's prominence as the country's financial center, as well as its political capital. Housed in a striking Greek Revival building designed by William Strickland, the bank now contains a gallery of portraits of American heroes, a veritable Who's Who of 18th-century America painted mainly by Charles Wilson Peale. Strickland also designed the Philadelphia Exchange, which is located only a stone's throw from the City Tavern. This traders' and merchants' meeting place has been called "one of the great creations of American architecture." Like the First Bank of the United States, only the outer shell of the Philadelphia Exchange has been restored. But don't feel cheated by these closed doors; there's enough history-searching to be done in Philadelphia to wear out many a pair of shoes.

BENJAMIN FRANKLIN'S PHILADELPHIA

If there is one name that will be forever associated with Philadelphia, it is that of Benjamin Franklin. Independence National Historical Park contains many sites associated with the life and work of this inventive American genius.

The young Franklin arrived in Philadelphia on October 5, 1723, a 17-year-old on the run from a harsh apprenticeship to a Boston printer. Franklin quickly began to make a name for himself as a printer, journalist and publisher. In 1732, he began to publish *Poor Richard's Almanack*, the famous compendium of common sense and homely virtues that made his fortune. After his retirement from printing in 1747, Franklin devoted himself to civic improvement, scientific research and diplomacy. He organized and financed Philadelphia's first lending library, its first hospital and fire insurance company, street lighting, local police and a militia.

He also was a leading light in the establishment of the American Philosophical Society, the oldest learned society in America, founded in 1743 "for the promotion of useful knowledge among the British plantations in America." Philosophical Hall on Independence Square remains the seat of the society today. The organization is still limited to only 300 members. Nearby stands Library Hall, a reconstruction of Philadelphia's oldest subscription library, which currently houses the library of the American Philosophical Society.

At nearby Franklin Court, the site of the great man's house, Franklin's presence is most keenly felt. The house occupied a rear courtyard off Market Street and was built from 1763-65. However, before he had a chance to live in it, Franklin was sent to England as official envoy of the colonies. He served as a diplomatic agent during and after the American Revolution and in 1785, at age 80, he returned to Philadelphia to live out his remaining years. He died in 1790, and the house was demolished about 20 years later. No drawings or architectural plans have survived, but a steel framework designed by Philadelphia architect Robert Venturi has been erected on the site to help tourists visualize the only house that Franklin ever owned. Franklin Court also contains the print shop once operated by Franklin's grandson, a colonial-style post office, the excavated remains of a tenant's house and an underground museum.

Philadelphia honors Benjamin Franklin in many different ways. Franklin is buried with his wife Deborah in Christ Church Cemetery, where it is a custom to toss pennies on his gravestone for good luck. His name is enshrined in the Benjamin Franklin Parkway and Franklin Square. A bust of Franklin, made from 80,000 pennies minted in Philadelphia and collected by schoolchildren, overlooks Arch Street; and an enormous marble figure sits in the foyer of the Benjamin Franklin National Memorial. This statue is surrounded by many of this multifaceted man's inventions and innovations, including the Franklin stove, the lightning rod, bifocal glasses and the odometer.

After a few days spent exploring the roots of America's history in Philadelphia, visitors may find that a question arises: How did it ever come about that Washington—in that arbitrary square of territory called the District of Columbia—should become the national capital? Why did Philadelphia, obviously the historic capital of the United States, ever let that happen?

NEARBY SITES & ATTRACTIONS

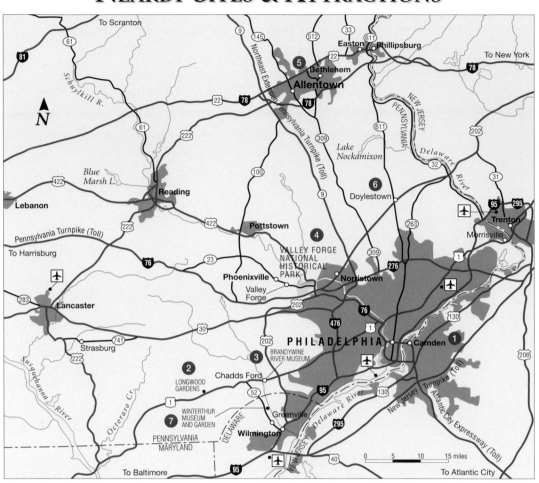

Longwood Gardens' four-acre glass conservatory, first opened in 1921, features different floral displays for each season, including spring bulbs in winter, bougainvilleas in summer, chrysanthemums in fall and a poinsettia gala at Christmas.

1 NEW JERSEY STATE AQUARIUM AT CAMDEN

The aquarium is set in a picturesque 4.5-acre park on the east bank of the Delaware River. Outdoor exhibits include a trout stream and a 170,000-gallon seal pool. Inside, a huge 760,000-gallon tank, which replicates the conditions of the open ocean, contains more than 400 fish of 40 different species including sharks, striped bass, sea robins and cow nose rays. Dive demonstrations can be observed through a window, and divers answer visitors' questions through a Scuba Phone system. Another tank features exotic fish from around the world. Located on Hwy. 676 via the Ben Franklin Bridge from Philadelphia.

2 LONGWOOD GARDENS

Acclaimed as one of the great gardens of the world, Longwood was started by the grandsons of George Peirce. Peirce bought the land from William Penn in 1700. In 1906, Pierre S. du Pont purchased the land, which he bequeathed to the Longwood Foundation for public use in 1946. Du Pont's legacy today is a 1,050-acre estate garden with exquisitely landscaped grounds and ornate flower gardens of lilies, azaleas, rhododendrons, begonias, ferns and orchids, as well as 700 acres of meadow and woodland. More than 11,000 different types of plants are grown here. Other highlights of the estate include

fountains, waterfalls and waterlily ponds. The formal Main Fountain Garden contains 380 fountainheads. Located 30 miles west of Philadelphia off Hwy. 1.

3 BRANDYWINE RIVER MUSEUM

Situated on the banks of the Brandywine River, this historic 19th-century gristmill has been transformed into an art gallery that houses works by some of America's foremost artists. On view are the illustrations of Howard Pyle, considered to be the father of modern American illustration, as well as a superb collection of N.C. Wyeth's illustrations for books by Robert Louis Stevenson and James Fenimore Cooper. A separate gallery displays major works by Andrew Wyeth; his son Jamie's works are in the gristmill. The museum also features still life and landscape paintings by William Trost Richards, John Frederick Peto and Edward Moran. Located in Chadds Ford on Hwy. 1.

4 VALLEY FORGE NATIONAL HISTORICAL PARK

George Washington's exhausted army spent the cruel winter of 1777-78 encamped at Valley Forge, 18 miles northwest of Philadelphia. Poorly fed and

Dressed in the uniform of the Continental Army, costumed interpreters reenact the cannon drills performed by Washington's troops during their winter at Valley Forge. This national historical park remains an enduring symbol of America's fight for independence.

clothed, more than 2,000 soldiers perished, victims mainly of disease. Despite these conditions, the survivors were transformed into a regiment of well-trained fighting men, thanks to the Continental Army's drillmaster "Baron" Friedrich von Steuben. Today, the 3,400-acre park includes the soldiers' original log barracks, the officers' quarters and the remains of earthworks and trenches. Artifacts, including George Washington's field tent, are on display in the visitor center. Located on Hwy. 23 near the junction of Hwys. 76 and 422.

5 BETHLEHEM MORAVIAN SETTLEMENT

Bethlehem's historic district is a unique complex of 18th- and 19th-century buildings, the legacy of the Moravian community from Germany, which settled in eastern Pennsylvania in 1741 to minister to the Native population. The Moravians are a Christian denomination, which holds that the Scriptures are the only rule of faith. The town's oldest structure, built in 1741, is the Gemein Haus (now the Moravian Museum), a five-story log dwelling. The museum contains a fine collection of the Moravians' crafts and handiwork. The Central Moravian Church, dedicated in 1806, is famous for the marvelous music played during services. Located northeast of Allentown, off Hwy. 78.

6 THE MERCER MUSEUM, DOYLESTOWN

This remarkable edifice contains more than 40,000 tools, everyday objects and crafts from pre-industrial America. These objects were collected over a period of 33 years by pioneering archeologist Dr. Henry Mercer. To house them, Mercer built the first all-concrete museum structure in the country. On exhibit are the tools commonly used by dressmakers, watchmakers, bakers, potters, wagon builders, blacksmiths, glass blowers and many other professionals and craftspeople. Located north of Philadelphia in Doylestown, off Hwy 611.

7 WINTERTHUR MUSEUM AND GARDEN

In 1926, Henry Francis du Pont inherited the family mansion, Winterthur, and began its conversion into a treasury of American furniture and decorative arts. To do so, du Pont purchased entire rooms of old houses in order to preserve their furnishings and ornamental details. Today, the museum's 200 period rooms show off his collection of furniture, glass, textiles, room paneling and silver. One room displays the Anglo-American rage for Oriental design with Chippendale "Chinese taste" furniture and wallpaper handpainted in China; another room contains a set of six silver tankards by Paul Revere. In stark contrast are an austere Shaker room and a recreated cabinetmaker's shop. Surrounding the house are 980 acres of gardens and parkland landscaped by du Pont himself. Located on Hwy. 52, 6 miles northwest of Wilmington, Delaware.

The Brandywine River Museum is housed in a former gristmill dating from the Civil War period. In 1971, the building was converted into an art gallery, and today houses an impressive collection of works by American artists and illustrators, particularly those associated with the Brandywine region. The museum boasts one of the largest collections of works by the Wyeth family. Glassed-in towers connect the floors of the museum, and afford panoramic views of the surrounding hills. The museum is administered by the Brandywine Conservancy, which also maintains superb wildflower and native plant gardens around the museum site.

CALIFORNIA MISSIONS

---

*Their adobe walls, red-tiled
roofs and flower-filled courtyards
speak of Spain's presence.*

In July of 1769, while American colonists
protested British taxation from Boston to
Charleston and planted the seeds of revolution,
history was unfolding on the western side of
North America as well. Near what is now San
Diego harbor, a Spanish friar dressed in simple
robes and sandals raised a cross and led a small
band of followers in singing a hymn and saying
a prayer. Their voices carried over the land, then
a wilderness, and filled the dry, summer air with
the promise of piety and prosperity.

The priest was Fray Junípero Serra, father-
president of the Franciscan friars in Alta
California. Serra had been entrusted by Spain
with bringing God and salvation to the Indians of
Alta California (today the state of California).
Though Serra was a small man, and no longer
young, he stood tall in vision and resolve. The
friar was ready to prevail over all obstacles. Failure
was out of the question.

Over the next 54 years, from 1769 to 1823,
Serra and his successors built 21 missions in a

chain from San Diego 650 miles north to San Francisco Solano in Sonoma. Each of the missions was within a day's travel of the next, most were near the coast, and all of them were small, self-sustaining islands of commerce and Christianity. Connecting this outstretched necklace of pearls was El Camino Real, The Royal Road, known more affectionately among those travelers who followed it as "the path of the padres."

PROTECTING SPAIN'S INTERESTS

With Serra at that first cross-raising stood Gaspar de Portolá, Spanish governor of Baja California. Portolá's presence was a sign of the importance that Spain had recently attached to the virtually unexplored territory of Alta California. Don José de Gálvez, Portolá's superior in Mexico City, understood the need to settle the territory. He reasoned that mission colonies, run by priests and protected by Spanish troops, would serve to discourage intruders, such as the Russian fur traders who had begun to venture south from Alaska.

Spanish soldiers accompanied the friars and built forts, called presidios, at San Diego, Santa Barbara, Monterey and San Francisco. While the missions were intended to convert the Indians to Christianity, they were also outposts of the Spanish empire. The Franciscans understood well that they were under royal authority. Their rivals, the Jesuits, had been expelled from Spanish territory a few years earlier due to conflict with the crown, and would be suppressed by papal order in 1773.

Serra himself lived to see the completion of only the first nine missions. But he died undaunted by the tasks ahead, convinced that his vision would continue.

And so it did. California's Indians, like the contours and climate in which they lived, were a gentle people, neither quick to work nor to fight, and it proved to be comparatively easy for the Spanish to assimilate them peacefully.

By contrast, about 250 years earlier, in 1519, the Spanish conquistador Hernán Cortés had splashed ashore with 508 soldiers near Veracruz, in present-day Mexico, and had conquered the entire Aztec empire—a highly civilized nation of 11 million who ruled an area larger than Spain—in a few short, bloody years.

Cortés and his men had ostensibly arrived in the name of God; in fact they had posed as gods for the superstitious Aztecs. But glory and gold was what they had desired most, and that they got. Thus began Spain's rapacious conquest of the Indians of North America; a beginning that hardly pleased the Franciscans. California, the friars reasoned, was an opportunity to do God's work properly, peacefully and respectfully; to perhaps make amends for the bloody past and begin a tradition of saving Indians rather than slaying them. Thus they built their missions.

Today, the Franciscan missions of California, most of them still standing in whole or in part, offer a portal into one of the most vibrant chapters in California's past. "To that composite American identity of the future," wrote poet Walt Whitman in 1883, "Spanish character will supply some of the most needed parts. No stock shows a grander historical perspective—grander in religiousness and loyalty, or for patriotism, courage, decorum, gravity and honor...Who knows but that element, like the course of some subterranean river, dipping invisibly for a hundred or two years, is now to emerge in broadest flow and permanent action?"

As the 20th century draws to a close and California's human population exceeds 30 million, a growing Hispanic culture finds its roots here. One in eight people in the United States lives in California, and many of them are of Spanish descent. Walt Whitman was right: a river has emerged—a river of humanity that struggles to maintain its cultural identity and pride, the headwaters of which can be found in the Franciscan missions along El Camino Real. While some of the missions stand today as enclaves within modern, thumping cities, others rest quietly in the countryside. Each bears witness to the past.

Their beginnings were humble: usually a simple thatched church flanked by a kitchen and storeroom and stockaded quarters for the friars, servants and single Indian women. In time, however, a tile-roofed adobe church would be built with a bell tower, or twin bell towers, made of sandstone and in some cases reaching more than 70 feet high.

And branching out from the church and sacristy, so that they created a quadrangle (with the church sitting in one of

PERFECT SETTING
Overleaf: San Miguel Arcángel Mission lies nestled in the rolling foothills of the Coastal Range. The mission's church and long monastery building are made of adobe, but the wood for the ceiling and roof beams came from the forest 40 miles away. Founded during the summer of 1797, the mission was built to fill the gap between Mission San Antonio de Padua to the north and Mission San Luís Obispo to the south. San Miguel's distinctive brick and adobe bell wall, right, is freestanding.

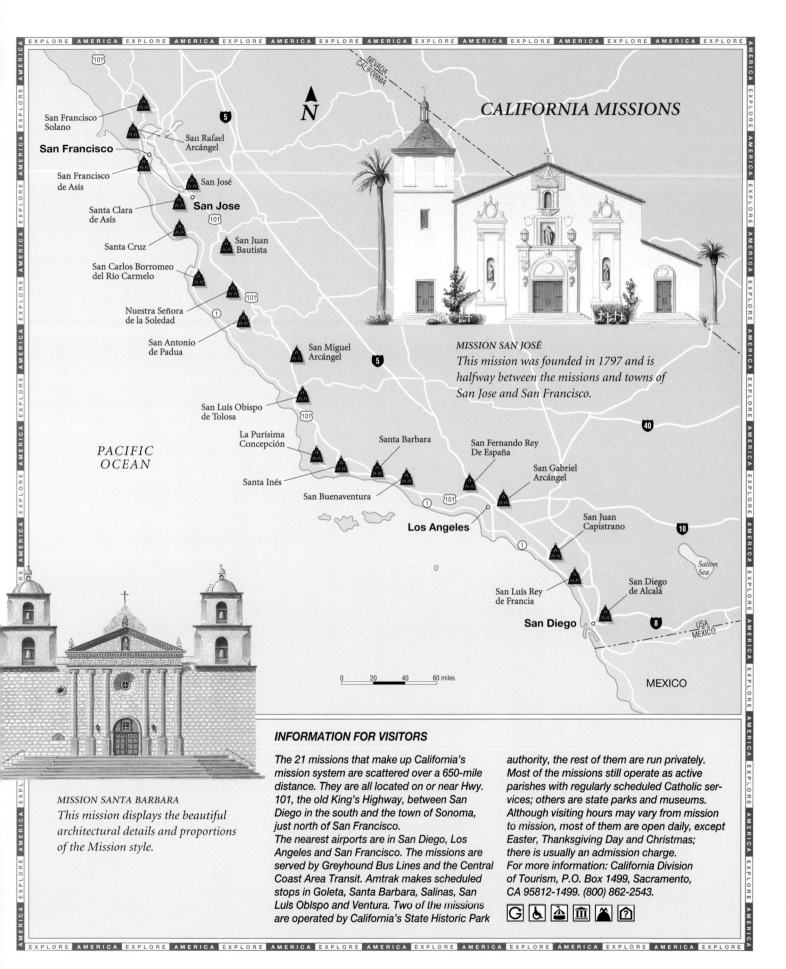

CALIFORNIA MISSIONS

San Francisco Solano

San Francisco

San Rafael Arcángel

San Francisco de Asís

San José

Santa Clara de Asís

San Jose

Santa Cruz

San Juan Bautista

San Carlos Borromeo del Río Carmelo

Nuestra Señora de la Soledad

San Antonio de Padua

San Miguel Arcángel

San Luís Obispo de Tolosa

La Purísima Concepción

Santa Barbara

San Fernando Rey De España

San Gabriel Arcángel

Santa Inés

San Buenaventura

Los Angeles

San Juan Capistrano

PACIFIC OCEAN

San Luís Rey de Francia

San Diego de Alcalá

San Diego

Salton Sea

MEXICO

NEVADA CALIFORNIA

USA MEXICO

MISSION SAN JOSÉ
This mission was founded in 1797 and is halfway between the missions and towns of San Jose and San Francisco.

0   20   40   60 miles

MISSION SANTA BARBARA
This mission displays the beautiful architectural details and proportions of the Mission style.

INFORMATION FOR VISITORS

The 21 missions that make up California's mission system are scattered over a 650-mile distance. They are all located on or near Hwy. 101, the old King's Highway, between San Diego in the south and the town of Sonoma, just north of San Francisco.

The nearest airports are in San Diego, Los Angeles and San Francisco. The missions are served by Greyhound Bus Lines and the Central Coast Area Transit. Amtrak makes scheduled stops in Goleta, Santa Barbara, Salinas, San Luis Obispo and Ventura. Two of the missions are operated by California's State Historic Park

authority, the rest of them are run privately. Most of the missions still operate as active parishes with regularly scheduled Catholic services; others are state parks and museums. Although visiting hours may vary from mission to mission, most of them are open daily, except Easter, Thanksgiving Day and Christmas; there is usually an admission charge.

For more information: California Division of Tourism, P.O. Box 1499, Sacramento, CA 95812-1499. (800) 862-2543.

the corners), would be the mission buildings: the friars' quarters, one or more storerooms, workshops and living areas for the converts.

The work was never done. Of paramount importance to the friars was the conversion of the Indians to Christianity. No sooner had construction of a chapel and crude dwellings of logs and boughs ended than did the proselytizing begin. Souls were to be saved, and the sooner the better. For enticement, the friars offered gifts of glass beads, clothing, blankets and food. However, once the Indians had embraced Catholicism, they were restricted to the mission grounds—an edict that was enforced by armed soldiers.

CONVERSION MEANT HARD WORK

The converts, called neophytes, tilled the fields, tended the livestock, and helped to replace temporary mission structures with permanent ones. Each year the Franciscans submitted a report summarizing the status of each mission. Among the entries were the numbers of cumulative baptisms, marriages and deaths; the current neophyte population; the numbers of cattle, sheep, goats, pigs, mares, other horses and mules; and the amount of wheat, barley, corn, beans, garbanzos, peas, lentils and oats planted and harvested. These meticulous reports were prepared in triplicate with copies provided for the Franciscan headquarters in Mexico City, the Spanish governor and the order's California archives.

The Franciscan master plan estimated that it would take 10 years to properly convert a neophyte from paganism to Christianity. What the master plan did not foresee—nor did the friars list this on their annual reports—was the number of Indians who died from the white man's diseases, mostly smallpox and measles. Some mission cemeteries soon contained thousands of victims, many of whom died young.

It should not have been surprising, therefore, when the Indians revolted. At Mission Santa Inés, for example, a one-day revolt in 1824 ended in the destruction of a statue of the mission patroness, Saint Agnes. Other revolts resulted in bloodshed.

PADRES AT WORK
This 1832 painting of Mission San Gabriel Arcángel by Ferdinand Deppe is one of the earliest known paintings of a California mission. Founded in 1771, the mission was one of the most prosperous; the padres and their converts worked hard at tilling the soil, tending cattle and managing the largest vineyard in the area.

SUNSHADE
An outdoor arcade runs the length of the friars' residence building at La Purísima Concepción Mission. The mission, destroyed during an earthquake in 1812, has been authentically restored. It is now run as a state historic park, complete with costumed interpreters who reenact the day-to-day life of the original mission settlement.

SHINING STAR
Situated at the mouth of the Carmel Valley and overlooking the sea, San Carlos Borromeo del Río Carmelo was the second mission to be built in the state. The Moorish style of its tower and its star window distinguish it from the other missions. It is considered by many to be the most beautiful of all the missions on The Royal Road.

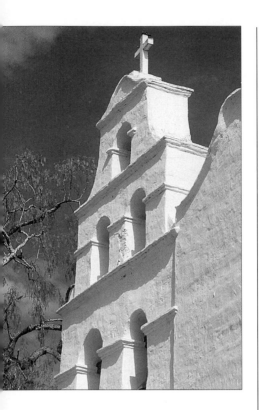

MISSION BELLS

Mission San Diego de Alcalá, the first of California's missions, was founded in 1769 by the Sacred Expedition, led by Gaspar de Portolá and Father Serra. Its adobe bell tower is just one of many that mark the path of the padres.

ARCHITECTURAL DETAILS

The ornate main chapel at Mission La Purísima Concepción, right, has been painstakingly restored. The colorful decorative details on the pulpit, walls and ceiling beams have been handpainted. Horses and cattle still graze outside the mission church, which is located in a small coastal valley near Lompoc.

Spanish soldiers retaliated, once killing 16 Indians at La Purísima Concepción. The revolts were sharp and sporadic. For the most part a peace prevailed in the California missions. Yet for the Indians it was often an uneasy peace.

What never fully dawned on the Franciscans, despite their good intentions and hard work, despite sweating in the fields side by side with their human flock, was the essential fact that they were a vanguard of one dominant culture imposing itself on another; a relatively kind vanguard, but dominant nonetheless. The friars were students of the Spanish Inquisition and practitioners of extreme asceticism. Using whips and chains as a means of persuasion was not common practice, but neither was it out of the question. The friars were in the business of executing deep cultural and spiritual changes, and their missions became the most effective way to implement those changes.

PALACES TO GOD'S GLORY

"In the still uncertain light of dawn," wrote a European visitor to Mission San Luís Rey de Francia in 1827, "this edifice has the aspect of a palace." Imagine what the Indians must have thought. Early settlers called San Luís Rey the "King of Missions." Located in a fertile valley near San Diego, the buildings covered more than six acres, and the church itself boasted a cruciform layout, an octagonal dome above the transept and lavish paintings inside on the pillars and ceilings.

Most of the missions were built facing east, to greet the sunrise. And a few, such as San Gabriel Arcángel, established fourth in line in 1771, contained elements of the Moorish architecture typical of southern Spain—capped buttresses and high, narrow windows. Attention to details was at times exquisite. Inside Mission San Miguel Arcángel, for example, a rainbow of colors brightened the ceilings and walls. And intricate paintings, completed by Indian neophytes as instructed by Spanish artist Estéban Munras, embellished the pillars, balconies, altar, pulpit and overhead beams.

There was pride in this creation, and harmony as well. Music became a focal point of mission life, as neophytes and friars would gather to play instruments at festivities, and sing songs into the dark hours of the pleasant California evenings. These were the happiest of times. The children delighted in ringing the church bells, and over the decades, as this new way of life was learned by the Indians, the old ways were forgotten. For better or worse, California would never again be the same; the Spanish were here to stay.

Despite drought, fires, even earthquakes, the missions survived. Some were destroyed and had to

CHURCH AND STATE
In the garden of Mission Basilica San Diego de Alcalá is a statue of Anthony of Padua, a 13th-century Franciscan. Sent by the Spanish government, the Franciscan padres had a mandate that was twofold: to convert the natives and to place them under Spanish rule.

The interior patio of San Carlos Borromeo del Río Carmelo is surrounded by the restored sandstone church and the mission's living quarters. The courtyard, with its splashing fountain and lush vegetation, was an oasis for the mission's friars and workers, offering them respite from the California sun.

be entirely rebuilt. They sit today where they always have, on some of the most active geologic fault zones in North America. Yet like faith itself, they stand defiant amid the changes around them. The brick and tile walkways that have felt a century of human feet shuffling over them will no doubt feel human feet for a century more. Some adobe walls and archways are cracked, moss grows on the rooftops, and the red trim is peeling, but a certain pride prevails, like the acceptance of growing old gracefully. History speaks with utter clarity here.

THE COMING OF A NEW CONQUEST

Father Serra's dream did come true. In 1829, 60 years after his first mission was founded, his friars were able to report a total of 17,000 Indian converts. The Franciscans' indoctrination of the native peoples of California—what they called "the great spiritual conquest of the wilderness"—had been achieved. But the tide would turn: a new conquest was coming. And the next chapter of California's history would belong to the Americans.

Though Mexico had won its independence from Spain in 1821, California would continue to suffer neglect as a half-forgotten outpost of a mismanaged empire. Funding for the missions grew scarce, and understaffing was commonplace. In the mid-1830's, the missions were secularized and the lands broken up for ranches. While many neophytes left the protection of the sequestered courtyards, the friars carried on with their divine mission as best they could.

It is ironic that the early Spanish inhabitants of California—descendants of the conquistadors who had plundered the gold and crushed the cultures of the Aztecs and the Incas—would themselves miss the gold veins and placer deposits of the Sierra Nevada. Those riches would go to the Americans who, like some incoming tide of historic retribution, would flood the California landscape and crush the Spanish culture.

In time, nearly every mission built by the Franciscans was abandoned to decades of disrepair. In the 1930's came resurrection, accomplished for one of the mission buildings, La Purísima, by the Civilian Conservation Corps. Thousands of California school children now visit the missions every year. Their laughter brightens the courtyards. As they step from the afternoon brightness into the cool dimness inside, they are asked to be quiet. They fall silent because something about the place commands respect. They look. They listen. They try to imagine a California of long ago; a California without television and shopping malls, a California that will never occur again, where friars and Indians worked together and played music on the edge of yesterday.

To imagine such a world can be difficult; without the missions it would be impossible.

The stretch of land between San Simeon and Carmel is framed by the crashing waves of the Pacific Ocean to the west and the stunning mountains of the Santa Lucia range to the east.

NEARBY SITES & ATTRACTIONS

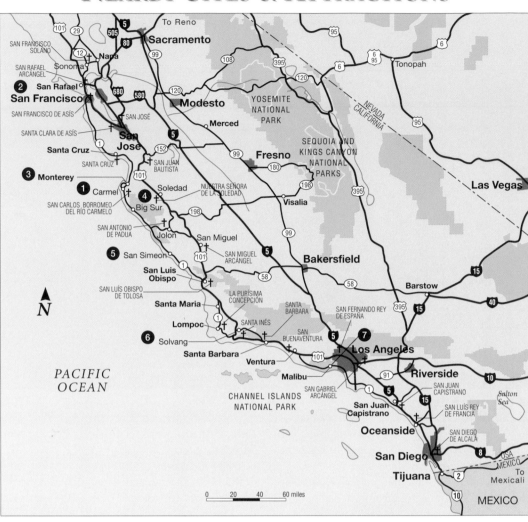

① CARMEL

Generations of artists and writers have flocked to this picturesque village since the turn of the century. Set on a sweeping bay, Carmel has been home to Jack London, Sinclair Lewis and William Rose Benét, among many others. Present-day residents strive to preserve the town's turn-of-the-century atmosphere. Streetlights and sidewalks are banned in the residential area, as are buildings of more than two stories. Carmel is the southern gateway to the Seventeen Mile Drive—a spectacular stretch of highway that winds along the Pacific Coast to Monterey. The road takes motorists past sandy beaches, wind-sculpted cypress groves and the pine woods of the Del Monte Forest. Located south of San Francisco on Hwy. 1.

② SAN FRANCISCO

In 1848, the cry of "Gold!" thundered from the Sierra foothills and changed the small trading post of San Francisco into a bustling metropolis. The city survived a devastating fire in 1906 and, with the opening of the Panama Canal in 1915, grew into the nation's great Pacific port. Century-old cable cars, still part of the public transport system, clang up the city's steep grades. The city is an eccentric mix of skyscrapers and ethnic neighborhoods that sprawl across 43 rumpled hills and fringe the city's colorful waterfront. Chinatown is the largest settlement of its kind east of Asia; store signs in Little Italy are written in Italian; and the landscaped grounds at the Japanese Tea Garden have been captivating visitors since 1894. The city contains many museums, including Alcatraz, which is open to the public. Located on Hwy. 101.

③ MONTEREY

White-washed adobe structures with red-tile roofs stand next to Victorian-era homes along Monterey's Path of History, a 2.7-mile walking tour of some of the city's historic buildings. One landmark building is the 1840 two-story adobe house where Robert Louis Stevenson stayed in the fall of 1879. Constructed in 1840, it is now a museum that displays some of the author's manuscripts, personal effects and diaries, and the desk where he penned *Treasure Island*. The adobe and wood Old Custom House, part of which was built in 1814, is the oldest government building in the state. Cannery Row, the setting of John Steinbeck's novel of the same name, is now a neighborhood of art galleries and shops, as is

The extravagant Neptune Pool at the Hearst San Simeon State Historical Monument is framed by a Greco-Roman temple facade, classical colonnades and Carrara marble statues.

Fisherman's Wharf, once a port of call for trading schooners and whaling ships. Located at the southern tip of Monterey Bay on Hwy. 1.

4 BIG SUR

Big Sur, defined as the stretch of coastline between Carmel and San Simeon, is one of the most beautiful in America. Hiking paths meander along the craggy shore and often touch the splendid beaches. The Big Sur coast is also the gateway to the 850-acre Pfeiffer Big Sur State Park, which itself is one of the entrances to the 400,000-acre Monterey District of Los Padres National Forest. The forest's network of trails weaves through the Big Sur River basin, past gorges, steep craggy slopes and tumbling waterfalls. Along the way hikers may catch sight of black-tailed deer, wild pigs, otters, minks and, very occasionally, bobcats and black bears. Although rarely sighted, brown pelicans, peregrine falcons, bald eagles and spotted owls also inhabit this area. American poet Robinson Jeffers claimed to have drawn inspiration for many of his poems from the rugged beauty of this region. Located 30 miles south of Monterey on Hwy. 1.

5 HEARST SAN SIMEON STATE HISTORICAL MONUMENT

William Randolph Hearst spent an estimated six million dollars to transform a barren hilltop into La Cuesta Encantada—a 250,000-acre complex of grounds and buildings. The palatial 115-room main house, aptly named La Casa Grande, displays his eclectic collection of ornate Renaissance, Baroque and medieval treasures. These include intricate mantelpieces, Roman sarcophagi, Persian carpets, choir stalls, one of the world's finest collections of Greek and Etruscan vases and 16th-century Venetian paintings. Some of the furniture pieces are massive. The walls of the Assembly Room are hung with precious Flemish tapestries; its 84-foot-long ceiling was carved for an Italian palazzo. Located at San Simeon on Hwy. 1.

6 SOLVANG

In 1911, Danish educators built a college on the site of the present-day town. They were followed by Danes who came here to farm the Santa Ynez Valley. The town grew up around the college, its buildings modeled on the Danish style of architecture. Today, visitors come to the town to soak up its Old European flavor. The narrow streets are lined with half-timbered houses crowned with shingled roofs and shops topped with copper roofs. One of the original windmills still works. Solvang is surrounded by rolling hills, manicured farms and stands of California oaks. Visitors to the region can tour one of the many nearby vineyards and visit Lake Cachuma, a county park famous for its large winter population of bald eagles. Located 30 miles northwest of Santa Barbara off Hwy. 101, Exit 246.

7 J. PAUL GETTY MUSEUM

One of the most richly endowed museums in the world is a monument to its founder, oil magnate J. P. Getty, who personally oversaw the purchase of the museum's collection. On display are Greek and Roman antiquities, English, Dutch, Italian and western European paintings from the 14th to 19th century, 18th-century French furniture and decorative arts, European sculptures, and illuminated Medieval and Renaissance manuscripts. Highlights of the collection are Rembrandt's painting entitled *St. Bartholomew* and Van Gogh's *Irises*. The collection is housed in a building that is modeled after a 1st century A.D. Roman villa found buried beneath the ashes of Mount Vesuvius's A.D. 79 eruption. Located in Malibu at 17985 Pacific Coast Hwy.

Golden Gate Bridge, which spans the mouth of San Francisco Bay, is held by many to be the most beautiful bridge in the world—even when the city's famous fog rolls in from the Pacific and almost blankets it.

FRONTIER SPIRIT

Entrepreneurs, including Abraham Lincoln, settled in the small Illinois town of New Salem in the 1830's.

This small cluster of log cabins in the woods never was much of a town. In fact, it was deserted not long after it was settled. Only one thing of historic importance ever happened here: in 1831 a young man named Abraham Lincoln stopped by on his way to New Orleans and decided to return to New Salem to settle down.

Lincoln's New Salem State Historic Site, 20 miles northwest of Springfield, Illinois, is an authentic recreation of the place where the 16th president of the United States grew into manhood. In his own words, he "came here as an aimless piece of driftwood." When he left, six years later, he was a lawyer and was on his way to becoming a statesman.

Lincoln's acquaintance with New Salem came about by chance. At the age of 19, young Abraham traveled by flatboat from Indiana down the Ohio and Mississippi Rivers to New Orleans. He and a friend were transporting produce and livestock to the city for sale. Lincoln enjoyed his taste of river life, and eagerly seized the opportunity

COOPER SHOP

The village cooper was an important cog in the economy. Aside from the buckets and tubs used in homes, the cooper turned out the barrels for the transportation of produce. Almost everything was shipped in barrels—whiskey and meat preserved in brine, as well as dry goods such as flour. Henry Onstot, New Salem's cooper, charged 40 cents for a flour barrel and $1.00 for a pork barrel. He moved his shop to Petersburg in 1840. In 1922 the business was relocated to New Salem.

CORNER STORE

Overleaf: William Clary's store was one of New Salem's first structures. It sold groceries, but did its briskest trade in liquor. Brandy, wine, gin, rum and whiskey sold for between 12 and 25 cents a pint. Villagers gathered here to wait for products from the mill, or for the ferry, also run by Clary. Wrestling matches and cockfights often filled the peaceful-looking glade with the shouts and cheers of spectators.

to repeat the adventure three years later. By this time the Lincoln family had moved from Indiana and had settled near Decatur, Illinois. Thomas Lincoln, Abraham's father, was never very successful at farming, and he had moved his family several times in search of a better life. In Illinois, Abe and two young relatives hired themselves to a merchant to pilot a flatboat down the Sangamon and Illinois Rivers to the Mississippi and then down to New Orleans. Their journey had hardly started when, without warning, they found their boat stranded on a dam in the Sangamon at New Salem.

The little settlement of New Salem was only a couple of years old. James Rutledge and a nephew, John Camron, had come to this area from South Carolina in 1828. They built a house, laid out a village on a ridge above the river and got permission from the state legislature to dam the Sangamon River in order to run a water-powered saw and gristmill. By the time Lincoln arrived, New Salem was a tiny but bustling hamlet counting a dozen or so structures. Most buildings doubled as places of business as well as residences.

Everyone in town turned out to watch the strangers try to pry their boat loose from its snag. It was Lincoln who eventually figured out how to solve the problem; the men simply shifted the load, drilled some holes to drain the hull, plugged the holes again and the boat slipped over the dam.

New Salem was so friendly that Lincoln and his companion Denton Offutt decided to return after their trip to New Orleans. It seemed to them that this was a place with a future. In the spring of 1831, Offutt opened a store in the village and hired Lincoln as a clerk. Abraham was then 22 years old, and this was his first home away from his parents.

In the 1830's central Illinois was raw, rough frontier country, perched on the dividing line between eastern forests and western prairie grassland. Illinois had been a state—the 21st in the Union—for only a dozen years. The 1830 census counted a little more than 150,000 people in the entire state; 10 years later the population had tripled. Settlers were on the move from east to west, flooding through Illinois in search of land and opportunity.

Villages like New Salem were very important to the opening up of the frontier. The government sold land in 40-acre lots for $1.25 an acre, but it took a lot of hard work to clear the trees, hack through the thick prairie sod, and then turn the fertile soil underneath into farmland that would support a family. The people who settled in New Salem were not farmers, but merchants and artisans who hoped to make a living as suppliers to the farmers. They offered goods and services that the farmers could not provide for themselves but which were essential to their survival. The village never

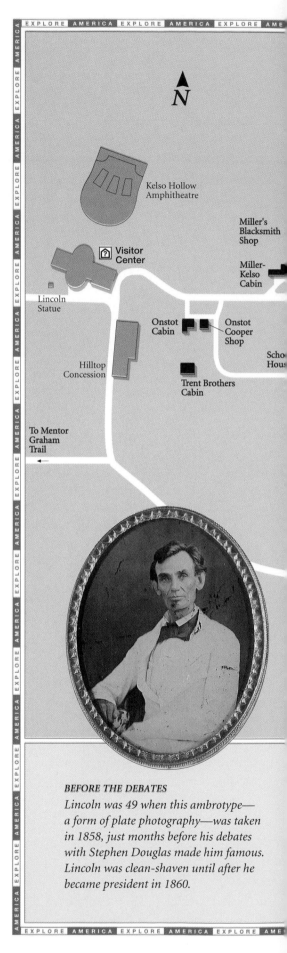

BEFORE THE DEBATES

Lincoln was 49 when this ambrotype— a form of plate photography—was taken in 1858, just months before his debates with Stephen Douglas made him famous. Lincoln was clean-shaven until after he became president in 1860.

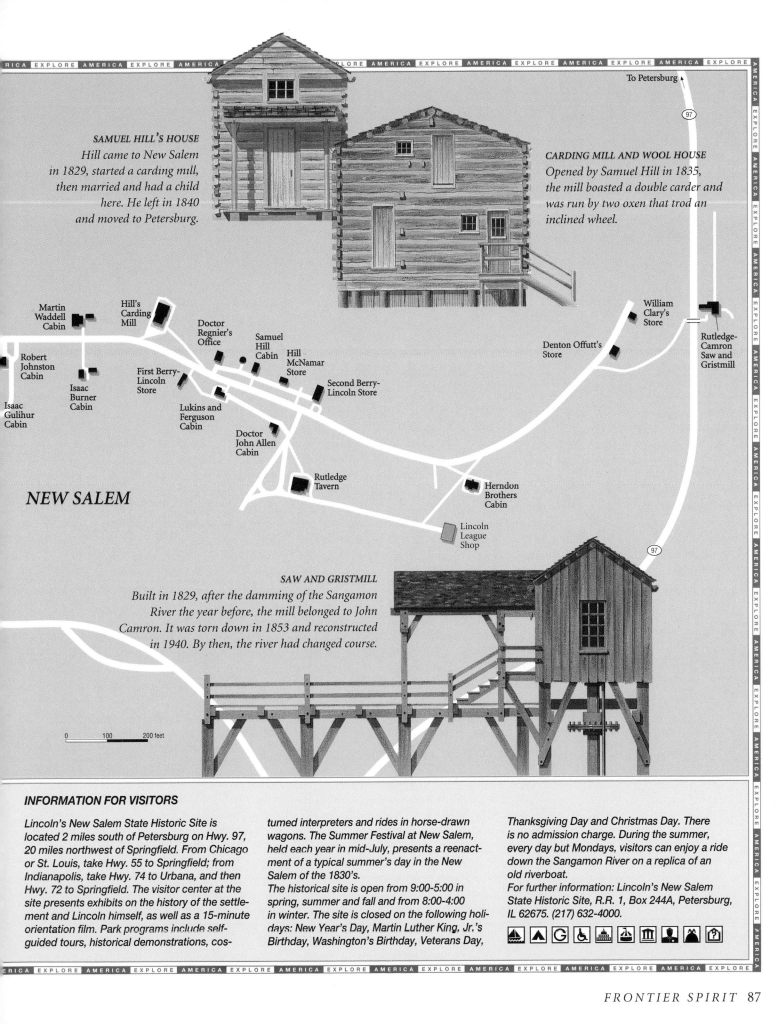

SAMUEL HILL'S HOUSE
Hill came to New Salem in 1829, started a carding mill, then married and had a child here. He left in 1840 and moved to Petersburg.

CARDING MILL AND WOOL HOUSE
Opened by Samuel Hill in 1835, the mill boasted a double carder and was run by two oxen that trod an inclined wheel.

To Petersburg

97

Martin Waddell Cabin

Hill's Carding Mill

Doctor Regnier's Office

Samuel Hill Cabin

Hill McNamar Store

Robert Johnston Cabin

First Berry-Lincoln Store

Second Berry-Lincoln Store

Isaac Gulihur Cabin

Isaac Burner Cabin

Lukins and Ferguson Cabin

Doctor John Allen Cabin

Denton Offutt's Store

William Clary's Store

Rutledge-Camron Saw and Gristmill

NEW SALEM

Rutledge Tavern

Herndon Brothers Cabin

Lincoln League Shop

SAW AND GRISTMILL
Built in 1829, after the damming of the Sangamon River the year before, the mill belonged to John Camron. It was torn down in 1853 and reconstructed in 1940. By then, the river had changed course.

97

0   100   200 feet

INFORMATION FOR VISITORS

Lincoln's New Salem State Historic Site is located 2 miles south of Petersburg on Hwy. 97, 20 miles northwest of Springfield. From Chicago or St. Louis, take Hwy. 55 to Springfield; from Indianapolis, take Hwy. 74 to Urbana, and then Hwy. 72 to Springfield. The visitor center at the site presents exhibits on the history of the settlement and Lincoln himself, as well as a 15-minute orientation film. Park programs include self-guided tours, historical demonstrations, cos-

tumed interpreters and rides in horse-drawn wagons. The Summer Festival at New Salem, held each year in mid-July, presents a reenactment of a typical summer's day in the New Salem of the 1830's.
The historical site is open from 9:00-5:00 in spring, summer and fall and from 8:00-4:00 in winter. The site is closed on the following holidays: New Year's Day, Martin Luther King, Jr.'s Birthday, Washington's Birthday, Veterans Day,

Thanksgiving Day and Christmas Day. There is no admission charge. During the summer, every day but Mondays, visitors can enjoy a ride down the Sangamon River on a replica of an old riverboat.
For further information: Lincoln's New Salem State Historic Site, R.R. 1, Box 244A, Petersburg, IL 62675. (217) 632-4000.

had more than about 24 houses, yet at its peak, historians estimate, there were nearly 200 residents.

The first business establishment in New Salem was probably William Clary's liquor store. Mr. Clary also operated a ferry service across the river. The mill owner, Mr. Rutledge, together with his wife and 10 children, ran a tavern where travelers could spend the night for a fee. Guests were given a meal and a bed for an amount fixed by law at 37 ½ cents. The conditions were cramped, however; all men, whether family or strangers, slept together in a loft and the women shared a small downstairs bedroom.

A CLEARING IN THE FOREST

By the time Offutt and Lincoln became citizens, the village had a post office, three or four stores, a shop licensed to sell liquor by the drink and a sawmill and gristmill. Residents included a doctor, a cooper and a cobbler.

Just as it appears today, New Salem was a tiny clearing in the deep woods. Deer, skunks, raccoons, foxes, rabbits and other animals roamed the forests and occasionally appeared in the village to raid the gardens. Settlers raised cows, pigs and chickens for food, and sheep for wool. All the buildings but one were made of logs — mostly white oak — cut from the forest. Other hardwood trees, such as black cherry and red oak, were used for furniture.

Samuel Hill, who ran the post office and the most successful general store in the village, built a carding mill and wool shop in 1835. The mill was powered by two oxen treading an inclined wheel. After the carding process, women and girls spun the wool into thread, dyed the thread with natural dyes made from wild and home-grown plants, and wove it into cloth on looms that could be taken apart and stored when not in use.

Spring was the time for "sugaring," tapping the maple trees in the woods and boiling the sap down for syrup and sugar. In summer and fall the women were busy, often from dawn to dark, with gardening, cooking and preserving foods. Besides the garden crops, they picked wild blackberries for jelly and cobbler and gathered sassafras twigs to use in making tea, candy and jelly.

More specialists settled in New Salem over the next few years, including a hatmaker, a blacksmith and a second doctor — this one licensed to practice surgery. Robert Johnston, who came to the village in 1832, was a particularly important artisan. He was a wheelwright, woodworker and cabinetmaker. He could repair all kinds of things, including the gears for the two mills.

Abraham Lincoln's six years in New Salem were the turning point in his life. He tried his hand at several jobs. He was the postmaster, but this did not pay very much. He and some friends served as soldiers in the Fourth Regiment of Mounted Volunteers during the Black Hawk War of 1832, during which he was elected captain of his company. He hired out as a farmhand, split rails for pay and worked at the gristmill. He learned how to do surveying work and spent some time at that. He opened a general store with a partner, but this enterprise soon failed.

Abe also found time for fun. Wrestling was a popular sport with young men, and he was pretty good at it. He also spent time in the company of Ann Rutledge, the tavern-keeper's daughter. When she died in 1835, he mourned her loss.

The law interested young Lincoln, and he spent many hours reading law books. In 1834 he made his

HOMESTEADER'S HEARTH
The interior of the Robert Johnston Cabin has been furnished as it would have been in the 1830's. Johnston, a wheelwright, woodworker and cabinetmaker, also repaired furnishings and tools for his neighbors, and made the wooden gears for the two mills in the village.

RAIL SPLITTER
Splitting rails was just one of the trades the young Abraham Lincoln tried in his six years in New Salem. The experience was put to good use in this poster created for his 1860 campaign for the presidency. The log cabin, rail-splitting image was so popular that entrepreneurs of the day sold canes and cigar holders made from "authentic" Lincoln rails.

start in politics when he ran successfully for the state legislature. Reelected in 1836, he helped to pass the legislation that moved the state capital from Vandalia to Springfield. In April 1837, one month after he had been admitted to the Illinois bar, the young politician left New Salem and went to live in the new capital city.

New Salem didn't last long after Lincoln left it. Few of the businesses there were very profitable. Several of them changed ownership as residents lost hope and drifted off in search of better opportunities. The final nail in the settlement's coffin was hammered in when nearby Petersburg was chosen to be the county seat.

By 1840 several citizens had moved their homes and businesses to the new county seat or had bought farms outside of town. Soon New Salem

was left to the birds and the squirrels and the deer, and over the next few decades, only a handful of people were aware of the historical importance of this site. One group, the Old Salem Chautauqua Association—a branch of the organization that promoted popular education—held summer meetings nearby, and in 1906 they persuaded newspaper publisher William Randolph Hearst to purchase the site and transfer it to them in trust. In 1919 the association transferred ownership of the site of New Salem to the State of Illinois.

Meanwhile, the Old Salem Lincoln League, formed in 1917, had been doing research on the history of the village. They found the Onstot Cooper Shop in Petersburg, where the family had moved it, and took it back to its original New Salem foundation in 1922. It is the only original build-

HOME AND BUSINESS
In 1835 Henry Onstot built this cabin located in the western part of town. Onstot, the local cooper, constructed his shop next door. The shop is the only original building in New Salem.

ing on the site. The League also built a road and erected several cabins, but they were not authentic reproductions.

A VILLAGE FROZEN IN TIME

In 1932 the Illinois state legislature appropriated $50,000 to begin construction of an authentic recreation of the village. Initially, 12 cabins were built. Later, the Civilian Conservation Corps completed reconstructions that included the Rutledge-Camron Saw and Gristmill, the Hill Carding Mill, Miller's Blacksmith Shop, the Church and the Schoolhouse, and built several public and service facilities. The Old Salem Lincoln League continued to collect furnishings, many of which actually had been used by New Salem residents.

Today visitors to New Salem find it easy to imagine the village as it was when young Abe Lincoln lived there. True, the dirt-colored roadways are no longer plain dusty soil, there are fewer animals underfoot and the yards are probably tidier.

But on a quiet summer morning, when the sun casts dappled shadows on the grass and birds are singing in the woods, it is as if time has stood still in New Salem. Interpreters dressed in period costumes are on hand to demonstrate the crafts and daily chores of the villagers in the 1830's. All of them are well read in the history and lore of New Salem, as well as the life of Lincoln. They explain the use of such articles as candle molds and dough chests, show how to tighten up a cord bed, and demonstrate the churning of butter. Expert quilters and weavers are busily creating works of art. Visitors chat with shopkeepers, watch a blacksmith at work, listen to a lady playing a dulcimer and singing songs from the 19th century.

One of the most popular interpreters plays the part of the schoolmaster, Mentor Graham, who taught local children in a round-log building originally located about a half mile southwest of where it now stands. Schools like his were called "subscription" schools, because parents subscribed for their children's education by promising payment in cash, food items or other services. The usual teaching method was by rote recitations. Several groups would be reciting out loud and in unison, each group reciting different words from the others. The resulting din gave these schools another nickname; they were known as "blab" schools.

A beautiful walk through the woods around the village is named the Mentor Graham Trail, in honor of the schoolmaster. Along this trail, away from the bustle of the village, visitors can see the same kinds of trees, smell the same types of wildflowers and hear the same species of warbling birds Lincoln must have observed as he tramped the paths and thought about his studies and his ambitions.

The most common view of Lincoln is that of a great leader beset with awesome problems, and with terrible decisions to make, an often melancholy man whose private life was less than blissful. But to visit New Salem is to see a different person — a sometimes carefree young man with his whole life ahead of him, on a search for his destiny. Visitors often come away with the feeling that they have actually been talking with Abe Lincoln's own neighbors and friends, and many of the site's employees and volunteers comment on the "sense of presence" they feel in New Salem.

The settlement existed for only ten years, and Abe Lincoln lived here for only six. Yet that brief period of time changed him, and altered the course of American history.

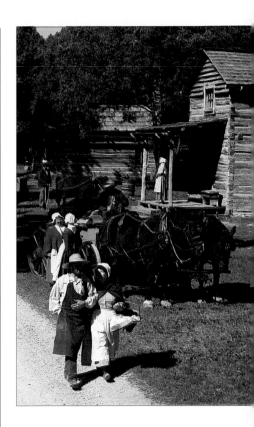

STREET SCENE
Villagers clad in 19th-century clothing carry out their day-to-day chores. Twelve timber homes, the Rutledge Tavern, 10 workshops, stores, mills and a school where Sunday church services took place line the only street in town. The interiors of the buildings have been furnished with contemporary furniture and furnishings.

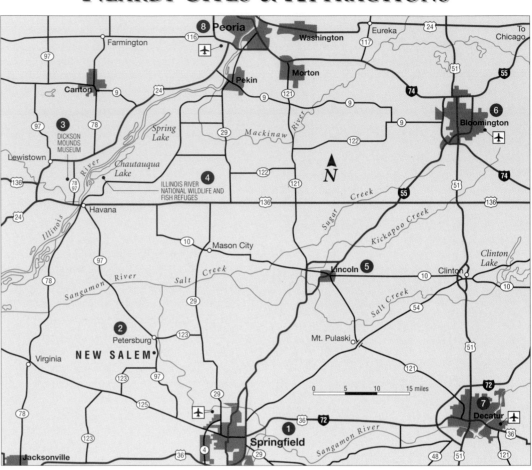

The Lincoln family home in Springfield has been maintained just as it was in Lincoln's day. Lincoln bought the house in 1844 soon after his marriage to Mary Todd. The needs of a growing family led him to add a second story to the house in 1856.

① SPRINGFIELD

Abraham Lincoln's journey into history began in Springfield. It was partly through his efforts that in 1837 the town was selected to become the state capital. There is still much here to bring him to life, starting with the plain wood-frame house built in 1839, where Lincoln and his family lived for 17 years. The bright and comfortable home was decorated by Mary Lincoln and displays family items such as Lincoln's shaving mirror, his wife's sewing box and their children's toys. The home is located in a restored four-block historic area that includes a visitor center and the homes of Lincoln's neighbors. Springfield's concentration of Lincoln historical sites includes the majestic Old State Capitol, where Lincoln gave his famous "House Divided" speech, the restored offices of Lincoln's law practice, the Great Western Depot, where the President-elect delivered his famous farewell address to his beloved city, and Lincoln Tomb, where he lies with his wife and three sons.

② PETERSBURG

Nearly half of Petersburg is listed in the National Register of Historic Places, and the town boasts many of the finest houses and public buildings in Illinois. In 1833 when George Warburton and Peter Lukins founded the new community, they accurately predicted it would someday eclipse New Salem. Legend has it that the two founders wagered on a game of cards to determine who the town would be named after. Lukins won the game and the town was christened Petersburg. The historic district's 56 homes, buildings and attractions range from a humble log cabin moved from New Salem, to spectacular Italianate-style homes. The beautiful Tiffany window in Central Presbyterian Church was almost not delivered by Tiffany because he had intended it for a west exposure and the church decided to install it on the north. Located 2 miles north of Lincoln's New Salem Historic Site on Hwy. 97.

③ DICKSON MOUNDS MUSEUM

The discovery of prehistoric Indian burial mounds on a high western bluff overlooking the confluence of the Illinois and Spoon Rivers has given archeologists important clues with which to unlock the early history of Illinois. Dickson Mounds, once a private farm owned by amateur archeologist Don. F. Dickson, is now a 162-acre National Heritage Site with a museum, five prehistoric American Indian villages, a major 2,000-year-old Middle Woodland mound burial site and the 10-mound Dickson cemetery, which is 1,000 years old. Using weapons, tools and pottery found on site, the museum traces the lifestyle, ceremonies and settlement patterns of the Indians in the

Illinois River valley. Festivals, workshops, tours and some archeological excavations demonstrate Native American culture and rural life. Located between Lewistown and Havana, off Hwys. 78 and 97.

4 ILLINOIS RIVER NATIONAL WILDLIFE & FISH REFUGES

The fertile lowlands, sandy bluffs and sedge marshes surrounding Lake Chautauqua are a major staging area for enormous concentrations of waterfowl and other birds that replenish themselves here during fall migration. Some 20,000 geese, 100,000 mallards, and large numbers of wood ducks, shovelers, mergansers and northern pintails are among the visitors. Eighty bald eagles winter here, and summer residents include herons and egrets, mourning doves and American finches. In all, some 250 bird species frequent the area. A walk along the sanctuary's interpretive trail offers the possibility of observing deer, foxes, opossums, and many other more elusive small mammals. The refuges' wide range of environments support an exceptional variety of wildflowers, grasses and trees. The gathering of blackberries, raspberries, nuts and mushrooms is allowed in designated areas. A boat launch at the recreation area serves sport fishermen. Located 6 miles northeast of Havana on Manito Road.

5 LINCOLN

In 1853, the good citizens of the Postville area asked their legal adviser, Abraham Lincoln, if he would agree to be chosen as a neighboring town's new namesake. He christened the town with the juice of a watermelon, cautioning that he "never knew anything named Lincoln that amounted to much." Though there are other Lincolns, this town is the only one named with the great man's consent and participation. The Lincoln College Museum houses one of the nation's most extensive collections of Lincoln memorabilia, displaying more than 2,000 volumes, manuscripts and other items. A tour of Postville Courthouse brings to life the legal system of Lincoln's time, and an interpretive program describes how Lincoln came to the town twice a year to practice law during the years when Postville was the county seat (1840-48). Located on Hwy. 55 between Bloomington and Springfield.

6 DAVID DAVIS MANSION STATE HISTORIC SITE, BLOOMINGTON

One of the most opulent Victorian homes still standing in the U.S. is Clover Lawn, a 20-room yellow brick mansion built in 1872 by David Davis, 8th Circuit Court judge and intimate of Lincoln. Davis was instrumental in securing Lincoln the Republican nomination in 1860, and was later appointed to the U.S. Supreme Court by the President. Clover Lawn was designed in the Italian style by architect Alfred Piquenard. The interior of the home is nothing short of dazzling, and includes eight marble fireplaces (one of sparkling white Carrara marble), walls patterned with stencil-painted designs and sumptuous furnishings. Several of the house's

features were innovations in their day: a central hot-air, coal-burning furnace, flush toilets fed by an attic water reservoir and closets with built-in drawers. Located at 1000 East Monroe in Bloomington.

7 DECATUR

Visitors to Decatur can enjoy a rich and diverse collection of architecture representing almost all the styles popular in Illinois from the Civil War to the Great Depression. Three walking tours explore an 80-acre tract of buildings listed in the National Register of Historic Places. For a look at some of the articles that graced these homes, the Birks Museum displays more than 1,000 pieces of porcelain, including some rare pieces dating back to the 15th and 16th centuries. At the Macon County Historical Museum Complex visitors can poke around a recreated prairie village with an 1860 log cabin, a working 1900 blacksmith shop, a train depot and an 1830 courthouse. The 1,343-acre Rock Springs Center for Environmental Discovery, at the southwest edge of the town, preserves an 1860's prairie farm where nature lovers can hike, fish and cross-country ski.

8 JOHN C. FLANAGAN RESIDENCE, PEORIA

Peoria, the oldest settlement in Illinois, is the only city over which four flags—those of France, Spain, Britain and the U.S.—have flown. The town's oldest standing residence, John C. Flanagan House, was built in 1837 on the bluffs overlooking the beautiful Illinois River valley. The primitive kitchen, children's room and carpenter shop are furnished with pre-Civil War and late 19th-century antiques, china, toys and textiles. Curtains, wallpaper, quilts and carpets of the period from 1830 to 1890 and a costume collection are highlights. The Federal-style brick home is maintained by the Peoria Historical Society and is its headquarters. Located on Glen Oak Ave., in Peoria.

More than 10,000 Canada geese touch down in the Chautauqua area of the Illinois River National Wildlife & Fish Refuges from late November to early December.

The present Postville Courthouse, in the town of Lincoln, is a replica of the original wood-frame building that was purchased by Henry Ford for his Greenfield Village Museum.

CONFEDERATE CHARLESTON

---

*This charming city of the
Old South played a starring role
in the War of the States.*

Scarlett O'Hara hated it. Josiah Quincy, a real-life visitor from Puritan Boston, clucked his tongue over its "magnificence, and ostentation." Others have called it arrogant, quick-tempered and stubbornly racist. It was, after all, the birthplace of the American Confederacy. But Rhett Butler, in the closing reel of *Gone With the Wind*, could not wait to get home to Charleston, "where there's a little bit of grace and charm left in the world." And Rhett was right.

No other city in America manages to carry the past with such easy, well-bred elegance. From the neo-classical porticoes of its antebellum mansions, its tree-shaded streets and marketplaces, to the modest stucco town houses of Catfish Row—inspiration for George Gershwin's *Porgy and Bess*—Charleston retains the magnolia-scented ambiance of a more gracious era. More than 2,000 houses in its historic district date from before the turn of the present century. Some are still occupied by descendants of their original owners. Not a single high-rise mars the skyline

IRON-CLAD DESIGN
The iron balconies, fences and stair rails which adorn Rutledge House, at 116 Broad Street, were made by Christopher Werner, one of Charleston's most skilled iron artisans. The house was built before the revolution, and was designed to be used for official functions by John Rutledge, president of the Republic of South Carolina. The ironwork, added in 1853, bears the state's palmetto tree symbol as well as the federal eagle. Legend has it a famous Charleston delicacy, she-crab soup, was invented here.

MANSIONS WITH A VIEW
Overleaf: A graceful row of mansions along the Battery glitters in the glow of a setting sun. Built by well-to-do merchant-planters from the 1820's to the 1850's, these year-round residences overlook Charleston Harbor. At 4:30 a.m. on April 12, 1861, homeowners had center-stage seats from which to view the Confederate assault on Fort Sumter.

and no structure reaches above the tip of the tallest church steeple.

The miracle is not that so much of Charleston's past survives, but that the city exists at all. Few places anywhere have been so beset by misfortune. Shortly after the first colonists arrived—in 1670—and set up housekeeping on a point of land between the Ashley and Cooper Rivers, a hurricane swept through, all but wiping them out. It was the first of many great storms. Then, in 1697, an earthquake hit. The next year it was fire, which destroyed one-third of the colony. Epidemics added to the misery. But much worse lay ahead.

| BRITISH BATTLES |

From The Battery, at the southernmost tip of the Charleston peninsula near the site of the early town, a park stretches back from the sea wall. Sunday picnickers spread their blankets there in the shade of live oaks. Behind rise the colonnaded piazzas of the great city homes, built by families with names such as Pinckney, Drayton, Rhett and Ravenel.

Seaward, across the expanse of Charleston Harbor and beyond a far spit of land, lie the grassy embankments of Fort Moultrie. Early in 1776, the colonists hurriedly constructed a redoubt of earth and palmetto logs on Sullivan's Island to defend the harbor from an impending British attack. It came on June 28, seven days before the signing of the Declaration of Independence. Fifty warships sailed into the harbor and began pounding Fort Moultrie with heavy guns. The defenders fired back, and the fleet sailed off. But victory was temporary.

Four years later the British returned, marching up the coast some 8,000 strong, and laid siege to Charleston. For an entire month British artillery bombarded the city, raining down fire and death. Then the redcoats moved in to take possession. When they departed, at the war's end, they carried off silver, books and the bells of St. Michael's Church. And the city lay in ruins.

Another citadel, on a small islet across the ship channel from Fort Moutrie, also guards the entrance to Charleston Harbor. From the vantage point on The Battery it can be made out—the low silhouette of Fort Sumter in the blue morning haze. It was built in the mid-1800's, one of a series of coastal defenses designed to protect the U.S. from attack by foreigners. But the first salvos came from Americans. In the wee hours of April 12, 1861, Confederate gunners at Fort Johnson and other nearby points opened fire at a Union garrison on Fort Sumter, launching the nation into the most bitter and devastating conflict of its entire history.

It seemed that no one wanted the Civil War, but no one knew how to avoid it. For well over a cen-

INFORMATION FOR VISITORS

To reach Charleston from Columbia, SC and Asheville, NC, take Hwy. 26. From Savannah, take Hwy. 95, which connects with Hwy. 17. From Myrtle Beach, SC and Wilmington, NC, take Hwy. 17 along the coast. Charleston's airport and Amtrak station are both located in North Charleston. The Visitor Center is located at 375 Meeting Street across from the Charleston Museum and is open 8:30-5:30 p.m., seven days a week; closed Thanksgiving, Christmas, New Year's Day. It provides information and tickets to many of the city's attractions, as well as tickets for the Downtown Area Shuttle (D.A.S.H.) service, which runs throughout downtown Charleston. Sightseeing tours are available by boat, bus and mini-bus, horse-drawn carriage, foot or by air. Boats to Fort Sumter National Monument leave from City Marina on Lockwood Blvd. and from Patriots Point Naval and Maritime Museum in Mt. Pleasant.
For more information: Charleston Area Convention and Visitors Bureau, P.O. Box 975, Charleston, SC 29402. (803) 853-8000 or (800) 868-8118.

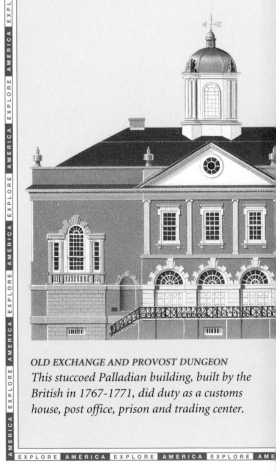

OLD EXCHANGE AND PROVOST DUNGEON
This stuccoed Palladian building, built by the British in 1767-1771, did duty as a customs house, post office, prison and trading center.

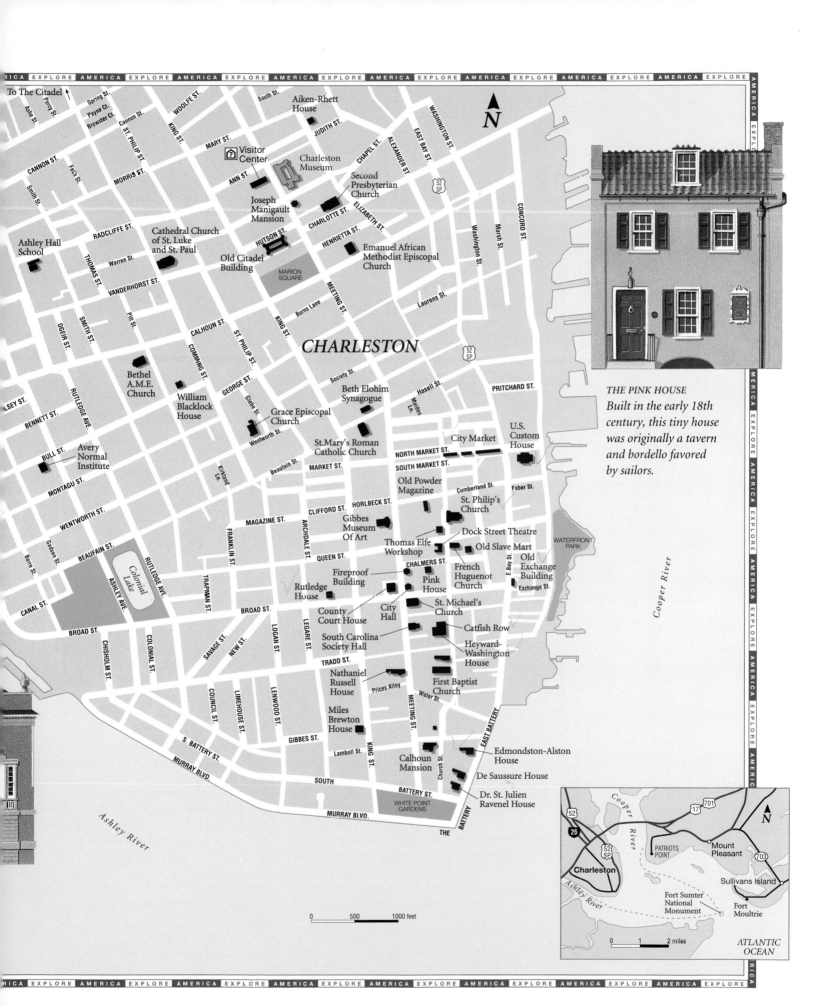

THE PINK HOUSE
Built in the early 18th century, this tiny house was originally a tavern and bordello favored by sailors.

RICA EXPLORE AMERICA EXPLORE AMERICA EXPLORE AMERICA EXPLORE AMERICA EXPLORE AMERICA EXPLORE AMERICA EXPLORE AMERICA EXPLORE

CONFEDERATE CHARLESTON 97

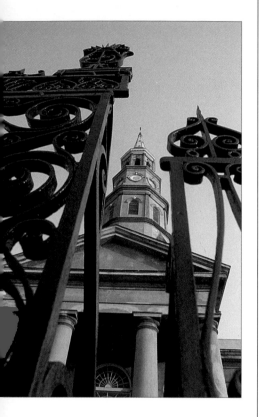

LIGHTHOUSE CHURCH
St. Philip's is known affectionately as "the lighthouse church." A light shining from its steeple helped to guide sailors into Charleston harbor. The federal government maintained the beacon until the early 1900's. St. Philip's has been a presence on Church Street since 1723. The present church was rebuilt from 1835-38, following a disastrous fire.

tury the prosperity of the Old South, and of Charleston especially, rested on the agricultural bounty produced by thousands of African slaves. Vast tracts of South Carolina lowlands were cleared and marshes drained in order to grow rice and indigo—the region's first cash crops. Black labor did the job. The profits went to plantation owners and to Charleston merchants who shipped the rice to England. The sums were enormous. By the time of the American Revolution, Charleston was the fourth-largest city in the Americas, and one of the richest. It was also a principal slave market.

SIGNS OF DECLINE

The system continued to flourish through the early 1800's with a new crop—cotton— edging out rice as the main export. But already there were signs of decline. New plantation lands in Alabama and Mississippi began yielding bumper crops and by the 1830's New Orleans had emerged as the South's busiest seaport. As Charleston's market share dwindled, the city took on a ragged, windblown aspect—too poor

to paint, and too proud to whitewash, as the saying goes. It reminded English actress Fanny Kemble, visiting in 1838, of "a distressed gentlewoman...a little gone down in the world, yet remembering still her former dignity."

Along with their declining bank accounts, Charlestonians faced an additional threat: a large and increasingly restless black population. Of the city's 24,780 inhabitants in 1820, more than half were either slaves or black freedmen. Persistent rumors of a slave rebellion began to circulate. One such plot came to light in 1822, sending the city into panic. The town fathers pushed through strict laws curtailing the movements of blacks. To maintain order, they opened an arsenal, The Citadel— still an important training school for military cadets.

Meanwhile, the institution of slavery itself was coming under attack. Already the slave trade from Africa had been banned by federal law. Now reformers in the North were calling for total abolition. Such a move seemed intolerable to Charleston. Not only was it no business of Northerners how the city conducted its affairs, but

freeing the slaves would bankrupt landowners and cause untold civil havoc—or so many white Charlestonians believed.

The debate raged in town meetings, in the halls of Congress and in editorial pages throughout the land. In 1847, John C. Calhoun—his grandson's mansion graces Charleston's Meeting Street— harangued the U.S. Senate in slavery's defense. Each state, he declared, had the right to control its own destiny. Other grievances, including a tariff that raised costs for planters, widened the split between North and South. As the voices grew louder, the battle lines hardened, and in 1860 South Carolina and several other Southern states called for the ultimate act of defiance: withdrawal from the Union.

Wiser heads urged caution. "South Carolina is too small for a republic and too large for an insane asylum," warned James Petigru, one of Charleston's last Unionists. Others predicted ruination and bloodshed. But as the clamor mounted, secession became all but certain.

South Carolina was the first to go. On December 20, 1860, following the election of Abraham Lincoln as President, the state's leading citizens met in Charleston's St. Andrews Hall, and voted to secede. The 10 other states of the Southern Confederacy followed suit. The deed was done.

A small Union garrison manned Charleston's harbor fortifications. Its commander, Major Robert Anderson from Kentucky, was himself a former slave owner. But above all Anderson was a soldier, sworn to defend his country. And the most tenable patch of U.S. soil in the area was the newly

PINK PALACE
The mansion at 5 East Battery was built around 1849 for the planter-scientist Dr. St. Julien Ravenel, whose son helped design a torpedo vessel for the Confederacy in the front room. The house is one of the great mansions built along the waterfront. Although the massive pink walls measure 32 inches in thickness, they were nearly destroyed during an earthquake in 1886. Colonnaded porches, called piazzas, were used as outdoor rooms, allowing Ravenel and his family to enjoy the refreshing ocean breeze.

PERFECT HARMONY
The ornate music room in the Calhoun Mansion at 16 Meeting Street boasts a 45-foot-high ceiling with a coved glass skylight. The 35-room house was completed in 1878 and later acquired by Patrick C. Calhoun, grandson of John C. Calhoun, the Charleston lawyer famed as a fiery nationalist and defender of slavery.

OPENING ACT
A hand-colored contemporary engraving shows Confederate soldiers at Fort Johnson bombarding Federal troops in Fort Sumter. The battle marked the beginning of the Civil War. Fort Sumter withstood the onslaught for 34 hours, until garrison commander Major Robert Anderson surrendered to Confederate forces under Pierre Beauregard.

erected bastion of Fort Sumter. Fort Sumter today is a peaceable outpost of the National Park Service, a 20-minute boat ride from the Charleston docks. But in 1860, it was formidable. It was one of the strongest fortresses in America. Anderson moved his troops—all 85 of them—to Fort Sumter and settled in to wait for help.

As the leading city in its own nearly independent state, Charleston found the Union presence intolerable. When the first Union relief ship approached the harbor, local shore batteries sent it fleeing. Weeks passed. Anderson's supplies ran low and the general in charge of Charleston's forces, Pierre G.T. Beauregard, encircled the fort with Confederate guns. Years earlier, when Anderson had taught gunnery at West Point, Beauregard had been his pupil; the two men had become close friends. Now Beauregard demanded Anderson's surrender.

A CITY AT WAR

Beauregard's final ultimatum reached Fort Sumter about midnight on April 12, 1861. At 4:30 a.m. a Confederate mortar shell arched through the sky and burst overhead. For 34 hours the shelling continued; more than 3,300 projectiles crashed down on Fort Sumter. Anderson fired back as best he could. Then he bowed to the inevitable. Down came a tattered Old Glory. Up went the Palmetto banner of South Carolina. The Civil War had begun.

During the war's early years, most of the fighting raged elsewhere—in Virginia to the north, and west along the Ohio and Mississippi Rivers. Charleston remained untouched, except for a fire that swept through in December of 1861 and burned up 575 houses. Rising above this misfortune, the city began a feverish round of drum-beating Southern patriotism. Always a party town, it held picnics and supper dances and fancy dress balls for the Confederate soldiers stationed there. It became a major supply port for the Confederacy, with swift blockade runners dodging past the cordon of Union warships that attempted to patrol its seaward approaches.

Then came the spring of 1863. Determined to enforce the blockade, a Union armada of nine iron-clad gunboats swept down in early April. Their target: Fort Sumter. Over the following months the Union navy returned again and again to unleash its fire. At the same time, Federal troops closed in from the south and set up siege guns in the nearby marshes. For two weeks in August the Federal artillery subjected the fort to almost incessant bombardment, reducing its walls to rubble and inflicting 323 casualties. And still the Confederate flag continued to flutter from ruined parapets.

If Fort Sumter stood as a symbol of Confederate valor and defiance, a second stronghold—Battery Wagner, on the tip of nearby Morris Island—took on another kind of significance. On July 18, 1863, three Union brigades hurled themselves against Wagner's guns. Leading the assault was the 54th Massachusetts Infantry, a regiment of free black volunteers under Boston abolitionist Colonel Robert Gould Shaw. "We shall take the fort or die there!" cried Shaw as he charged across the sands. And die he did, along with half of his troops. But even in defeat, the 54th won a victory for the Union cause. From then on, no one disputed the bravery of the black soldiers or their eagerness to lay down their lives for freedom.

The ultimate Federal goal was Charleston itself. Between volleys at Fort Sumter, the Union gunners turned their sights on the city, taking their range from the steeple of St. Michael's Church. Most of the beautiful mansions in the downtown

CANNON POWER
A row of Civil War cannons point through Fort Sumter's moldering breastworks toward the shipping channel beyond. When war broke out, only 15 of the 135 guns planned for the fort had been mounted. Some 70,000 tons of rock were used in the fort's construction, including 10,000 tons of granite (some shipped from as far away as the granite quarries of Maine). Its five-foot-thick masonry walls rose 50 feet from the ground, to more than twice their present height. The fort's living quarters, now in ruins, could accommodate as many as 650 men.

The Dock Street Theatre stands on the site of one of the nation's first playhouses. The original theater of 1735—simply called the New Theatre—was demolished early in the 19th century to make way for the old Planter's Hotel. (Legend has it that the planter's punch cocktail was invented in the hotel bar.) The present Dock Street Theatre, which reopened on February 12, 1936, encompasses the restored hotel and a reconstruction of an early Georgian playhouse.

area, the docks, the slave market, the Exchange Building where President Washington had danced the night away in 1791, were raked by Union fire. Residents moved north of Calhoun Street, beyond the reach of the guns. Any excursion to their old homes, said one, was "like going from life to death."

In February of 1865, Charleston finally surrendered. By then the tide of war had turned decisively against the South. The armies of General William Tecumseh Sherman had captured Atlanta, and put it to the torch. Now they were in Columbia, South Carolina's capital, leveling it to the ground. "Should you capture Charleston," a friend had written Sherman, "I hope that by some accident the place may be destroyed."

A TIME OF RECOVERY

Sherman bypassed Charleston, but an accident did occur—a fire that broke out at a railroad depot on the Cooper River and raged uncontrollably through the northeast part of town. It was the war's grim parting gesture. By early April the conflict was over. It had caused untold misery and devastation, and taken the lives of 620,000 Americans. Five days after the South capitulated, Robert Anderson—now General Robert Anderson—returned to Fort Sumter to raise the same torn Stars and Stripes he had lowered four years earlier.

As after so many other disasters, both natural and self-inflicted, Charleston began picking up the pieces. New dwellings replaced the debris of war. The mansions that survived—the Nathaniel Russell House, for example, and the Joseph Manigault Mansion, both now open to public view—had their brickwork patched and their columns restored. The port was rebuilt and trade resumed.

But recovery would take many decades. Most of the great plantation houses in the surrounding lowlands, with the spectacular exception of Drayton Hall, built in 1742 and now a National Historic Landmark, had been demolished by Union troops and their croplands laid waste. Starvation threatened. Even the city's most patrician families faced years of poverty. But, like Scarlett O'Hara, they looked ahead to another day.

They also looked back. Theater had always played a starring role in Charleston's social life: the old Dock Street Theatre, built in the 1730's, was a leading center of dramatic arts in colonial America. Now, a new Academy of Music opened on King Street. (Charleston continues the tradition with its Spoleto Festival U.S.A., held each year from late May to early June.) The St. Cecilia Society, founded in the 18th century to encourage music, resumed its annual full-dress party.

Understandably, the social pace was a bit less frenetic than in earlier times. No one could equal the great spread that Mrs. Charleston Alston had laid out for her 200 guests in the 1850-51 winter season: 50 partridges, 12 pheasants, 22 ducks, 10 quarts of oysters, plus turkeys, hams, pyramids of coconut and crystallized fruits and an endless flow of champagne. She had the space for it, to be sure, as a visit to the Edmondston-Alston neo-Classic mansion on East Battery will attest.

Perhaps that is just as well, given Charleston's early reputation for high living. "Cards, dice, the bottle and horses engross prodigious portions of time and attention," groused old Josiah Quincy, down on a visit from Boston just before the Revolution. A guest in the antebellum period was shocked to note that "their principal amusements in the City in the morning is Billiards...and in the Evening cards and Segars," all accompanied by herculean amounts of refreshment.

But even as Charleston struggled to recover, new cycles of disaster caught the city with jarring regularity. A hurricane roared through in 1885, with 125-mile-an-hour winds and a tidal surge that caused 21 deaths and flooded the houses along the Battery to a depth of six feet. The following year, the city was shaken by one of the largest earthquakes in national memory. Some 12,000 chimneys toppled to the ground, 100 buildings were destroyed beyond repair, and 2,000 more suffered substantial damage. One hundred and ten people died.

Partly because of such great setbacks, the economic decline of the post-Civil War era lingered on until well into the present century. In one sense, this was the city's salvation: lack of funds helped save it from the bulldozers of modern development. Then, in 1920 a local citizen's group formed the Society for the Preservation of Old Dwellings, which was committed to saving what remained of the city's former glory. Its Old and Historic District Ordinance, passed a decade later, was the first zoning law in America designed to protect a community's architectural heritage. And so Charleston remains a delight to the visitor—"unrepentant and proud," in the words of local historian Robert Rosen, and a living, vibrant heir to a gracious and heroic past.

HOLY CITY
Charleston deserves its nickname of "the Holy City"—its skyline is defined by the soaring spires of churches such as St. Michael's, seen here. It is the city's oldest house of worship. The church was completed in 1761, and its 182-foot-tall octagonal steeple has done double duty as the city's fire lookout. The steeple's eight bells have tolled the hour for more than 200 years, interrupted only by the Revolutionary War, when they were carried off by the British, and during the Civil War, when they were removed to Columbia, South Carolina, and later damaged by fire.

NEARBY SITES & ATTRACTIONS

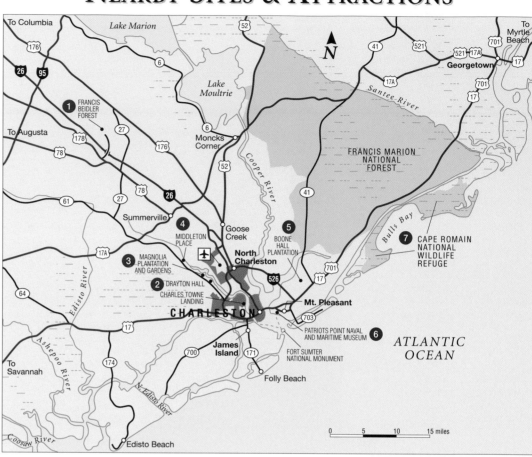

❶ FRANCIS BEIDLER FOREST

This 6,000-acre refuge, located in Four Holes Swamp, contains the world's largest virgin stands of bald cypress and tupelo gum trees. Some of the ancient cypresses tower 120 feet above the flooded forest and are estimated to be up to 1,500 years old. A 1½-mile boardwalk allows visitors to explore a small portion of this watery, mysterious maze; interpretative signs provide information on the local flora and fauna, which includes alligators, watersnakes and fish-eating spiders. Naturalist guides take experienced canoeists to the interior of the swamp (reservations needed). Northwest of Charleston off Hwy. 178.

❷ DRAYTON HALL

John Drayton built his plantation home adjacent to his father's estate between 1738 and 1742. It was owned by his descendants until 1974. The red brick mansion is one of the finest examples of Georgian Palladian architecture in America, and is the only home on the west side of the Ashley River to have survived both the Revolutionary War and the Civil War intact. Tours of the house highlight the two-story portico, intricate door and window moldings, and an ornate, hand-molded, 18th-century plaster ceiling. Located 10 miles northwest of Charleston on Hwy. 61.

❸ MAGNOLIA PLANTATION AND GARDENS

This plantation was built by the Drayton family in the 1680's, but the manor house burned down twice, the second time when General Sherman's troops set it afire. The current pre-revolutionary house was moved to the plantation from Somerville. Magnolia Plantation is renowned for its 50 acres of lawn and garden—the country's oldest colonial estate garden. During spring, 250 varieties of azaleas bloom; the gardens include camellias so old they are trees, a topiary garden, an 18th-century herb garden and, of course, magnolias. Located 10 miles from Charleston on Hwy. 61.

❹ MIDDLETON PLACE

The oldest, and unquestionably the most beautiful, formal landscaped garden in the U.S., Middleton Place was begun in 1741 by Henry Middleton, president of the First Continental Congress. The 65-acre garden comprises ornamental waterways and lakes, sweeping sculptured terraces and spectacular displays of exotic flowers. A walkway leads to an ancient "Middleton Oak," believed to be 1,000 years old. Other highlights include the original springhouse (built in 1741), a prerevolutionary rice mill, and the tomb of Middleton's son Arthur, one of the signers of the Declaration of Independence. Most of the original Georgian mansion was destroyed during the Civil War. The south wing, which survived, is a museum

Rustic bridges draped with wisteria and pathways that meander along the Ashley River help to weave Magnolia Plantation's unique spell. In addition to the estate's famous flower gardens, Magnolia Plantation includes a replica of a maze designed by King Henry VIII.

housing priceless silver, china, furniture and works of art collected by the Middleton family. Located 14 miles northwest of Charleston on Hwy. 61.

⑤ BOONE HALL PLANTATION

The quarter-mile approach to Boone Hall is lined by stately moss-draped live oaks, and is appropriately known as "Avenue of Oaks." The vista is one of the most beautiful in the South, and the famous home to which it leads has been featured in several television series. Major John Boone, one of Charles Towne's first settlers, established a 17,000-acre cotton plantation here in 1681. Today, the plantation's 738 acres still grow timber and wheat. In 1935, the house was completely rebuilt with vintage bricks made on the plantation. One room was rebuilt with the original flooring and handhewn beams. Among the original plantation buildings still standing are nine slave cabins dating to 1743, a circular smokehouse and the cotton gin house. Located 8 miles east of Charleston off Hwy 17 North.

⑥ PATRIOTS POINT NAVAL AND MARITIME MUSEUM

The mighty *USS Yorktown* saw active duty from 1943 to 1970. Today, the aircraft carrier is the star attraction of Patriots Point, the world's largest naval and maritime museum. *USS Yorktown*'s vast hangar deck houses bombers and fighter planes, along with historical displays and memorabilia collected by the crew. An Academy Award-winning film, *The Fighting Lady*, shown on board, describes the ship's illustrious military history. The flight deck provides a magnificent view of Charleston with Fort Sumter in the distance. As well as the huge flattop, the museum's collection includes a destroyer, a submarine, a Coast Guard cutter and the nuclear-powered cargo ship *Savannah*. Tour boats for Fort Sumter leave from here. Located at Patriots Point, Mount Pleasant, at the east end of the Cooper River bridges.

Boone Hall's Avenue of Oaks was planted in 1743 by the son of the estate owner, Captain Thomas Boone.

⑦ CAPE ROMAIN NATIONAL WILDLIFE REFUGE

Most of the 20-mile stretch of barrier islands and salt marshes that make up this remote wildlife sanctuary are inaccessible by land, making it an excellent habitat for close to 300 bird species, including almost every species of Atlantic shorebird. Threatened sea turtles and pelicans lay their eggs on the beaches here, and dolphins explore the streams and inlets. Before the days of European settlement, the area was a popular hunting and fishing domain for the Seewee Indians. Today, the area remains an unspoiled refuge not only for birds, but also for white-tailed deer and raccoons. Visitors can take a day trip by boat to Bull Island, where they will enjoy excellent bird-watching opportunities, nature walks and fishing. Located 20 miles northeast of Charleston off Hwy. 17.

Middleton Place's blend of Georgian architecture, carefully landscaped gardens and ornamental lakes was created by a landscape architect brought over from England by the estate's owner, Henry Middleton. Legend has it that it took 100 slaves 10 years to complete the gardens.

Gold Rush Country

A fabulous discovery in a Montana valley brought fame and fortune to Virginia City.

On a late afternoon in May, 1863, Bill Fairweather and his companions were feeling down on their luck. Earlier they had run into trouble with Crow Indians who had kept them captive for three days before ordering them to leave the territory. Hungry and tired, they were stumbling back toward the gold camp of Bannack, in what would become Montana, when they stopped beside a stream to do some prospecting. Scooping up a little dirt, Fairweather said to his friend Henry Edgar, "See if you can get enough to buy some tobacco when we get to town."

Tobacco indeed. There was gold in that dirt—more than those early prospectors could imagine. They named the valley Alder Gulch, and it turned out to be the richest placer deposit in history, eventually giving up an estimated $130 million worth of nuggets and flakes and dust. At today's prices, the value would approach $2.5 billion—all from the gravel of a single stream bed only 17 miles long and in places less than 100 yards wide. It was a fabulous find. Once news got

TOWN WITH A PAST
Overleaf: Virginia City seems to be in a state of suspended animation, perhaps waiting for the Wells Fargo stagecoach to pull in. This preserved western mining center recalls the days when gold fever gave birth to hastily constructed towns whose fortunes rose and fell with the amount of dust and nuggets the land gave up.

JUST REWARD
Outlaw Boone Helm was tried and hanged from a beam of an unfinished building by the Alder Gulch Vigilantes. Several other outlaws of the day were buried near him in "Boot Hill" just outside Virginia City. Townsfolk stopped using the cemetery in 1867, either because it was getting crowded or because they felt that its occupants were bad company to keep into eternity.

out, thousands of hopeful prospectors poured into the gulch. By the end of the summer of 1863, a string of towns had popped up—Summit, Ruby, Adobetown, Nevada City, Central City, Virginia City and others.

Then, as happened in so many other western gold camps, the lights gradually went out. Mining returns diminished, and people drifted away to new centers of activity. It's an old story, but here with a different twist. By a lucky set of circumstances, much of the original Virginia City, as built that long ago summer, remains standing—the largest number of original buildings on their original sites surviving in any town in America.

The discovery of Alder Gulch came during the Rocky Mountain gold rush, a period of frantic activity lasting only about 10 years. The excitement began in 1858, when rumors of Colorado gold brought thousands of prospectors swarming into the tent city that was to become Denver. There was no gold in Denver, but the next spring when George Jackson let it leak out that he had found paydirt up in the mountains along Clear Creek, the rush was on for real.

Jackson's discovery was the first Rocky Mountain bonanza. It set off a decade-long dance, a sort of frenzied western two-step performed by thousands of men hoping to take a whirl with Lady Luck. She smiled on the first few to arrive at Clear Creek, but latecomers found all claims taken, and no room to sink a shovel. But there were other valleys, other mountain ranges, other chances. As one gold camp filled with miners, the overflow ran west, over the ridges, deeper into the mountains, north to Idaho, south to New Mexico—wherever rumors and chance happened to lead.

Around campfires and along the trails, the men heard stories of strikes yielding gold by the pound and even the ton. The stories fed their enthusiasm but made them anxious because they knew opportunities were limited, that the gold would run out, and that only a few would strike it rich.

The best thing to do was keep on the move, keep digging for gold, and listen for news. And in the summer of 1863, the big story was Alder Gulch in the sage-covered foothills of a place that wasn't yet named Montana.

Within a year of discovery, there were 30,000 people strung out along the gulch, an ebullient mix of miners, hustlers, merchants and hangers-on. The miners dug the gold while the others, through a variety of stratagems, dug the miners. In effect, the towns were secondary mining operations designed to harvest the rich supply of "pocket gold."

And harvest it they did. Miners needed food, clothing and entertainment. They bought ready-made clothing. They ate in restaurants. They drank

'NEW' MASONIC TEMPLE
Made of cut stone, the temple was built in 1867. The U.S. Post Office has been on the ground floor since 1916.

INFORMATION FOR VISITORS

From Hwy. 90, take Hwy. 287 south to Ennis, then Hwy. 287 to Virginia City. From Hwy. 15, take exit 59 for Dillon, and proceed along Hwy. 41 to Twin Bridges, which connects with Hwy. 287 to Virginia City. From West Yellowstone, Hwy. 20 connects with Hwy. 287 to Ennis and Virginia City. The nearest airports are at Butte and Bozeman. Hwy. 287 connects Virginia City

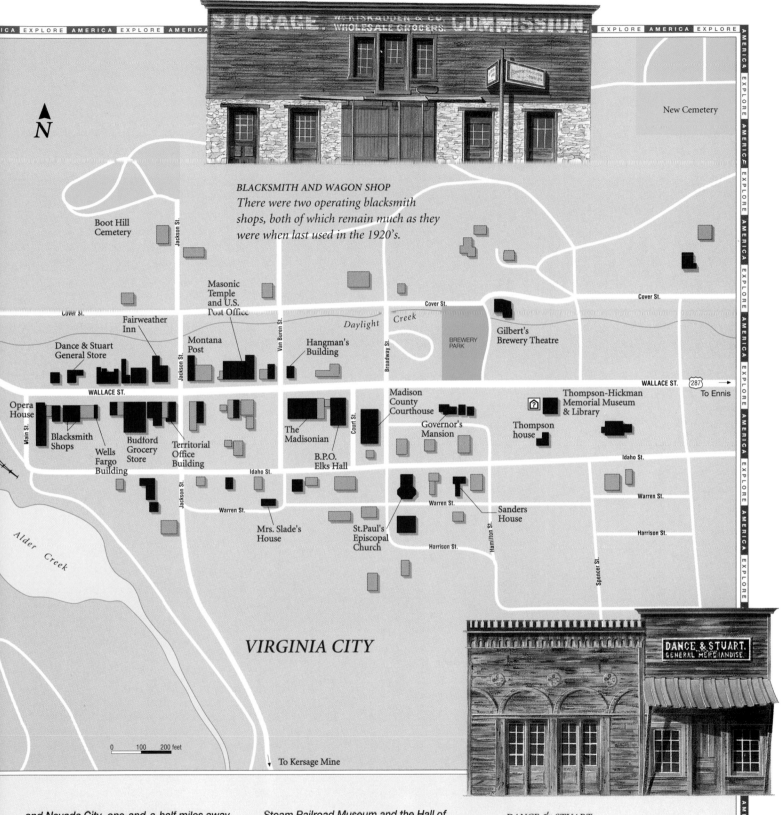

STORAGE. Wm RISKADDEN & Co. WHOLESALE GROCERS. COMMISSION.

N

New Cemetery

BLACKSMITH AND WAGON SHOP
There were two operating blacksmith shops, both of which remain much as they were when last used in the 1920's.

Boot Hill Cemetery

Jackson St.

Masonic Temple and U.S. Post Office

Cover St.

Fairweather Inn

Daylight Creek

Cover St.

Dance & Stuart General Store

Montana Post

Van Buren St.

Hangman's Building

Broadway St.

BREWERY PARK

Gilbert's Brewery Theatre

Cover St.

Cover St.

WALLACE ST. 287 To Ennis

Opera House

Main St.

WALLACE ST.

Madison County Courthouse

Thompson-Hickman Memorial Museum & Library

Blacksmith Shops

Budford Grocery Store

Wells Fargo Building

Territorial Office Building

The Madisonian

B.P.O. Elks Hall

Court St.

Governor's Mansion

Thompson house

Jackson St.

Idaho St.

Idaho St.

Idaho St.

Warren St.

Mrs. Slade's House

St. Paul's Episcopal Church

Warren St.

Sanders House

Warren St.

Harrison St.

Harrison St.

Hamilton St.

Spencer St.

Harrison St.

Alder Creek

VIRGINIA CITY

0   100   200 feet

To Kersage Mine

and Nevada City, one-and-a-half miles away, and a working narrow-gauge railroad runs between them. Both cities offer visits to period buildings. A theater in Virginia City puts on 19th-century melodramas nightly during the summer. Visitors can pan for gold at the Alder Gulch River of Gold, located a half mile from Virginia City, just off Hwy. 287. The Alder Gulch Short Line

Steam Railroad Museum and the Hall of Mechanical Music Machines are in Nevada City. The sites are open from May to September. For more information: Virginia City Chamber of Commerce, P.O. Box 217, Virginia City, MT 59755. (406) 843-5555.

DANCE & STUART, GENERAL MERCHANDISE.

DANCE & STUART
James Stuart, one of the partners in this general store, was panning for gold in Alder Gulch before the gold rush began.

ICA EXPLORE AMERICA EXPLORE AMERICA EXPLORE AMERICA EXPLORE AMERICA EXPLORE AMERICA EXPLORE AMERICA EXPLORE AMERICA EXPLORE

GOLD RUSH COUNTRY 109

great quantities of anything with alcoholic content, and sought bordello pleasures to compensate for the hard life of the mining camps.

They paid for it all with loose gold carried in leather pouches and measured more or less accurately by the ounce. Stories tell of shopkeepers who grew long fingernails so they could trap extra dust when weighing out payments; and of Chinese laundrymen who panned their washwater and made extra on the gold that was in the pockets and cuffs of miners' clothes. Later, when saloons went out of business, people ripped up floorboards to recover gold that had fallen through the cracks.

There was one other way to obtain gold, and Alder Gulch was to become famous for the practitioners of this alternate method. The method was robbery, and the chief robber was none other than the sheriff. He was an ex-convict named Henry Plummer, a smooth-talking ladies' man who had come to Virginia City by way of New England, California and Idaho. Behind him he left a trail of ruined families, dead bodies and highway robbery.

BOOMTOWN BREW
Many of Virginia City's inhabitants met regularly at Gilbert's Brewery. Built in 1864 during the town's heyday, the brewery operated until Prohibition.

SUPPLIES AND SPIES
Today the interior of Dance and Stuart's general store is much as it was except for the absence of the desperadoes who once gathered here. Clubfoot George Lane had a shoe repair stand in the store where he would gather information on the quantities of gold stored on the premises and pass it on to his thieving cohorts.

In the mining camps he joined with men of his ilk, desperate characters running loose beyond the reach of lawful authority. Witness Boone Helm. According to one story, he had left Idaho with five other men, but none of them survived the trip. There were rumors of cannibalism on the trail, and stories of Helm's gruesome bone collection.

Plummer was a bad apple in a rotten barrel, and in the course of their Alder Gulch depredations, he and his gang killed perhaps 100 people and made off with untold quantities of gold. Plummer kept his dual identity a secret, playing the upright peace officer on one hand, and tipping off his confederates with inside information on the other. They had the run of the gulch. One of their hangouts, a saloon now called Robber's Roost, can be seen on the highway north of Nevada City.

At last, the more honest citizenry had suffered enough. Incensed by the murder of a young teamster, the townspeople organized a miner's court and went after George Ives, one of the gang and the man they accused of killing the teamster. Ives was hauled back to Nevada City, tried and condemned by the light of a bonfire. He was hanged in the moonlight.

QUICK WORK BY THE VIGILANTES

Following that event, a vigilante committee was organized to finish the job. Before it was over, they hanged at least 22 men. Five, including the notorious Boone Helm, were taken in Virginia City in January of 1864. Tried in a matter of hours, they were hanged that afternoon from the beam of a half-completed building that still stands on Wallace Street, its famous timber exposed for inspection. Above town stands "Boot Hill," where those five were buried. Unmarked, the graves were later identified when the bodies were exhumed, and the unique foot of Clubfoot George Lane was removed to the local museum, where it remains on exhibit. Plummer was hanged in nearby Bannack on a gallows that he, as sheriff, had intended for others.

The real significance of Virginia City lies not in its Wild West antics, but in the way it developed from a boisterous mining camp into a community with respectable, long-range dreams—a good example of how the Rocky Mountain region came to be settled. The system of industry, agriculture and transport that grew up to support mining eventually became the dominant economy of the region, and Virginia City figured to be at the heart of things. In 1864, it became Montana's first territorial capital. It boasted the territory's first school, its first newspaper, its first published book, and it expected to become the state capital once Montana was admitted to the Union. Alas, the bright future faded rather quickly.

After about 10 years, the placer gold of Alder Gulch began to diminish. The easy pickings had been taken, and many successful miners and business owners took their winnings and left town. Some moved to Helena, the state capital, or to Butte, site of the world's largest copper mine.

This is not to say that gold mining died in Alder Gulch after its first decade. It took some 60 years to exhaust the possibilities, and even then mining never totally disappeared. Almost from the start there was underground mining in the nearby mountains (the richest mine of all was Kearsarge, said to produce quartz ore worth thousands of dollars a ton). When white miners got impatient with diminished yields, they sold out to Chinese miners who were content with smaller but steady profits. After that, enormous dredges collected millions from paydirt that the pick-and-shovel miners had missed. Yet none of this could support the activity of those first heady years and eventually, of all the gulch towns, only Virginia City survived as a func-

PANNING FOR PAYDIRT
Panning for enough gold dust to buy tobacco in 1863, two weary prospectors hit paydirt in Alder Creek. Within a year, thousands of miners flooded the area. Today visitors can still try their luck in the creek.

tioning—but much shrunken—community. By 1960 its residents numbered a scant 192.

All but forgotten, Virginia City drifted into a sleepy stagnation, a picturesque little town tucked in the foot hills of the Tobacco Root Mountains. The story might have ended right there, except for a lucky set of circumstances that saved one of the town's most important features—its history.

Today, the gray, weather-beaten stores and houses fronting on Wallace Street remain much as they were nearly a century-and-a-half ago. The structures and their contents survive because for one thing, the boom came and went quickly. The population fell so fast that there was never a demand for newer buildings to replace the old ones, as happened in places like Butte and Helena. Also, the dry, cold Montana climate prevented deterioration of existing structures. Buildings stood vacant and neglected, but they did not rot, and somehow they never burned. But most important, Charles Bovey came to town.

Bovey was a Montana wheat farmer with a passion for his state's history and enough money to preserve some of it. He drove through Virginia City in 1944, recognized the value of its old structures, and began buying them to keep them from being torn down. Before long, he owned nearly every building at the west end of Wallace Street—livery stables, blacksmith shops, general stores, saloons, a grocery, a tobacco store, a newspaper and printing shop, a cobbler's shop, a bordello and various houses.

HISTORY WITH DUST

Some of the buildings look as though their last owners just stepped out, locked the doors and never came back. In fact, that's just about what happened with some of them. Bovey bought buildings with all their contents, and touched almost nothing it seems, not even the dust.

Besides the structures in Virginia City, Bovey found buildings in other parts of the state. No one else wanted the structures and if he wouldn't move them, he was told, they would be torn down. So Bovey took them apart and reassembled them on the former site of Nevada City (about two miles from Virginia City) where only about a dozen original structures remained. The assemblage, laid out to form a small town, includes important landmarks from Montana's history. Among them are the state's oldest wooden building, the first school, and the oldest standing post office. The site has been used as a location for several films, including *Little Big Man.*

LILAC LANE
Lilacs in the lane behind Virginia City's Fairweather Inn bow to a June snow. At the height of the gold rush, the inn was called the Anaconda Hotel and housed a restaurant, a bar, a billiards room and a basement bowling alley.

Bovey was always on the lookout for complete businesses. From Fort Benton he brought the entire shop of a saddle maker. From Butte came the equipment and stock of a carriage works. From Basin came a fire station, complete with a large alarm bell. He bought the Wa Chai Tau Chinese supply house in Butte, and used its contents to furnish Nevada City's Chinese village.

Except for a grocery in Virginia City, none of the buildings has been restored to a like-new condition. They all look old and dilapidated, much as they did when Bovey first acquired them, some 50 years ago. He wanted it that way. He liked a coating of dust on his history, and cultivated an atmosphere that he called a suspended state of deterioration. But the deterioration has been slowed, not stopped. And the private company established by Bovey to care for this rich slice of history lacks the funding needed for really effective protection of buildings and artifacts—or interpretation of what we see. But by their very decay, these relics resting anonymously in their dusty context provide us with a measure of time passing. Peering through the original glass windows at dim interiors, you can almost hear the dry crackle of decades past, and imagine Bill Fairweather buying all the tobacco he ever wanted.

A Maiasaura pebblesorum ("good mother lizard") and her babies, members of the duck-billed dinosaurs, are recreated in the Museum of the Rockies' Dinosaur Hall.

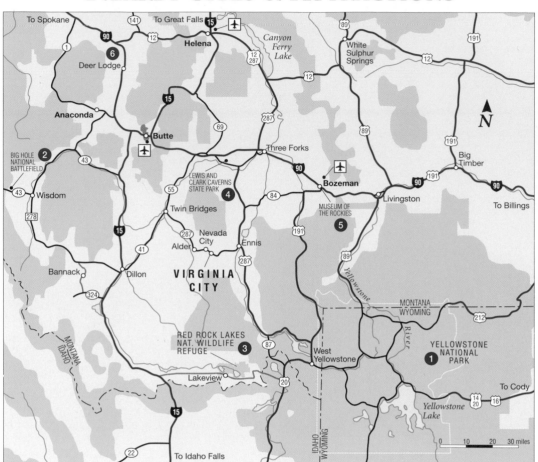

① YELLOWSTONE NATIONAL PARK

The world's first national park is famous for its spouting geysers, bubbling mud pots, jewel-like geothermal pools, canyons and abundant wildlife. Along the breathtaking Firehole and Gibbon Rivers lies the world's greatest concentration of geysers. Old Faithful, the most well-known geyser, never fails to attract crowds for its regular eruptions, while the irregular eruptions of Steamboat Geyser, the largest on the planet, vary from days to years. Yellowstone's scenery is awe-inspiring: Summit vantage points reveal panoramic views of Grand Canyon, Yellowstone Lake and Hayden Valley. The park's 2.2 million acres of scenic beauty are home to a dense concentration of wildlife, including American bison, elks, grizzly and black bears, and many bird species. From Virginia City, the closest of Yellowstone's three Montana entrances is West Yellowstone on Hwy. 287.

② BIG HOLE NATIONAL BATTLEFIELD

This battlefield marked the turning point in the 1877 Nez Percé War. On August 9, U.S. Army troops staged a pre-dawn attack on a sleeping band of 800 Nez Percé Indians. The Indians had refused to sign an 1863 treaty which would have reduced their Idaho reservation to less than one-quarter of its size. Before the battle was over, 30 to 60 Indian women,

children and old people, as well as 30 warriors lay dead. Several Nez Percé chiefs led the survivors in a desperate attempt to reach the Canadian border, but the band was forced to surrender to the U.S. Army two months later. Visitors to Big Hole can learn more about the Nez Percé War at the Visitor Center, which displays relics from the battle and presents audiovisual and interpretive exhibits about 1870's Indian and military life. The Nez Percé National Historic Trail follows the route of the Nez Percé War for 22½ miles. The site offers excellent fishing, cross-country skiing and wilderness hiking. Located 12 miles west of Wisdom on Hwy. 43.

③ RED ROCK LAKES NATIONAL WILDLIFE REFUGE

This remote 44,000-acre wildlife refuge is located on the northern edge of the Continental Divide in the unspoiled Centennial Valley. The refuge is famous as one of the primary nesting sites of the rare trumpeter swan. In 1935, the largest of North America's waterfowl—the majestic trumpeter—neared extinction, dropping to only 100 known swans. In the same year, the refuge was established to protect the species. Today, about 100 trumpeter swans arrive at this sanctuary to build their nests and rear their young. During peak migration periods, 23 different species of waterfowl can be observed among the refuge's lakes, creeks and marshes. Other migrant birds include falcons, hawks, sandhill cranes and eagles. Wildlife that can be spotted along the area's hiking trails include moose, deer, elk and pronghorns. Located off Hwy. 15 near Lakeview.

4 LEWIS AND CLARK CAVERNS STATE PARK, THREE FORKS

A labyrinth of corridors, passages and chambers lies 326 feet below the Montana grasslands. About 80 million years ago, the geological force of uplift fractured the limestone layers beneath the grasslands and created the nearby Tobacco Root Mountains. Rainwater seeped through the cracks and hollowed out the caverns. When the water level subsided, air filled the caverns, creating ideal conditions for the formation of a variety of speleothems (mineral formations), including stalactites, stalagmites, columns and crystal formations called popcorn. The site is located along the Jefferson River, in the northern foothills of the Tobacco Root range. The park is named for explorers Meriwether Lewis and William Clark, who traveled along the river in 1805 and 1806—unaware of the existence of the caves—during their great expedition to the Pacific. In 1937, the site became Montana's first state park. Guided tours are available during the summer. Highlights of the tour include the pillared Spiral Staircase Room, the domed Cathedral Room, the Garden of Gods and the Paradise Room, whose formations are still slowly growing. Located 20 miles west of Three Forks off Hwy. 90.

5 MUSEUM OF THE ROCKIES

This exceptional museum interprets 4 billion years of history of the northern Rockies. Its world-famous paleontology exhibition houses many of the discoveries made by Jack Horner, the dinosaur pioneer whose discovery of the nests and eggs of hadrosaurs (duck-billed dinosaurs) rocked the paleontological world. Visitors can examine the fossilized eggs and babies of these creatures from the Mesozoic era, as well as fossils of many other dinosaurs that once roamed the region. The museum presents evidence that these creatures, which may have been warm-blooded, nurtured their young. On permanent display is a life-size robotic recreation of a mother triceratops and her babies. Other exhibits shed light on the geological history of the Rockies, the arrival of man, and the art, history and culture of the Plains Indians. The museum's Taylor Planetarium employs computer graphics to simulate travel among the stars. Located on the Montana State University campus in Bozeman, off Hwy. 90.

6 DEER LODGE

The Old Territorial Prison, established in 1871 and in use until 1979, has been preserved as a reminder of Montana's outlaw past. The first territorial prison to be established in the western United States, the imposing stone structure of Deer Lodge was built by the labor of the convicts themselves. It is the centerpiece of a cluster of historic sites in the center of Deer Lodge, seat of Powell County. The prison also houses the Montana Law Enforcement Museum and the Towe Ford Museum, whose collection contains more than 100 Ford and Lincoln automobiles. On the grounds of the prison, the Powell County Museum displays the geological, mining and railroading history of the area around Deer Lodge. Across the street from the prison building is "Yesterday's Playthings," housing the Hostetter collection of early dolls and toys. Located on Hwy. 90.

The Grand Canyon of the Yellowstone River is one of the most famous sights in Yellowstone National Park. The park is the largest in the contiguous United States.

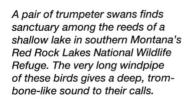

A pair of trumpeter swans finds sanctuary among the reeds of a shallow lake in southern Montana's Red Rock Lakes National Wildlife Refuge. The very long windpipe of these birds gives a deep, trombone-like sound to their calls.

Casa Rinconada, in New Mexico's Chaco Culture National Historical Park.

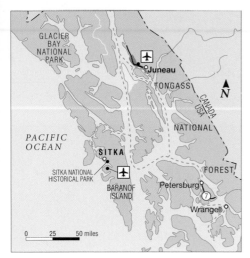

When the Russian empire extended to the shores of Alaska, Sitka was the flourishing capital of the Tsar's American territories. For more than half of the 19th century, this scenic settlement was the hub of a Russian colonizing and trading effort that stretched down the Pacific shoreline as far as Fort Ross on the northern coast of California. Sitka was a jewel of cultivation in the wilderness, and was dubbed by one writer "the Paris of the Pacific" for its opulence and sophistication.

Russian activity in North America began in 1741, after Russian-employed Danish navigator Vitus Bering made landfall on the coast of Alaska. Russian trappers and traders soon began to exploit the region's wealth of fur-bearing mammals, notably fur seals and sea otters. In 1804, Alexsandr Baranof, the manager of the Russian-American Company, defeated Tlingit Indians at their settlement of Shee Atika, close to Sitka's present site. Shee Atika was renamed New Archangel, and quickly became a chief port of call for ships carry-

ing valuable otter skins to China. By the 1850's, the seal and otter populations had been decimated by over-hunting and the local economy faltered. Interest in the colony waned as Russia faced increasing challenges at home. This lack of interest led to the land deal of the century: On October 18, 1867, the Russian government sold Alaska to the United States for $7.2 million—two cents an acre. The official transaction took place in Sitka on what is now known as the Castle Hill Historic Site. Each year, on Alaska Day, the town proudly reenacts the transfer ceremony. Yet Sitka's glorious past is evident on every day of the year. A walking tour of the streets of this community of 9,000 people reveals echoes of Tsarist Russia and raises the ghosts of another America.

THE SPRUCE PALACE

The Russian Bishop's House still stands as a reminder of the days when the Russian empire dominated the North Pacific. Built of Sitka spruce by Finnish shipwrights in 1842, the house was first occupied by the Russian Orthodox Bishop Ivan Veniaminov. After a massive restoration carried out by the National Park Service, this rough-hewn ecclesiastical palace is open to visitors. So, too, is St. Michael's Cathedral, a replica of the 1848 onion-domed structure that was destroyed by fire in 1966. While the bronze bells in the spire had to be recast from originals that were melted by the intense blaze, a fascinating collection of artifacts survived the flames, including icons, chalices and robes.

Just outside Sitka stretches the 106-acre Sitka National Historical Park. The park contains the battleground where the Tlingit Indians were driven off by Baranof and his settlers in 1804, as well as two miles of

A totem pole in Sitka National Historical Park conjures up an image of the time when Tlingit clans occupied this part of Alaska.

wooded pathways that are lined by totem poles. Many of them are copies of deteriorating originals first brought to Sitka from southeastern Alaska in 1905 by Territorial Governor John G. Brady.

At the park's visitor center, which encompasses the Southeast Alaska Indian Cultural Center, native artisans demonstrate a variety of traditional crafts. Close by, the Sheldon Jackson State Museum (established in 1888) features exhibits on the history and culture of Alaska's native peoples: Eskimos, Aleuts, Haida and Athabaskans and Tlingit.

Sitka's very isolation has helped to preserve the community's heritage. The town is accessible only by cruise ship, Alaska State Ferry or airplane. But once ensconced in this delightful outpost, the visitor can travel by taxi, tour bus or bicycle. The weather, though hardly hospitable, is not fiercely cold. Chilly, rain-drenched winds are typical of the southeastern panhandle.

FOR MORE INFORMATION:
Superintendent, Sitka National Historical Park, P.O. Box 738, Sitka, AK 99835. (907) 747-6281.

St. Michael's Russian Orthodox Cathedral is a tangible reminder of Sitka's past.

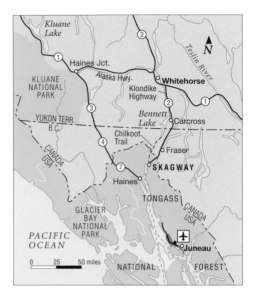

During the gold rush, Sheep Camp was called "City of Tents." Thousands of prospectors ascending the Chilkoot Trail camped here.

In July 1897, wild-eyed men ran through the streets of America's Pacific port cities yelling "Gold! Gold in the Klondike!" It was a cry that preceded the 19th century's greatest stampede for riches, a stampede that ended in despair and an early grave for many. When the dust had settled, barely 300 miners had made their fortune.

But the giddy months that followed the discovery of gold saw some 100,000 hopefuls set off on the long trail northwards. More than 30,000 of these flocked to the Alaskan tent and shack settlements of Skagway and Dyea—springboards for the trek through the Chilkoot Pass to the headwaters of the Yukon River in Canada's Yukon Territory. From there, boats carried the miners and their equipment to the goldfields.

Boisterous pioneers quickly turned Skagway (originally Skaguay, "home of the north wind" in Tlingit dialect) into a brawling, bawdy boomtown of boardwalks and honky-tonk saloons. Spread beneath soaring snowcapped mountains, Skagway still contains a remarkable number of buildings associated with the gold rush era. These include saloons, hotels, railroad and steamer offices, a bakery and a jewelry store. Today, Klondike Gold Rush National Historical Park helps preserve part of Skagway's historic district as a living monument to the gold rush that ended as abruptly as it began.

A popular walking tour of the town starts at the park's visitor center, housed in a former railroad depot. One of the tour's most intriguing stops is the Arctic Brotherhood Hall, the facade of which is made of more than 20,000 sticks of driftwood. Captain Moore's Cabin was built in 1897 by the town's original settler, Captain William Moore, a resourceful seaman whose ingenuity contributed to Skagway's brief reign as the largest city in Alaska.

The Trail of '98 Museum showcases ceremonial parkas, relics of local history and native culture exhibits. The Gold Rush Cemetery holds local villain Jefferson Randolph "Soapy" Smith, whose reign of crime ended when he was killed in a shootout with town surveyor Frank Reid in 1898.

THE CHILKOOT TRAIL ✓

Weather permitting, intrepid travelers can hike the 33-mile Chilkoot Trail, which winds from the nearby—but now nearly obliterated—site of Dyea, Skagway's rival outpost. At the time, the trail was the shortest and best known route to the Yukon. It quickly became crowded with fortune-hunters who carried all their supplies on their backs. Outfitters in Skagway and Seattle made fortunes by supplying the prospectors with food and hardware, since the North West Mounted Police—who maintained a customs post at the Chilkoot summit—refused to allow anyone into Canada who was not carrying a year's supply of provisions. Many reminders of their struggle are still visible along the trail, in the form of telegraph wire, boots, rusty tin cans, bullets, bedsprings, broken china and fragments of tent canvas. Visitors are urged not to disturb these poignant relics of the prospectors' broken dreams.

With difficulty, animals could negotiate the rocky White Pass Trail, which left from Skagway. But many desperate prospectors overloaded their mules and horses and then beat them until they dropped. More than 3,000 animals died on this trail. In 1899, the construction of the White Pass and Yukon Route Railroad made the Dyea-Chilkoot route obsolete and ensured Skagway's survival. The route affords spectacular views of the precipitous terrain, and a narrow-gauge railroad offers excursions between Skagway and Fraser, in British Columbia. Skagway is accessible year-round by airplane, ferry service and cruise ship, as well as by road via the Alaska and Klondike Highways.

FOR MORE INFORMATION:
Skagway Convention and Visitors Bureau, P.O. Box 415, Dept. B, Skagway, AK 99840. (907) 983-2854; Klondike Gold Rush National Historical Park, P.O. Box 517, Skagway, AK 99840. (907) 983-2921.

Driftwood adorns the facade of Skagway's 1899 Arctic Brotherhood Hall.

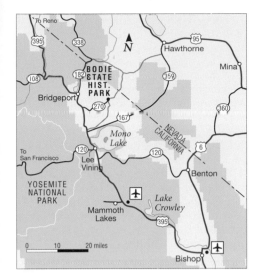

Amid the scrub of the eastern slopes of the Sierra Nevada, a collection of 100 or so ramshackle wooden buildings is all that remains of the town of Bodie, a gold mining boomtown that in 1879 boasted a population of 10,000. Today, Bodie State Historic Park preserves what is left of the town in a state of arrested decay, and the town appears much as it would have done when the last of its residents moved away. Bodie is one of the largest ghost towns still standing, and a stroll through its streets is a walk into the past, where the legends of the Old West still live; the shootouts, saloons, outbreaks of gold fever and tales of riches found and lost all emanated from towns like this one.

Bodie was named after Waterman S. Bodey, a prospector who discovered gold here in 1859. The town fathers later changed the spelling of his name to avoid mispronunciation. Following Bodey's discovery, the town became the scene of a frantic gold rush, and its population swelled from over 500 to more than 10,000 seemingly overnight. Like most boomtowns, Bodie eventually went bust, but by the time the veins of ore ran out, more than 100 million dollars worth of gold had been mined in the area. At the height of the town's prosperity, there were 30 mines in Bodie. One stagecoach that left town packed with 500,000 dollars worth of gold for the trip east was guarded by no less than six men.

SIN CITY
The rapid influx of fortune hunters transformed Bodie. The town garnered a reputation for wickedness that saw the expression "Badman from Bodie" slip into the lexicon of the Old West. It was a lively, dangerous place, where shootings were common, street brawls an everyday occurrence, and the jail generally filled to over-

flowing. Its reputation became such that one little girl, upon finding out her family was moving to the town, wrote in her diary, "Goodbye God, I'm going to Bodie."

In its heyday Bodie could count an impressive total of 65 saloons within the town limits, and three breweries were kept busy supplying the thirsty miners. There was also a thriving red-light district and several opium dens. Bodie's reputation for raw and rowdy behavior led one minister of the time, the Reverend F.W. Warrington, to condemn the town as "a sea of sin, lashed by tempests of lust and passion."

But Bodie was not all sin and lawlessness. It was here in 1892 that the first long-distance electric power line was introduced, which brought electricity to power Bodie's ore mills from a hydroelectric plant on Green Creek, some 13 miles away. The use of cyanide to extract gold from ore was perfected in Bodie, which greatly increased the amount of gold that could be extracted from the rock.

Today, about five percent of Bodie's buildings still stand. The town lies at the end of a deserted 13-mile stretch of

highway (the last 3 miles of which are unpaved). With its sawmill, schoolhouse, jail, morgue, houses and places of business, it is easy to imagine the town as a thriving community. The miners' union hall is the only building actually open to the public, and it contains a fascinating collection of mementos of Bodie's past.

In 1962, Bodie was set aside as a state historic park, to be an example of the way things were. As a result it has not undergone major restorations or renovations. Visitors see the same buildings that existed here 100 years ago. The passage of time, devastating fires and the harsh winters of the Sierra Nevada have all taken their toll. But these weatherbeaten structures can still spark the imagination, recalling days of adventure, tall tales and the fever inspired by gold.

FOR MORE INFORMATION:
Bodie State Historic Park, P.O. Box 515, Bridgeport, CA 93517. (619) 647-6445.

The James Stuart Cain House was home to Bodie's principal property owner. Cain made his fortune when a patch of ground he had leased with a partner from the Standard Mine and Mill yielded gold. Cain later acquired the company.

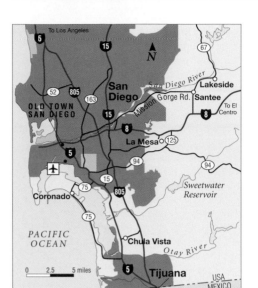

From its beginnings as a Roman Catholic mission on a hill north of a sheltered harbor, San Diego has developed into the nation's sixth-largest city. Old Town San Diego State Historic Park preserves a six-block area of the city's old Spanish quarter, established in the 1820's when San Diego began to grow beyond its original walls. Today, strains of mariachi guitar and the cool elegance of rich adobe haciendas evoke memories of the days of Spanish and Mexican rule, while markets and restaurants breathe life into a district that was left in decline for almost a century.

San Diego enjoys a long and venerable history. It was here in 1542 that the Portuguese sailor Juan Rodriguez Cabrillo came ashore and claimed possession of the California coast for the King of Spain. By 1769, San Diego was the meeting point for the land and sea expeditions sent to bring California under Spanish control and establish Franciscan mission settlements all the way up the coast. Don Gaspar de Portolá established a presidio (fort) on a hill to protect Father Junípero Serra's first mission, San Diego de Alcalá.

When Mexico gained its independence from Spain in 1821, the soldiers of the former Spanish regime moved down from their Presidio Hill garrison to set up farms on the slopes below, aided by grants of land and cattle from the Mexican government. A scale model on view at the park headquarters shows their adobe homes, which formed the nucleus of Old Town. But the flavor of the boom days that followed the end of Spanish rule is best appreciated by taking a walking tour through the streets, and visiting the old buildings themselves.

OLD TOWN PRESERVED

Since the state of California bought Old Town San Diego's six blocks in 1967, several historic buildings have been reconstructed or restored to provide a glimpse of life in the Mexican and early American periods, which lasted from 1821-72. In the quaint one-room Mason Street School, visitors sitting at antique desks hear how California flourished as a world center for the cowhide and tallow trade.

The Mexican pots for sale at several shops in Old Town reflect the area's historic role as a marketplace.

Four original adobe homes still stand in the park, two of them restored and open to the public. The most spectacular is the Casa de Estudillo on Mason Street, a sprawling whitewashed hacienda, which is now the area's showplace. Built in the late 1820's by a retired Presidio commander, the mansion is lushly furnished in late Spanish-period style. After its restoration in 1910 by sugar baron John Spreckels, the hacienda gained new fame for its evocative resemblance to "Ramona's Marriage Place" in a popular romantic novel. For years couples flocked to the house's chapel to be married. If a party was not on at the Estudillo house, activity often centered on the Casa de Bandini at Calhoun and Mason streets. Juan Bandini arrived as a skipper and stayed to marry the daughter of a local notable.

Other significant sights in the area include Whaley House, a luxurious brick mansion that was once San Diego's seat of government. Seeley Stables, originally built in 1867 as a stagecoach terminal, now houses a collection of horse-drawn vehicles, branding irons, saddles and Indian artifacts. The frame-style Casa de Altamirano on San Diego Avenue looks the way it did when the first issue of the San Diego Union rolled off the presses here in 1868. A museum in the house chronicles the newspaper's history.

California became part of the United States in 1847, but it was not long after this that Old Town went into decline. By the 1860's, drought had contributed to the decline of ranching in the area, while San Diego began to develop a new downtown core nearer the bay and its growing port. By coincidence, in 1872 a fire destroyed several major buildings in Old Town. In recent decades, however, the revived Old Town has attracted increasing numbers of visitors. The bustling Bazaar del Mundo—where ranchers once bartered for their treasures with cowhides known locally as California bank notes—is once again the center of Old Town's intriguing mixture of Hispanic and American cultures.

FOR MORE INFORMATION:
Old Town San Diego State Historic Park, 4002 Wallace Street, San Diego, CA 92110-2743. (619) 220-5422.

Mason Street School was San Diego's first publicly owned school. The one-room wooden schoolhouse was built in 1865.

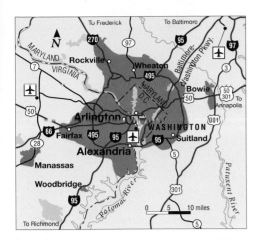

The Capitol building has been the seat of the U.S. Congress since 1800.

The nation's capital lies in a roughly diamond-shaped parcel of land at the confluence of the Potomac and Anacostia Rivers. A city of broad avenues, monumental plazas and magnificent public buildings, Washington is the repository of the history and democratic traditions of the United States.

George Washington selected the site for the city that was to be named for him, and land was ceded by Maryland and Virginia to create the new federal district. A French military engineer, Pierre Charles L'Enfant, was commissioned by Washington to plan the new capital. L'Enfant conceived of a city on a grid pattern, with broad avenues criss-crossing the grid in a network of diagonals. Spacious squares or circles marked the intersection of avenues, creating sweeping views and providing significant sites for public monuments.

L'Enfant based his plan around two focal points: the residence of the president, now known as the White House, and the seat of government, the domed Capitol building.

L'Enfant's most daring innovation was a mile-long, 400-foot-wide mall running west from the Capitol to the Potomac River. He called it the Grand Avenue, but it is known today as the National Mall. Today, the National Mall is lined by museums and galleries, including the Smithsonian Institution, which administers 13 museums and galleries in Washington. From the Capitol, the serene vista of the National Mall extends to the Washington Monument, with the Lincoln Memorial in the distance.

Reality soon caught up with L'Enfant's grand plan. He himself was dismissed after a year for attempting to demolish the house of Daniel Carroll, a prominent local resident. Construction of the city proceeded slowly. By the time the federal government moved to Washington from Philadelphia in 1800, Washington was only half-built.

During the War of 1812, a British column burned every public building except the Patent Office.

During the Civil War, government buildings served as hospitals, and the city's open spaces were used to graze cattle to feed the troops. President Abraham Lincoln remained in the city throughout the war. Only a few days after the war's end, Lincoln was felled by an assassin's bullet as he sat with his wife in a box at Ford's Theatre. The Lincoln Memorial, built from 1911 to 1922 to honor the martyred president, is the most famous of Washington's many public monuments.

The Three Servicemen, a life-sized bronze sculpture honoring Americans who served in Vietnam, is one of Washington's many memorials and monuments.

THE WHITE HOUSE AND THE CAPITOL

A nationwide competition to design the residence of the President was won by Irish-born James Hoban. Construction began in 1793, and in 1800 President John Adams and his wife set up housekeeping in the still-unfinished building. Today the White House is the oldest public building in the District of Columbia. Major renovations over the years have included the construction of a third story, the West Wing and the Oval Office. From 1948-52, the White House was completely rebuilt.

The Capitol building is the seat of the legislative branch of government. L'Enfant sited it on Jenkins Hill, which he dubbed "a pedestal waiting for a monument." Originally designed by Dr. William Thornton, the present structure is the product of much rebuilding and expansion. The length of the building doubled in the 1850's, when Thomas U. Walter enlarged the wings, and commenced the construction of the massive cast-iron dome.

Millions of visitors come to Washington every year to visit its many museums and monuments, and the city is home to more than 600,000 people. Washington has grown tremendously since the 18th century, but it is L'Enfant's elegant plan that remains the foundation of this great city.

FOR MORE INFORMATION:
Washington D.C. Convention and Visitors Association, 1212 New York Avenue N.W., Washington, DC 20005. (202) 789-7000.

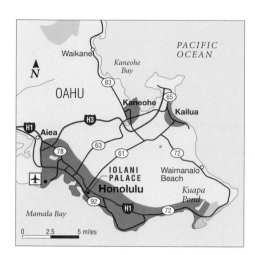

In the center of Honolulu stands stately Iolani Palace, the only royal residence on American soil. From 1882 to 1893, the palace was the residence of the Hawaiian monarchy, and the scene of a never-ending succession of balls, galas, pageants, musicals and social activity. Here politicians, diplomats, visiting royalty, prominent writers and artists of the day were all guests of King Kalakaua and Queen Liliuokalani.

Kalakaua, the last king of Hawaii, initiated the building of a palace that would reflect the aspirations of his tiny nation. The new palace was to replace an earlier structure that had been found to be infested by termites. Completed in 1882—at a cost of nearly $360,000—the palace certainly lived up to the king's dreams.

Four architects had a hand in its design, and skilled craftsmen from all over the world were assembled for its construction. The architecture was European, but the wide verandas surrounding the building were typical of many other government buildings constructed in tropical and subtropical climates during the late Victorian era. While Iolani honored history and tradition, it was also a modern building, reflective of King Kalakaua's interest in things new and innovative. For example, electric lights were installed only seven years after Edison perfected the first incandescent electric bulbs, and telephones were installed only four years after they were invented by Bell. A vein of artesian water was tapped to provide water for the palace's modern plumbing system.

FIT FOR A KING

The lavish interior was a perfect setting for the life of the monarchy, and featured etched glass portals, elegant woodwork (much of it constructed from the native Hawaiian woods of koa, kou and kamani), and a large collection of Davenport furniture. In the Grand Hall, oil paintings of former kings and queens of Hawaii were displayed, as well as porcelain vases from England and Japan, brass from India and statuettes from France.

The long tables in the State Dining Room held up to 40 guests, and the room was adorned with flowers in silver vases, a massive epergne (an ornate, tiered centerpiece), several candelabra and portraits of European royalty. At state dinners, the tables were laid with china from France, crystal from Bohemia and silverware from England and France.

The Throne Room was the scene of many formal state occasions and of the charming musical evenings that King Kalakaua so dearly loved. On these occasions the traditional feathered cloaks of the Hawaiian monarchs were placed on display, and the king would greet his guests while the Royal Hawaiian Band played classical music. Hundreds of incandescent lights in crystal

Even the exterior of Honolulu's Iolani Palace reflects the splendor of the court of King Kalakaua, Hawaii's last monarch.

The restored coat of arms of the Hawaiian Kingdom is mounted on each of Iolani Palace's four gateways. When translated, the motto reads "The life of the land is perpetuated in righteousness."

chandeliers illuminated the rich crimson-and-gold silk draperies and the Wilton carpets imported from England.

After the death of King Kalakaua in 1891, his sister Liliuokalani reigned for a scant two years before the monarchy was overthrown, and the palace was converted into government offices.

Hawaii became a republic, then a U.S. Territory, and finally, in 1959, it became the 50th state of the United States. When a new capital building was constructed in 1969, the decision was made to restore Iolani Palace to its former glory.

Today the restored palace displays the same elegance and grace as it did during the days of King Kalakaua and Queen Liliuokalani. The palace's restorers spared no effort in recreating its furnishings and decor, and curators scoured the world for relics from the palace. Eventually, more than 1,000 items were restored or duplicated, with attention being paid to even the smallest detail, so that the fabrics and colors matched as close to the originals as possible.

FOR MORE INFORMATION:

Friends of Iolani Palace, P.O. Box 2259, Honolulu, HI 96804. (808) 522-0832.

Hawaii ▪ PUUHONUA √

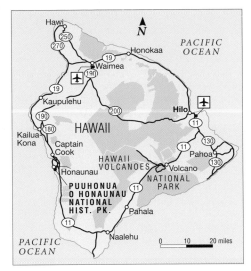

On the west coast of Hawaii, largest island of the Hawaiian chain, a high stone wall at the base of a lava promontory conceals a sanctuary where disgraced warriors and lawbreakers could make a new start. Amid spectacular coastal scenery, Puuhonua o Honaunau National Historical Park preserves one of the sacred sites of Hawaiian culture, at the heart of which was the ancient system of tribal law known as kapu—the sacred rules of life.

Kapu was a set of taboos and prohibitions that governed every aspect of life. Kapu forbade anything from men and women eating together to commoners walking in the chief's footsteps, or even casting a shadow on the chief's palace grounds. Breaking the kapu meant risking the wrath of the gods, and invariably carried the death penalty. Luckily, there was a loophole.

Hawaiian kings were buried in the Hale o Keawe Heiau (temple), which has now been reconstructed. The Hawaiians believed that the spiritual energy of the chief survived in his bones and could increase the holiness of the puuhonua.

In English, puuhonua means place of refuge, and Puuhonua o Honaunau was exactly that. The kapu-breaker had to reach the puuhonua, where the kahuna pule (priest) could grant him absolution. This could be tricky, as mainland access was blocked by the chief's compound, and the shrine was built on a peninsula accessible only by water. Once there, however, the transgressor was safe, and could return home after only a few hours with a total and unconditional pardon, and begin his life again.

THE GREAT WALL

Many of the structures at Puuhonua o Honaunau have not been accurately dated, but the Great Wall, which separates the chief's compound from the shrine, is known to have been built around 1550. The Great Wall was originally intended to be a monument to the reigning chief. No mortar was used in its construction. The stones were taken from a nearby lava flow, and fitted together perfectly. With a length of 1,000 feet, a height of 10 feet, and a width of 17 feet, the wall guaranteed protection from the mainland. Giant ohia-wood kii, or statues of temple gods, faced the sea to ward off any naval attacks. These kiis have been recently restored.

At the end of the Great Wall is the Hale o Keawe Heiau, which dates from around 1650 and was the last temple built here. It was here that the priests placed the bones of the chief, who achieved godlike status upon his death; 23 chiefs were interred here. Hale o Keawe Heiau is the only temple that has been substantially restored; two others, A-lealea Heiau and Old Heiau, are ruins.

Many of the rocks at the puuhonua have historical or mythological significance. Keoua Stone is named for a high chief famed for his great height. Legend has it that he could lie across the stone with his arms and legs stretched out and equal its length—some 20 feet. There are also petroglyphs, or carvings etched in rock long ago by unknown islanders, as well as several stone konane "tables," where visitors can play an ancient Hawaiian board game.

In 1819, King Kamehameha II abolished the kapu system, ending the need for puuhonuas. Most of the islanders were converted to Christianity over the next few years, and Puuhonua o Honaunau was abandoned, because it was seen as a symbol of the old ways. The Great Wall and the foundation of the temple, however, were left intact. Later these were reconstructed from sketches made by the early European explorers.

The royal canoe landing at Keoneele Cove was forbidden to all commoners. Today, visitors can swim here, and explore the reconstructed palace grounds nearby.

The residential section of the park is not to be missed. The reconstructed royal village is made up of wooden houses designed for the chiefs or for commoners. Swimming is allowed at the royal canoe landing, a site originally forbidden to anyone except nobility. Puuhonua o Honaunau is no longer isolated by water and the royal compound. Visitors are permitted to wander around the site at their leisure. Yet, once inside the puuhonua, the daytrip seems to take on the significance of the long-ago pilgrimage.

FOR MORE INFORMATION:

Puuhonua o Honaunau National Historical Park, P.O. Box 129, Honaunau, HI 96726. (808) 328-2326.

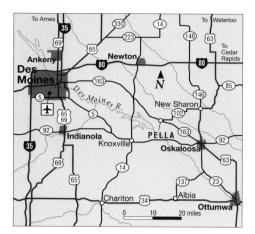

A hundred and forty-six years ago, a band of Dutch Separatist families descended upon a tract of virgin prairie wedged between the Skunk and Des Moines Rivers in the heart of Iowa. Disgruntled by an 1845 Dutch ruling on compulsory allegiance to the state church—and eager to escape the Netherlands' high taxes—hundreds of church-goers abandoned their homeland. The promise of religious freedom, and the great expanse of land in the Midwest, lured droves of these Dutch immigrants.

The group that settled in Pella were led by Dominie Henry Peter Scholte. Scholte's flock came from all social strata—they were wealthy professionals, craftsmen, artisans and farmers. In 1847 they boarded four sailing vessels and set out to cross the Atlantic. Two leaders on each ship maintained order, conducted prayer meetings and organized English classes. According to one captain, the immigrants scrubbed and prayed during the entire voyage. They landed in Baltimore and traveled by train, horse-drawn canal boats, river steamboats and horse-drawn wagons to their final destination. The arduous journey took them five months.

DUTCH SETTLERS

Their inimitable leader, Dominie Scholte, had purchased the land—18,000 acres at $1.25 per acre—from the United States government. He and his 800 followers laid out a village and named it Pella—the "city of refuge." Their first dwellings in the New World were simple affairs, mostly sod huts and log shanties. Pella was nicknamed Strawtown, an allusion to those first straw-roofed dugouts. Dominie Scholte's first church was crudely built and bitterly cold. Worshippers would bring their own braziers to keep their feet from freezing during the three-hour sermons. Later that first church was replaced with a brick structure. Most of the parishioners upgraded

their own homes as well, supplanting them with wood-frame homes and barns. Within a year of their arrival, Dominie Scholte had built a 22-room house for his wife, Mareah. It was furnished like any well-to-do European manor, complete with grand piano, silver tea service, paintings and chandeliers. Wallpaper was ordered from Paris and carpets from Brussels. Gardeners were hired to design a nine-acre formal garden, a unique feature on the endless grasslands of the prairies.

Pella's tulip gardens, windmills, houses with sculptured corbels and small leaded windows are a constant reminder of the town's Dutch heritage. Graceful courtyards and gloriously bright Dutch gardens are awash with color from May to October. Some of the homesteaders' houses can be toured. One of them, an old log cabin, is filled with typical Dutch household furnishings and an old loom. In another building, costumed craftsmen turn out Holland's famous wooden shoes. Nineteenth-century merchandise is on display in the Van Spankeren general store. One of the legends of the American West spent 14 years of his early life in Pella. Wyatt Earp came here with his family when he was two. (His gunfighting fame came much later, after the family moved farther west.) The Van Spankeren house, next door to the store, took in tenants, including young Wyatt's family. Artifacts and furnishings from the Earp era fill the rooms. Scholte House is

also open to the public. Besides its exceptional collection of French and Italian furniture, many of Scholte's original writings are displayed in the library.

Pella's annual Tulip Time, a festival held in May, commemorates the town's forefathers. Each year 75,000 tulips are planted and up to 500 costumed clog dancers parade through town. Traditional Dutch delicacies are served by sidewalk vendors.

FOR MORE INFORMATION:
Pella Historical Village, 507 Franklin St., Pella, IA 50219. (515) 628-2409.

A costumed craftsman, right, shows off Pella's Dutch heritage. Dutch dancers wear the traditional wooden shoes during Pella's popular Tulip Time festival. Below is Beason Blommer's gristmill, restored in 1967. The mill still grinds corn on festival days.

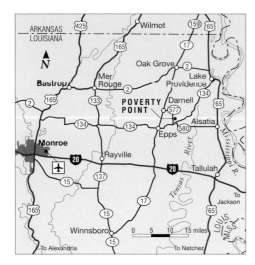

An aerial view of Poverty Point reveals the man-made earthen ridges that were built at least a thousand years before the birth of Christ.

Eight centuries after the Egyptians built the Great Pyramids, the inhabitants of a site in what is now northeastern Louisiana were erecting a complex structure of earthen mounds that overlooks the Mississippi River flood plains. The earthworks consisted of six rows of concentric horseshoe-shaped ridges surrounding a 37-acre plaza. Each ridge was originally 5 to 10 feet high (today 2 to 4 feet high) and the diameter of the outermost ridge measures three-quarters of a mile. Despite countless clues from artifacts found at the site, archeologists have not been able to fathom the reason for the configuration.

One very large mound and three smaller ones surround the six concentric ridges. The largest mound is shaped like a gigantic bird with outstretched wings. It measures 710 by 640 feet and is 70 feet high. The other three mounds are conical in shape and range from 3 feet to approximately 20 feet in height. The largest conical mound covered a human cremation.

Although Poverty Point's name comes from that of an 1840 plantation, the site was a major prehistoric city with about 4,000 to 5,000 inhabitants who lived in the area from 1800 to 500 B.C. Archeologists have discovered that these people imported raw materials that were not available locally. Dart points and other stone tools found at Poverty Point were made of copper from the Great Lakes area, lead ore from Missouri, soapstone from the Appalachian regions of Alabama and Georgia, and different types of stones from Arkansas, Tennessee, Mississippi, Alabama, Kentucky, Indiana and Ohio. It has been conjectured that Poverty Point was a religious and ceremonial center where spiritual services were bartered for raw materials for tools and weapons. The 3,000-year-old remnants include darts and spear points (bows and arrows were not used for another 1,000

years), knives, stone figures in a variety of shapes, including bird effigies and pregnant women, and small stone tools such as microliths—tools with serrated edges that were particular to this culture.

SURVIVAL STRATEGIES

In order to survive, this ancient culture had to adapt to its environment. One of the most interesting adaption techniques concerned the method of cooking food. Typically, heated stones, placed in earth ovens or hearths, cooked food. But there were no stones at Poverty Point; instead, these people made thousands of molded clay balls, rolled by hand and hardened by firing, and placed them in earth ovens—simply holes in the ground—producing an efficient, energy-saving method of cooking. A great number of these clay cooking balls have been found at the site, along with countless smaller objects far too small to have been of any practical use. They may have been ornaments.

The 400-acre site was acquired by the State of Louisiana in 1972, and in 1975, Poverty Point was designated as a National Historic Landmark. A museum now tells the story of these Native Americans through permanent displays and a video. Seasonal guided tram tours and a self-guided hiking trail provide a closer view of these incredibly interesting man-made structures. There are still many unanswered questions about Poverty Point, and archeologists are continuing the quest for answers. Amid the ancient earthen ramparts, the imagination

is bound to take over. Who was this complex society that held sway here for 1,000 years, and what motivated them? And when will Poverty Point reveal more of its secrets?

FOR MORE INFORMATION:
Poverty Point State Commemorative Area, P.O. Box 276, Epps, LA 71237.
(318) 926-5492.

Countless small artifacts, such as those above, have been found at Poverty Point. Some of them seem to have been ornamental; others had practical uses.

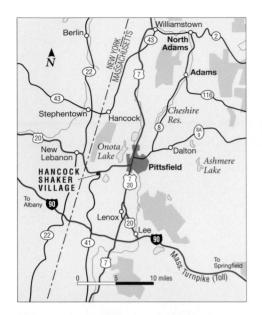

The Tan House, in the foreground, supplied the leather for the village's shoemakers, harnessmakers and hatters. The Sisters' Dairy and Weave Shop, middle ground, produced the community's dairy products. In 1820 the dairy was enlarged and a two-room weaving loft was added so that the sisters could keep busy while they waited for the milk to arrive from the barns. The Brick Dwelling, nestled in the trees, housed nearly 100 Shakers.

The Elders' Room in the Brick Dwelling displays some of the finely designed and crafted furniture made by the Shakers.

Hancock Shaker Village, set among 1,200 acres of meadows and woodland near Pittsfield, was the third of 18 Shaker communities to be established in New England, New York, Ohio and Kentucky between 1776 and 1836. An offshoot of the dissident English Quakers, the Shakers took their name from the trembling and shaking some members experienced when the spirit moved them during their meetings.

In 1774, reacting to the goad of persecution in England, Shaker founder Mother Ann Lee and eight followers came to America. They first settled near Albany, New York, and set about the work of gathering converts. Soon afterwards, Mother Ann and several followers made a missionary trip to Massachusetts and, in 1783, preached in a house in Hancock. As the list of converts in the area grew, Hancock became an established Shaker community, respectful of the fundamental tenets of Shakerism: celibacy, separation from mainstream society, sharing of goods, confession of sins, equality for all people regardless of race or sex, and pacifism.

The Shaker village at Hancock, deep in the Berkshire Hills of western Massachusetts, sprouted and thrived from 1790 through 1959. At its peak in the 1830's, the village was inhabited by some 300 Shakers who farmed, sold seeds and herbs, manufactured medicines and produced crafts. The walls and floors of their buildings no longer tremble with their fervent devotion. Instead, the community that was once called The City of Peace in the belief that it would emulate heaven on earth, is a walk-in museum, devoted to the Shakers' simplicity, and resourcefulness.

SKILLFUL WORKMANSHIP
Every building, every article of furniture, and every plowed furrow was made to express worship of God. The Shakers themselves have slipped into obscurity, but interest in their beliefs and lifestyle has multiplied. In particular, the quiet elegance of Shaker design and successful organic farming methods appeal to people today.

The standards laid down by Mother Ann Lee still prevail in the village. "Do all your work," she declared, "as if you had a hundred years to live and as if you were to die tomorrow." Craftspeople and interpreters now populate the village, tending the 20 restored buildings, the whitewashed fences and orderly gardens. They explain the farming and manufacturing methods of yesteryear, make reproductions of 19th-century furniture and furnishings, and use original devices to prepare food from Shaker Sisters' recipes. The village has America's largest public collection of Shaker artifacts.

The hallmark of the village is the Round Stone Barn, built in 1826. The barn was designed to stable 50 cows in stanchions radiating from a central haymow like the spokes of a wheel. Nearby, a five-story brick dwelling, constructed in 1830, once housed 100 Brothers and Sisters on separate sides of the building, reflecting the segregated but equal status of the sexes in Shaker society. The sect was administered by equal numbers of men and women.

Hancock Shaker Village is open daily for self-guided tours from May 1 through October 31. In April and November there are guided tours of the five most significant buildings. Interpreters explain Shaker worship and sing in the Meetinghouse each day. A cook's tour, talks on Shaker artisanship, and a Children's Discovery Room all contribute to the atmosphere. Special events include shearing days, textile demonstrations and candlelight suppers.

FOR MORE INFORMATION:
Hancock Shaker Village, P.O. Box 927, Pittsfield, MA 01202. (413) 443-0188.

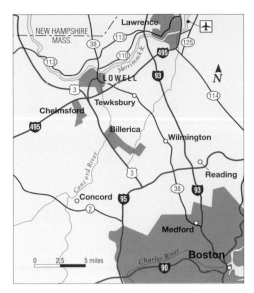

I n the history of the United States, there have been two revolutions: the American Revolution and the Industrial Revolution. There are hundreds of sites commemorating the former; for the birth of modern American industry, however, there are few. Lowell, Massachusetts, is the first large planned industrial city.

When Francis Cabot Lowell visited England in 1811, the British were the runaway leaders of the textile industry. They had entered the machine age towards the end of the 18th century, guarding their technological secrets closely to avoid competition. Lowell visited English textile factories and studied the design of their machines; upon his return to the U.S., he began working with a mechanic to duplicate them. By 1815, the men had progressed enough to open a mill in Waltham, Massachusetts. Lowell died soon after, but his backers continued with his work: a site in East Chelmsford, on the Merrimack River, was deemed capable of supporting 60 Waltham-scale mills, and in 1826 the town was rechristened Lowell in honor of Francis Lowell.

If Lowell was the town's father, then its children would have to be the waves of workers who passed through its gates. The Lowell mills first hired New England farmgirls to work the looms; they worked for lower pay than men would, and the mill owners believed that they would only work for a few years until they got married. The "mill girls" lived five or six to a room in company-owned boardinghouses, working 14 hours a day, 6 days a week. The company took great pains to provide strong moral and intellectual underpinnings to their workers: the dormitories the girls lived in were watched over by matron keepers, and their free time was often filled

with religious and educational occupations. The *Lowell Offering* was among the first women's literary magazines in America, appearing in 1840. The Women's Lowell Female Labor Reform Association led the movement for the 10-hour day.

IMMIGRANT CITY

The expansion of the mills, combined with an increasing number of wage strikes by the mill girls, gave rise to an influx of immigrant workers. They flocked to Lowell in droves, willing to work and face long hours and slight salaries. Individual immigrant communities built up and became a part of the mainstream, giving Lowell an exceptionally diverse ethnic background and tradition which continues to the present day. The town is an excellent example of the American immigrant city, with Irish, French-Canadian, Portuguese, Jewish and Greek cultures, among others.

The growth of the mills, while bringing economic prosperity to the town, also indirectly caused its decline. The influx of immigrant workers marked the beginning of a new era, one that stepped farther and farther away from the original intents of Lowell's founders and closer to the ugly realities of the English mill system where the workers had become a permanent underclass of exploitable cheap labor. Lowell was economically devastated as the mills moved south because of lower taxes, fewer regulations, cheaper land and a lower wage scale. By 1930, most of Lowell's original mills were finished.

In the 1970's and 1980's, however, the mills were designated a National Historical Park, and the long road to restoration began. Today, at the Boott Cotton Mills Museum, visitors can witness a recreation of what an early 20th-century textile factory was like, complete with the ear-shattering clattering of the looms. Almost everything here has been rebuilt from original parts— from the pulleys that drive the machines to the overhead line shafts. The museum also features exhibits on the history and future of industrialization.

Guided tours by bicycle, trolley and canalboat show off Lowell and its canals. At the Tsongas Industrial History Center, visitors can participate in interactive workshops, ranging from working a hand loom to building waterwheels and patenting inventions to experiencing the immigrant story through role-playing.

The town is also known for its contributions to the arts. The hometown of Beat writer Jack Kerouac, Lowell served as the subject of his first book, *The Town and the City*. Folk culture is amply represented

here, with the yearly Lowell Folk Festival. The Festival features traditional American music and dance, covering everything from bluegrass to zydeco. The Festival also showcases storytelling; Tunes and Tales is a long-running program that brings the town's history to life through stories and songs played on authentic folk instruments. In addition, Lowell hosts a variety of ethnic festivals every summer.

The Industrial Revolution opened a new chapter on American history, one that broadened the economic and cultural base of the nation. Its importance hinges on two things crucial to the American spirit: labor and technology. Nowhere in the United States can these two aspects of society be better understood than in Lowell.

FOR MORE INFORMATION:
Lowell National Historical Park, 246 Market Street, Lowell, MA 01852. (508) 970-5000.

Strategically located beside a Lowell canal, Boott Cotton Mills Museum is a recreation of a turn-of-the-century textile mill.

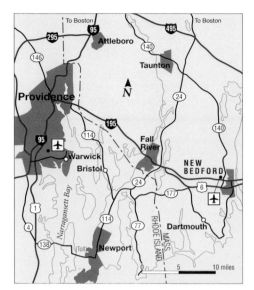

I n the mid-1800's, tall-masted schooners were tied up, hull-to-hull, along a waterfront loud with the clamor of sailmakers, ropemakers, carpenters, blacksmiths, coopers and candlemakers. The great writer, Herman Melville, lived among these men and joined crews that ventured far out to sea in pursuit of precious sperm whales. In *Moby Dick*, Melville immortalized the brave salts of New Bedford—America's whaling capital during the golden era of whales, whaleships and whalemen.

During the 1840's and 1850's, 80 percent of American whaling ships sailed from this New England harbor. The zenith of this dangerous yet profitable enterprise was reached in 1857 when New Bedford was a haven for 329 ships employing 10,000 men who reaped a multi-million dollar harvest of whale oil and whalebone from the sea. Then—in 1859—petroleum was discovered in Pennsylvania and the great whaling port went into decline, languishing briefly until

new mercantile activity was discovered—in textiles and glass.

OLD NEW BEDFORD
Today, New Bedford remains a major Atlantic deepsea fishing port and, in fact, produces more revenue from fishing than any port in the nation. Although the whaling days are long gone, there is a lingering atmosphere generated by those men, armed only with harpoons, who risked their lives to take on the sleek Leviathans of the deep. Fourteen blocks of New Bedford, which Melville asserted was "perhaps the dearest place to live in all New England," have been restored to look much as they did when whaling brought wealth and renown to the community. Gaslit, cobblestone streets evoke the waterfront of yesteryear. The County Street historic district, located on a ridge overlooking the harbor, is graced by stately mansions built for sea captains and merchants. Sailors used to love to walk the shaded streets of this town, saying that a stroll was as refreshing as a visit to the country.

The New Bedford Whaling Museum is dedicated to local history. Visitors can board a half-size replica of the fully-rigged whaling ship, the *Lagoda*, which at 89 feet in length is the largest ship model in the world. During the long whaling trips, sailors spent their leisure time engraving intricate designs on the teeth of sperm whales, or whittling away on pieces of whalebone. The museum has a compelling collection of this maritime art known as scrimshaw. An epic panorama, eight-and-a-half feet high and more than a quarter-mile long, depicts a worldwide whaling voyage. Another part of the museum concentrates on the supporting industries of whaling. On display are a chandlery, tin and cooper

shop, blockmaker, cooperage and countinghouse.

Across the street from the museum on Johnny Cake Hill—named originally Journey Cake Hill by early Quakers who stopped there briefly to eat cornmeal "journey cakes" on their way to and from meetings—stands the Seamen's Bethel (built in 1832), which Melville called the "Whaleman's Chapel," a mission dedicated to the sea. A three-masted whaling schooner sits atop the church, symbolic of the many sailors who knelt in prayer to prepare themselves for ocean voyages that sometimes lasted as long as four years. There is a prow-shaped pulpit, and the pews are made of sail canvas; one of them was occupied occasionally by Herman Melville himself. Cenotaphs on the walls perpetuate the memory of lone seamen, and in some cases entire crews, who lost their lives at sea.

FOR MORE INFORMATION:
Tourist Information Center, 70 North Second St., New Bedford, MA 02740. (508) 991-6200.

The Historic District of New Bedford, above, takes in 14 city blocks of cobblestone streets and 18th- and 19th-century buildings, which evoke the days when the town was the second-largest whaling port in New England. The chandlers, tavern owners, ropemakers and candlemakers set up shop in the Waterfront District, left.

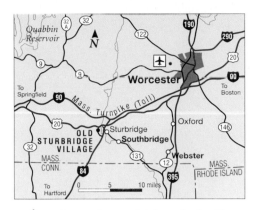

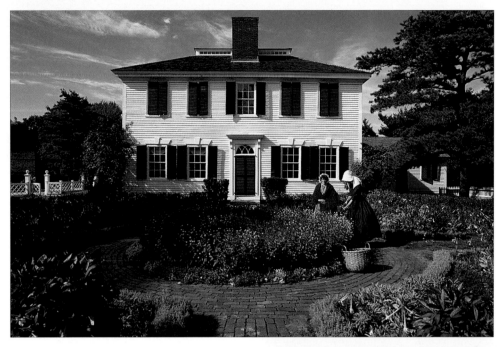

As a horse-drawn sleigh packed with revelers jangles past in winter, or a sturdy ox trudges through a field hauling a farmer's plow in spring, visitors to Old Sturbridge Village experience a strange sense of time warp. This typical New England town of the 1830's, set amid 200 acres of rolling terrain, has been transformed with scrupulous care into an outdoor museum of living history.

Wandering sheep crop the village green and roads are rutted by wagon wheels and hooves, but in spite of authentic detail this town did not exist in the period it depicts. Its 40 buildings have been moved from towns throughout New England and restored on site, or painstakingly reconstructed on the basis of historical evidence.

At Freeman Farm a costumed interpreter cooks soup from vegetables grown in the farm garden, pausing as she works to explain cooking techniques of the time to visitors who have dropped into the kitchen. The Asa Knight store, moved from Vermont complete with original shelving, counters and drawers, is stocked with recreated period merchandise, right down to the label on a packet of pins.

LIFE IN THE 1830'S

A stroll through the Village is a lesson in the economics and technology of the first half of the 19th century. Storekeepers explain how customers traded their farm products and homemade crafts for imported manufactured goods that they no longer made locally. The shoe shop reflects the dawn of a market economy. The shoes you can watch being cut and sewn were no longer made to individual order, but prepared in quantity for a wider, often distant market. Water powers the cast-iron wheel at the sawmill, setting in motion a blade that noisily rips planks from giant logs.

The various social strata of this community are reflected in the village's six houses, ranging from the white-frame structure owned by prosperous farmer and village leader Salem Towne, with its fashionable

Two women, dressed in the garb of the day, tend the gardens outside the Salem Towne House. The gardens are planned and planted to replicate garden designs and plant varieties that were typical of 1830's New England.

furniture and neatly kept flower beds, to the simpler home of Bixby the blacksmith. The center of every home is the cooking hearth, tended today as it was long ago by women, who also spent their time spinning, sewing and gardening.

The seasonal cycle is marked at Old Sturbridge Village. In March, as villagers plan and plant their gardens, green-thumbers can sign up for workshops geared to creating old-time effects. April brings the Spring Town Meeting where anyone can voice an opinion on local issues of the period. Summer visitors can try their hand at haying contests, and stay over for Sunday service at the meetinghouse to sing hymns and listen to sermons of the time. Harvest weekends provide an opportunity to pitch in digging potatoes and husking corn.

Activities often relate to special days: Independence Day, when the Declaration of Independence is read; Militia Day, an occasion for firing of guns and a mock battle; Thanksgiving, when quaking plum pudding cooks at the hearth and everyone goes to church. During the winter at Richardson Parsonage on the Village Common, history buffs willing to pay a fee can help prepare and eat a hearth-cooked meal. Other hands-on activities are making tin cookie cutters, craft workshops and early 19th-century dance. A

Oxen are put to work plowing a field in the village. Reenactments such as this depict the typical way of life for people living in farming communities.

special year-end holiday week includes lively games and reenactment of court cases from the 1830's.

A single day is not enough for many of the more than 500,000 annual visitors, so tickets can be validated for a free second day. During vacation, children can stay a whole week for "summershops" offering crafts and old-time games.

FOR MORE INFORMATION:
Old Sturbridge Village, Old Sturbridge Village Rd., Sturbridge, MA 01566. (508) 347-3362. Telephone Device for the Deaf (508) 347-5383.

Mississippi ■ NATCHEZ

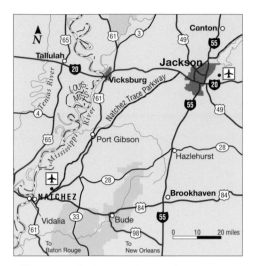

The formal triple parlor of Stanton Hall is beautifully furnished with Natchez antiques.

Situated high atop the bluffs overlooking the Mississippi River, Natchez has been a vibrant port of call since it was first settled by the French in 1716. The flags of five nations—France, Britain, Spain, the Confederacy and the United States of America—have flown over the town since then. For many years Natchez was the only port on the Mississippi between New Orleans and the mouth of the Ohio River. With the dawning of the steamboat era in 1812, the resulting river trade brought vast fortunes to many Natchez citizens. Between 1820 and 1860 the plantation owners accrued great fortunes from which they built massive homes, some in the imperial Greek Revival style, others reflecting the Spanish and French colonial look imported from the West Indies. By the Civil War,

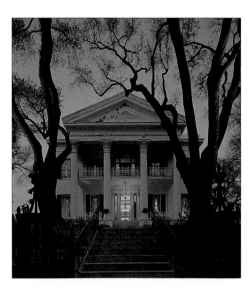

Stanton Hall, like many of Natchez's great antebellum homes, was built in the Greek Revival style. It is named for its builder, Frederick Stanton, who spared no expense on its construction.

Natchez had more millionaires per capita than any other city in the nation. It now boasts one of the best-preserved concentrations of antebellum properties in the country—almost 50 elegant mansions and a host of smaller but distinctive homes. The town's stunningly beautiful architecture is more than complemented by nature's own gifts: shady streets harbor live oaks draped with lacy networks of Spanish moss, sweet-smelling olive trees and boxwood hedges. The brilliant canopy of azaleas, daffodils and dogwood, and the velvety hues of the creamy white magnolia produce a visual feast. The city seems to exude Southern-style memories of romance, chivalry and duels at dawn.

SOUTHERN BELLES
During Spring and Fall Pilgrimages, 36 antebellum mansions are open to the public, while 20 are open year-round. All the houses have their own story, frequently told by a hostess in Southern-belle attire, complete with tight bodice, hoop skirt and a lilting accent. Stanton Hall, built in 1857 in the Greek Revival style, is one of the most magnificent and palatial residences, and captures perfectly the essence of early Natchez with its antiques and objets d'art. Longwood, constructed in 1860, is a red brick building, with arched windows, an onion dome and gingerbread trim. Fair Oaks, lived in by the same family since 1856, typifies a Southern planter's residence and contains some wondrous heirlooms.

Melrose House and the William Johnson House are owned by Natchez National Historical Park. Surrounded by 80 acres of landscaped parkland, Melrose is a Greek

Revival mansion, complete with the original furnishings. Besides conducted tours, presentations on 19th-century Natchez including the cotton industry, slavery and the role of women in the plantation household are given. The William Johnson House, built in 1840, was home to a prominent free African-American who left an extensive diary on daily life in Natchez from 1835 to 1851. Currently undergoing restoration work, the house will profile African-American history in Natchez.

Natchez Under-the-Hill was the original river port, and for many years, the main trading center for Natchez. Three, mile-long streets ran parallel to the river, connected by hundreds of narrow crossroads. Innocent travelers disembarking from river steamers were easy prey for boatmen, gamblers, river pirates and highwaymen. Not surprisingly, by the early 1800's Natchez Under-the-Hill was renowned as a place of ill repute. In recent years, the historic buildings and wharfs have been renovated and cater to 20th-century visitors in a more kindly fashion. Modern adventurers can still arrive in Natchez by luxurious steamboats, and with much of the city so lovingly restored, it does not seem so long ago that Southern belles and their beaus danced to dawn whilst all manner of dastardly shenanigans took place Under-the-Hill.

FOR MORE INFORMATION:
Natchez Convention & Visitors Bureau, P.O. Box 1485, Natchez, MS 39121. (601) 446-6345 or (800) 99-NATCHEZ.

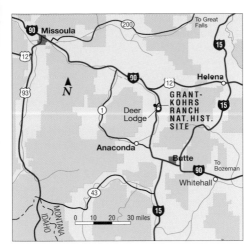

When cowboys rode the range during the heyday of the Northern Plains cattle boom, the Grant-Kohrs Ranch headquarters covered 25,000 acres and its range operations stretched across more than 10 million acres of grazing land located in four states and two Canadian provinces.

Johnny Grant, a Canadian trapper and trader, was the first person to settle in the Deer Lodge Valley region. Grant, who also ran a trading post, had moved into the wilderness when Indian bands roamed the hills, long before the coming of the railroad. He arrived in the late 1850's and began to build up a herd of cattle. By 1862, he had a herd of about 2,000 cattle and he decided to set down roots near the present town of Deer Lodge, building a two-story log ranch house for his large family. Grant soon returned to Canada. He sold his ranch in 1866 for $19,200 to Conrad Kohrs, a German immigrant and former butcher. By the 1870's, beef was the big market item on the eastern seaboard and Kohrs, a shrewd entrepreneur, worked hard to capitalize on the opportunity. He soon owned 50,000 head of cattle and at least 1,000 horses. Each year he would ship 8,000-10,000 cattle to the Chicago stockyards—more than any other rancher in the country.

THE DEATH KNELL

Kohrs and his partner and half-brother, John Bielenberg, survived the fierce winter of 1886-87 that wiped out close to half the cattle on the High Plains. But the open-range cattle industry prospered only for three decades. Few of its pioneering men and women—drawn to Montana's frontier by dreams of wealth—made their fortunes, and fewer still are remembered today. The death knell of the cowboys' lifestyle was rung in the late 1880's when the freewheeling days of nomadic grazing gradually gave way to more settled ranching. It was not long before cowboys were spending more time growing feed and repairing fences than herding cattle. The coming of homesteaders before World War I signaled the end of the open range. By the time Kohrs and Bielenberg died in the early 1920's, all but 1,000 acres around their ranch house in Deer Lodge Valley had been sold. The remnant of their empire was maintained for many years by Conrad Kohrs Warren, a grandson. And Augusta Kohrs, Conrad's widow, whom he had married when she was just 19, contributed to the ranch's upkeep as best she could until her death in 1945 at the age of 96.

After a movement grew to preserve Deer Lodge Valley's historical holdings, Congress announced in 1972 that the ranch would be set aside as a National Historic Site to provide "an understanding of the frontier cattle era of the nation's history."

Now visitors can wander through a variety of buildings on the restored Grant-Kohrs spread and soak up the lingering atmosphere of the Old West. The main attraction is the 23-room ranch house, one of the finest in the entire territory. The home's sumptuous furnishings provide a striking contrast to the austere bunkhouses where cowboys chewed tobacco, played cards and spun yarns around the stove. There is also an icehouse, buggy shed, a granary, several barns and a collection of old wagons.

Today, the ranch—with cattle, horses and poultry— covers 1,500 acres. Latterday ranch hands tend the livestock, brand the new calves in summer and mend and preserve the old buildings and fences.

FOR MORE INFORMATION:
Grant-Kohrs Ranch National Historic Site, P.O. Box 790, Deer Lodge, MT 59722. (406) 846-2070, weekdays; (406) 846-3388, weekends.

Once a prosperous cattle ranch, Grant-Kohrs Ranch is now a National Historic Site. The barns, outbuildings and the original house still stand and cattle and horses still graze.

The bunkhouse was home for the cowboys and ranch hands who worked on the ranch. They ate their meals in the bunkhouse dining room, played cards when the weather was bad, and slept in the simply furnished bunkroom.

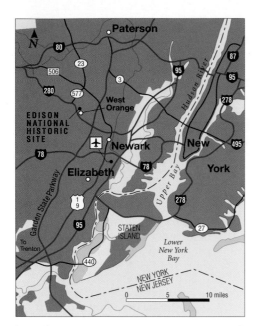

Thomas Alva Edison once joked that he stocked his celebrated West Orange laboratories with "everything from elephant's hide to the eyeballs of a United States senator." Edison patented 1,093 inventions in his lifetime, so if he was joking he wasn't being entirely flippant— his research compound at West Orange, New Jersey was staggering in its range. Unsmilingly, Edison boasted that his "invention factory," as he called West Orange, could build anything from "a lady's watch to a locomotive."

The laboratory complex that Edison left behind was an invention in its own right and was the much-copied prototype of the modern industrial research laboratory. The red brick buildings are now a National Historic Site where each year 75,000 visitors witness the extraordinary legacy of America's greatest inventor.

THE INVENTION FACTORY

When he built the West Orange laboratories in 1887, Edison was already famous for his work at the Menlo Park lab, where he had invented the phonograph and the first practical incandescent lamp. His new workplace, which Edison devoted to "the rapid and cheap development of inventions," was staffed by skilled experimenters charged with turning his dreams into reality. It wasn't long before one invention after another was leaping from the drawing boards at the new labs—the world's first movie camera, the storage battery, the fluoroscope used in America's first X-ray operation, the first movie studio, called "the Black Maria," and many, many more.

Touring Edison's "invention factory," visitors are left incredulous as to how this prolific, groundbreaking genius could have been withdrawn from school after being called "addled" by his teachers. By the age of 10, young Edison had developed a passion for chemistry. By his late teens, telegraphy and other inventions were commanding his attention and, at the age of 22, he took out his first patent—for an electric vote recorder.

The West Orange complex, now girded by a bustling urban area, is today a quiet enclave in which it is easy to imagine the feverish excitement that must have attended technology's infancy. The main laboratory, three stories high and 250 feet long, still contains machine shops, stock rooms, offices, and Edison's two-tiered library/office, which holds 10,000 volumes. Park rangers lead visitors through Edison's chemistry laboratory, machine shop and library. Many original inventions are on display, among them the tinfoil phonograph of 1877, the strip kinetograph and other motion picture apparatus, and early electric light and power equipment.

A visitor center, located in the former powerhouse of the main laboratory building, is open daily from 9:00 a.m. to 5:00 p.m., except on Thanksgiving, Christmas and New Year's Day. The center includes introductory exhibits, a bookstore, a kinetoscope parlor and a video theater that features the 1903 Edison motion picture, *The Great Train Robbery*, one of 1,700 silent movies made by the prolific inventor's company.

Less than a mile from the laboratories lies Glenmont, Edison's 23-room Victorian mansion, which today appears much as it did during the inventor's lifetime. Located in expansive grounds, Glenmont is open for tours Wednesdays through Sundays throughout the year. Edison lived there with his second wife, Mina (his first wife, Mary, died of typhoid fever) until his death at the respectable age of 84 in 1931.

The desk Edison called his "thought bench" is on display in the second-floor sitting room. Ensconced there, Edison conjured up many of the inventions that helped lead America from the age of steam into the age of electricity.

FOR MORE INFORMATION:
Edison National Historic Site, Main Street and Lakeside Avenue, West Orange, NJ 07052. (201) 736-0550.

The phonograph room at the West Orange laboratories contains a selection of original phonographs illustrating the history of Edison sound recording from 1877 through the 1930's.

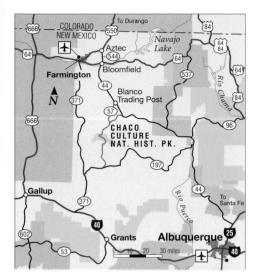

Pueblo Bonito, "pretty village" in Spanish, is the largest ruin in Chaco. Built of hard sandstone quarried from the cliff behind it, the town covered three acres and was home to about 1,000 inhabitants.

Highway 57 first appears to be the kind of dusty, narrow gravel road that is ubiquitous in northwestern New Mexico: bone-jarring and basically a dead end. The intrepid traveler, however, soon finds out that this stretch of highway leads to Chaco Canyon—and a superb collection of prehistoric ruins left there by the Ancestral Pueblo Indians.

From about A.D. 900 to A.D. 1200 Chaco was the economic, political and religious hub for a branch of the Ancestral Pueblo. Archeologists estimate that between 5,000 and 7,000 Indians lived along the Chaco River on the flat tops of the high desert mesas. They irrigated the fields and grew corn, beans and squash. This vast pre-Columbian civilization covered an area bigger than California, stretching across what is now the Southwest's Four-Corner states. Now this hardscrabble land can barely support vegetation; and the dry riverbed of the Chaco River snakes through the wide and shallow 15-mile sandstone rift like a scar of memory.

MYSTERIOUS PAST

It is a mysterious memory indeed: the Chacoans left behind no written record. That has meant that archeologists must rely on ruins, artifacts, carbon dating and tree ring-counting to help them paint a chronologically accurate portrait of these ancient people. Some of the earliest inhabitants were basketmakers who soon turned to masonry, using a mosaic-like style of small-cut stones laid with mortar to build communal dwellings, or pueblos. By A.D. 1000 they had constructed multistory

Pueblo Bonito had 800 interior rooms and 37 kivas—round underground chambers that were used for ceremonial events.

dwellings, many subterranean ceremonial rooms, called kivas, a sophisticated road network connecting more than 75 satellite communities, and a complex irrigation system. Rock paintings carved into the soft sandstone are still visible at various sites. Many of the buildings are in remarkable condition, others are little more than a

pile of rubble. For most of the 11th century Chaco flourished as a center of agriculture, trade and art. Then the Ancestral Pueblo began to leave, and the canyon was deserted by the end of the 13th century. Archeologists believe that a drought may have provoked the exodus. At any rate, the abandoned pueblos stayed silent for hundreds of years.

Today Chaco Culture National Historical Park contains 13 major ruins within an eight-mile area, mostly accessible by car or foot. Five self-guided trails and four backcountry trails lead to isolated sites. At Pueblo Bonito, one of the Ancestral Pueblos' most complex structures, visitors must stoop to pass through doorways interconnecting dozens of rooms. The walls of this sandstone desert citadel once rose five stories; some of the original timber beams are still intact.

For now, archeologists have called a moratorium on new excavations with the hope that future scientists, with improved technology and techniques, can better solve the riddle of this mysterious past.

FOR MORE INFORMATION:
Superintendent, Chaco Culture National Historical Park, P.O. Box 220, Nageezi, NM 87037. (505) 786-7014.

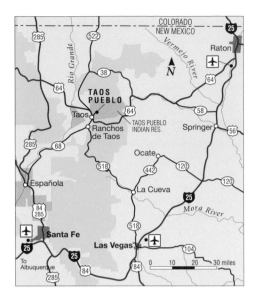

Pueblo people still occupy some houses in Taos, which has the oldest continuously inhabited multistoried dwellings in North America.

Spanish conquistadors, led by Francisco Vasquez de Coronado, were the first Europeans to see Taos Pueblo. The year was 1540 and the gold-hungry Spaniards were tempted to believe that the multistoried structures rising from the desert might just be one of the fabled seven golden cities of Cibola.

They didn't find gold, but they did stumble across what was the oldest continuously inhabited multistoried community in the United States. Positioned 7,000 feet above sea level, the settlement occupies a plateau of lush meadowland at the foot of the Sangre de Cristo Mountains. The two five-story structures that make up the village, *Hlauuma* (North House) and *Hlaukwima* (South House), are believed to have been built between A.D.1 000 and A.D. 1450, long before Christopher Columbus set eyes on the New World. Today, Taos Pueblo looks much as it did to those first Spaniards.

ADOBE VILLAGE

The village is constructed entirely of adobe—earth mixed with water and straw that is then poured into forms or made into sun-dried bricks. The roofs of each story are supported by thick logs felled from nearby mountain forests, and smaller slats of wood placed perpendicular to the logs. The wooden roof structure is filled in with a layer of packed dirt. To give exterior walls a facelift, a thin coat of mud is smoothed over them. Interior walls are maintained with thin coats of white earth.

Tradition dictates that neither electricity nor running water be allowed within the pueblo walls. The tiny village still provides housing for about 150 people and serves as the cultural and administrative center for about 1,500 Taos Indians in the surrounding areas.

Visitors are welcome in the earthern plaza or courtyard that lies between North House and South House. Rio Pueblo de Taos, a trout stream, runs through the courtyard. This central area, considered by inhabitants to be a sacred place, is the traditional ceremonial dance ground. Signs in the courtyard remind visitors to respect the restricted areas of the pueblo and the privacy of residents and the sites of religious practices. No photographs may be taken without permission, and fees are charged to anyone wishing to photograph, paint or draw within the village. A succession of feast days and ceremonial processions are open to the public, but cameras are not allowed during these festivals.

Mica-flecked pottery, silver and turquoise jewelry, beadwork, tanned buckskin moccasins and drums are local specialties.

The pueblo's six kivas, or religious centers, are off limits to visitors.

Throughout the town's history, the kivas have served as a meeting place for planning revolutionary action. In 1680, a massive revolt against the Spanish was hatched. The Spanish were driven back into Mexico so that all of New Mexico—including the Spanish capital of Santa Fe, 70 miles away, was once more in Indian hands. This rebellion remains the only time in American history where extensive territory was recovered and retained by native people through force of arms. A consortium of Indians ruled the region until Sante Fe was captured by the Spanish in 1692.

Two miles south of Taos Pueblo lies the town of Taos, a world-famous art colony and ski resort. Taos was founded in 1615 around a central plaza, which serves as the focal point of artistic interest. Taos became firmly established as an art colony when the Taos Society of Artists was formed in 1915. The long list of celebrities who visited—sometimes taking up residence—includes Ansel Adams, Georgia O'Keeffe, Thomas Wolfe, Frederic Remington, Aldous Huxley and D.H. Lawrence. Overawed by "the vast amphitheatre of lofty, indomitable desert," Lawrence wrote of his temporary home: "What splendor! Only the tawny eagle could really sail out into the splendor of it all."

FOR MORE INFORMATION:
Taos Pueblo, P.O. Box 1846, Taos, NM 87571. (505) 758-1028.

The main buildings rise in a tiered fashion to a height of five stories, each story set back about 15 feet from the floor below it. Ladders provide access to the upper stories.

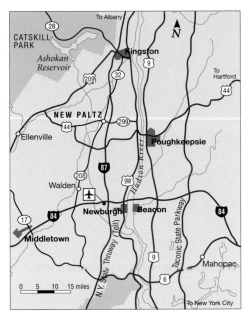

In 1677, 12 men and their families, united by religious and blood ties, purchased a large tract of land—almost 40,000 acres—from the Esopus Indians in New York State. These early settlers were French Huguenots (Protestants) who had been exiled from France by King Louis XIV for their religious beliefs. They hauled all their worldly goods from the nearby village of Old Hurley on three ox carts and immediately began to build a fledgling log settlement on the east bank of the Wallkill River.

The pioneers, known as Patentees, named their tiny village New Paltz in honor of Pfalz on the Rhine River, where they had previously found refuge from persecution by French Catholics.

Their settlement, the haven where they could worship God as they pleased, lies nestled between the Hudson River to the east and the majestic Shawangunk Mountains to the west. The settlers built log cabins along what is now called Huguenot Street. In 1692 they began to replace them with one-room stone dwellings. The rough, uncut stones were gathered from the fields and cemented with mud, clay or mortar. Additions were added to the houses as the families grew. Six of these first fieldstone buildings still stand.

STONE STRUCTURES

By 1712, Huguenot Street boasted six stone houses, a fort and a church. Not surprisingly, the buildings resembled those the Huguenots had left behind in France. Today, Huguenot Street, with its original stone homes, is the oldest street in America; visitors can tour the houses, which are maintained by the Huguenot Historical Society. Some of them feature original furnishings, farm machinery and tools. The newest of these stone houses is well over 250 years old. Their furnishings illustrate the continuity of the Huguenots' French heritage. Heirlooms brought from Normandy by the original settlers are on display, along with early treasures purchased by the settlers after their arrival.

The jewel in the crown of Huguenot Street is the Jean Hasbrouck Memorial House. It was built in 1712 by Jean Hasbrouck, one of the original settlers, and has escaped modern "improvements."

The rugged stone walls of the house are capped with a high, steeply pitched roof, and the plain entrance door is protected by a primitive shed-stoop. The interior has a typical central hall plan with two rooms on each side of the hallway. In the hall, visitors can see the mud plaster, wattle-and-daub construction used in the building. Three small garret rooms are located in the attic, but the rest of the space was used to store grain. The house has earned a citation as America's most outstanding example of medieval Flemish stone architecture.

The DuBois Fort was constructed in 1705 and, at the insistence of the English governor, it was to be "a place of Retreat and Safe-guard upon Occasion." Though it was never needed for protection, the building was well used as the main meeting place for the town's administrators. The building was enlarged, and the interior refitted, in 1835.

The French Church (1717) was reconstructed in 1972 after 10 years of research ensured the historical integrity of the work.

The community of New Paltz prospered under the administration of the Duzine—the original 12 men—who allocated land by lot and established all rules and regulations. The townsfolk held common ownership of the land and the products produced by them went into the common store. Until 1785, when the town was chartered by state legislature, succeeding Duzines were chosen annually at town meetings from descendants of the original dozen. It says much for the quality of their authority that no appeal against their judgment was ever recorded.

In fact, it was written that "so fine and free from animosity and greed has been the life of the people of New Paltz that previous to 1873 no lawyer ever found a permanent residence there."

Guided tours of New Paltz's stone houses start each year on the Wednesday following the Memorial Day weekend and continue until September 30. Both apple blossom time and harvest time are popular with visitors because of the orchards in the area.

FOR MORE INFORMATION:
Huguenot Historical Society, P.O. Box 339, New Paltz, NY 12561. (914) 255-1660.

The sturdy stone walls of Abraham Hasbrouck House show off the stonework of 17th-century New Paltz. The family kitchen did double duty as the center of village social life.

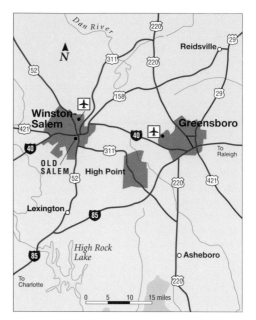

O ld Salem was founded in 1766 by settlers who trace their faith to the Bohemian Protestant martyr Jan Hus, who was burnt at the stake in 1415 for standing firm against Roman Catholic corruption. A band of his followers, called Moravians, began settling a large tract of land in what was then the wilderness of North Carolina. In 1766, Salem was planned as the central town in the tract. These founding fathers believed that by

producing finely crafted goods they could demonstrate and enhance their spiritual growth. And so they prospered, both spiritually and materially.

In the early days, a "choir" system of communal living was practiced in which people of like age, sex and marital status lived and worshipped together. The Moravians believed that this arrangement led to greater spiritual growth. At God's Acre, the graveyard opened in 1779 for Salem's congregation, people were buried with their fellow choir members rather than with their families. Eventually the church decreed that members could build their own homes, although the church owned the land on which they stood.

HISTORIC HOMES

This tiny wedge of 18th-century tranquility, which is locked within the modern-day city of Winston-Salem, once teetered on the brink of annihilation. In the 1950's, a non-profit educational corporation rescued about 90 of the original buildings from the wrecker's hammer. Vying for attention are large, half-timbered houses with tile roofs and central chimneys. Most of the restored homes are private residences, but 12 houses and several public buildings, set in a 16-block area of Moravian-style 18th- and 19th-century buildings, are open to the public.

Salem Tavern, the settlement's first brick structure, dating back to 1784, was operated by the Brethren for non-Moravian visitors. George Washington was a guest there for two days in 1791. The Single Brothers House, where bachelors lived and learned a trade after the age of 14, has been restored to match its original 1769 specifications. The Miksch Tobacco Shop, built in 1771, is reputed to be the oldest of its kind still standing in America. Amid the wealth of architecture, more than 17 gardens with 30 plots have been grown to bloom as they did two centuries earlier. Craftspeople— blacksmiths, gunsmiths, silversmiths, carpenters, potters and shoemakers, to name a few—still thrive in Old Salem as traditional skills are practiced for the edification and delight of today's visitors.

Walking the streets, visitors cannot help but notice the Brethren's ingenuity: a rotisserie's iron spit turns by weights and chains; a brick oven holds enough cast-iron pots to cook food for 60 people; a coin-operated tobacco dispenser dubbed "the honesty box" relied upon smokers to retrieve just one pipeful at a time. The Brethren made sure Salem was one of the first communities to boast stoves of ceramic tile and, by fashioning and aligning hollow logs, they engineered one of the nation's earliest piped water systems.

Each house in Old Salem was allotted a family garden to grow the household's yearly supply of fruits and vegetables. And each household had a larger parcel of land outside of the town, where field crops of corn, wheat, pumpkins and sweet potatoes were grown and the family cow was pastured. In 1972-73, a restoration program began to restore the gardens of the old settlement. Today, the fruits, vegetables, herbs and flowers that grew in the gardens of the Moravian town now thrive in these authentic utilitarian family gardens and fields. The local gardens are open to the public, and horticulture and domestic skills demonstrations can be arranged at the visitor center.

Old Salem's restored buildings and the Museum of Early Southern Decorative Arts are open year-round. The museum's galleries and period rooms feature authentic Southern furnishings, and pastel paintings by Henrietta Johnston, America's first professional female artist.

FOR MORE INFORMATION:
Old Salem, Inc., Box F, Winston-Salem, NC 27108. (910) 721-7300.

Costumed interpreters prepare a family meal in a carefully restored 18th-century kitchen. Cooking, baking and sewing are some of the domestic activities that are reenacted in this colonial town.

A full-scale replica of the Wright brothers' 1903 flying machine, called The Flyer, is on display in the visitor center.

On the morning of December 17, 1903, on a remote, windswept beach on North Carolina's Outer Banks, five witnesses at a nearby lifesaving station were the only observers of the first flight made by man in a heaver-than-air machine. After four years of intensive research and experimentation, two brothers, Orville and Wilbur Wright, had finally taken to the air.

In the first of four flights that morning, Orville piloted *The Flyer* as it flew for 120 feet without losing speed and landed gently 12 seconds later. By the fourth flight, *The Flyer* had covered 852 feet in 59 seconds, with Wilbur at the controls. Shortly after, a strong gust of wind blew the flying machine over, damaging it beyond repair. Although history had been made, recognition was to be slow in coming.

Those first flights took off near Kill Devil Hills, a 90-foot-high sand dune now part of the Wright Brothers National Memorial. The Memorial is located on the Outer Banks of North Carolina. A visitor center tells the story of the Wright brothers through exhibits and full-scale reproductions of their 1902 glider and the 1903 powered flying machine. There is a reconstruction of their spartan camp: one building that was used as a hangar and another that functioned as a combined workshop and living quarters. A large granite boulder marks the site where their first airplane left ground, and numbered markers show the increasing distance of each of the flights.

THE WRIGHT THING

The brothers ran a small, successful bicycle business in Dayton, Ohio, yet were fascinated by the concept of air travel. Unsuccessful trials with manned flights in Europe during the 1890's inspired them to look for their own solutions. Extensive reading about the experiments of others led to the building of kites and gliders. The Wrights built a wind tunnel and tested more than 200 wing surfaces, then began to design the wings, body, engine and controls of an airplane.

In 1900 they selected an isolated spot at Kill Devil Hills for their trials, close to the

The 60-foot-high Wright Memorial sits atop Big Kill Devil Hill and indicates the spot of the many glider flights that preceded the Wright brothers' first powered flight.

community of Kitty Hawk. Between 1900 and 1903, they made more than 1,000 glides from the top of four dunes, acquiring piloting skills which played a crucial role in their final invention. By December of 1903, the brothers were ready to mount a 12 horsepower engine and two propellers onto their newly built 605-pound biplane, which had a wingspan of 40 feet, 4 inches. The afternoon of their historic flight, a modest telegram to their father in Ohio alerted a newsman in Virginia to the story of their success. He promptly offered it to 21 newspapers throughout the country, yet only three deemed it newsworthy.

Despite a great deal of public skepticism, the Wright brothers continued their work and built an improved flyer. By 1905, they were flying circuits of up to 38 minutes, yet the U.S. Army refused to recognize their accomplishment. Reluctant to share their secrets unless they had a contract, the Wrights stopped flying for three years. Eventually a contract was signed with the U.S. Army in 1908. The fledgling industry caught up to the Wrights in 1910, and the brothers refined their design. A 1911 Wright Model B is still the prototype for modern planes.

FOR MORE INFORMATION:
Wright Brothers National Memorial, Cape Hatteras National Seashore, Route 1, Box 675, Manteo, NC 27954. (919) 441 7430.

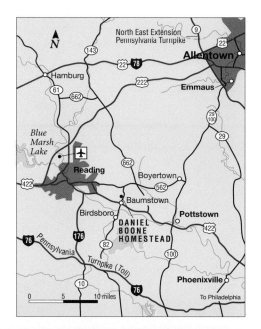

The barn—an example of the Pennsylvania German bank barn—and blacksmith shop are part of the 579-acre Daniel Boone Homestead site, which houses seven 18th-century structures.

Famed explorer and frontiersman Daniel Boone grew up on a farm in a small settlement in southeast Pennsylvania's Berks County. Before the Boone family moved south in 1750, young Daniel had learned the arts of survival in the rolling wooded hills that surrounded the family homestead. Today, a cluster of reconstructed stone and log houses forms Daniel Boone Homestead, a living museum of life in 18th-century Pennsylvania.

By 1730, when a Quaker by the name of Squire Boone purchased a 250-acre tract near the town, this area was no longer raw frontier country. The country around the little settlement was known as Oley (from an Indian word meaning kettle or bowl), and was home to pioneers of many backgrounds—English, French, German and Swedish among them. Many of them were Quakers, Moravians or Huguenots (French Protestants), beneficiaries of Pennsylvania's policy of religious tolerance.

Daniel was the sixth child of Squire Boone and his wife Sarah, but there would eventually be 11 Boone children. The family lived in a one-room, one-story log house. A large stone addition was made about 1750. It was probably finished by William Maugridge after the Boone family moved on. A later owner, John DeTurk, replaced the walls of the log house with stone utilizing the original foundation. All that remains of the original Boone home is the cellar of the Boone House, excavated by Squire with the help of his father's family. The flagstone cellar was built over a natural spring that supplied water for the house.

Squire Boone farmed here, but he was both a weaver and a blacksmith by trade. The Homestead's Blacksmith Shop dates from 1769, and was moved to the site from nearby Amityville. It is an exact reconstruction of the type of workshop that Squire Boone would have used to forge, weld and mend guns and wagons.

A FOLK HERO

Daniel Boone grew up in the little township. Although his formal schooling was limited, his Quaker upbringing gave him a respect and compassion toward all human beings, particularly for the Shawnee Indians who frequented the hills around Oley. From his father, the young Daniel learned farming, cattle raising and the skills of the blacksmith and the gunsmith.

Above all, Daniel acquired a spirit of adventure as he roamed the Pennsylvania woods. In 1744, Squire Boone purchased a few acres of grazing land about four miles west of the homestead. Young Daniel cared for his father's cattle, but also explored the

region's steep hills and wet bottom lands. From woodsmen and Indians, he learned how to shoot and trap deer and beaver.

In 1750, Squire Boone and his family left Pennsylvania to make the trek south to North Carolina's Yadkin River. Squire Boone had been disowned by the Oley Quakers, because several of his children had married outside the Quaker community. Furthermore, his lands had never been very productive. Perhaps he hoped to make a new start. For young Daniel, then only 16, the move was the start of a lifetime of wandering, exploration and adventure. In 1773, Boone would lead the first white settlers over the Appalachians to Kentucky via the Cumberland Gap. By the end of his life, Boone had explored vast tracts of the West, and is rumored even to have reached Yellowstone country and the Rockies.

Daniel Boone Homestead enshrines the explorer's humble beginnings. The site boasts seven original 18th-century structures, of the type that would have been used by neighbors such as the Bertolet and DeTurk families. Many are built in the Pennsylvania German style, with steeply pitched roofs, clay roof tiles and casement windows. The 579-acre area also includes a lake, picnic areas and a wildlife refuge. The site has been a state-owned historical site since 1938, and is administered by the Pennsylvania Historical and Museum Commission.

FOR MORE INFORMATION:
Daniel Boone Homestead, 400 Daniel Boone Rd., Birdsboro, PA 19508. (610) 582-4900.

Squire Boone was a blacksmith by trade, and his shop would have contained all the tools needed to shoe horses and oxen. This structure was moved to the site from a nearby village.

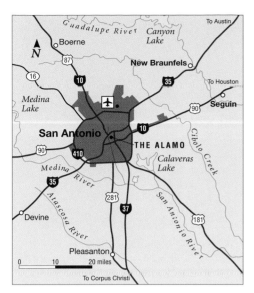

Headed by the figures of William Travis and David Crockett, the Alamo Cenotaph is inscribed with the names of all those who fell in battle at the Alamo.

San Antonio's Alamo is the most famous of the five missions established by the Spanish along the San Antonio River during the 18th century. The settlement was founded to save souls, and became a battleground in the fight for Texan independence.

The Spanish first moved into what is present-day Texas in the 17th century, but they never reaped great fortunes from their new lands. It was only when the French began to penetrate westward from Louisiana that the Spanish decided to strengthen their hold on Texas. Franciscan missionaries, who had reached the frontier in 1690, played a vital role in Spain's imperial design. The missions brought the word of God to the Indians, and extended Spanish rule over their thinly settled northern territory. In all, 38 Franciscan missions were established in the state of Texas between 1680 and 1793.

In 1718, Father Antonio Olivares was sent by the Spanish government to start a Franciscan mission on the San Antonio River. He established Mission San Antonio de Valero—better known as the Alamo. Four other missions followed; Mission San Jose was founded in 1720, and three others—Concepcion, San Juan Capistrano and San Francisco de la Espada—were relocated to San Antonio in 1731 from malaria-ridden eastern Texas.

REMEMBER THE ALAMO

Of all the missions, it is the Alamo that is the most renowned. Located in the heart of San Antonio, the mission was moved to its present site in 1724. The stone church, now known as the Shrine, was completed in 1756, after a hurricane destroyed the original structure in 1744. From 1801 to 1825, a Spanish cavalry unit was stationed within

the mission walls, and the name of their hometown, El Alamo (meaning cottonwood), became that of the mission itself.

The name passed into immortality during the struggle for Texan independence from Mexico. In 1836, 189 Texan patriots were besieged within the fortified mission for 13 days by more than 5,000 Mexican troops under the command of General Antonio Lopez de Santa Anna. The Alamo's defenders, a mixture of Texans of Spanish and Mexican descent as well as American settlers, were led by the fiery Colonel William Travis and by the legendary Jim Bowie. Their spirits were greatly strengthened by the arrival of frontiersman Davy Crockett and his 15 Tennessee volunteers.

The Texans' fight for freedom came to a tragic end on March 6, 1836, when Mexican troops breached the walls of the mission. The victorious Mexicans massacred every single one of the defenders. Texan patriots adopted the rallying cry of "Remember the Alamo." Under the leadership of Sam Houston, they won their independence just six weeks later by defeating a much larger Mexican force at the battle of San Jacinto.

The Alamo memorial is a four-acre compound that includes the stone mission church and the Long Barracks, where the last desperate fighting took place. The site contains a museum of the Alamo battle and of the 10 years of Texas independence before the United States annexed the territory.

By contrast, San Antonio's Mission Trail provides a vivid picture of the peaceful,

productive society that was created by the Franciscan brothers. The Trail encompasses four of the city's missions, which together make up the nearly 2,000-acre San Antonio Missions National Historical Park. All the mission except the Alamo remain active parish churches today.

FOR MORE INFORMATION:

The Alamo, P.O. Box 2599, San Antonio, TX 78299; (210) 225-1391. San Antonio Missions National Historical Park, 2202 Roosevelt Ave., San Antonio, TX 78210; (210) 229-5701.

The battle-scarred chapel of the Alamo is today a shrine to the Texans who fell in its defense. The upper story was never completed by the Spanish.

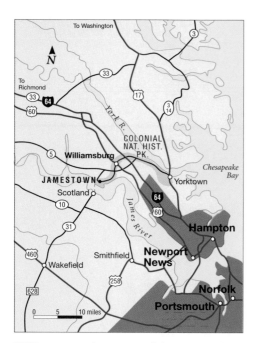

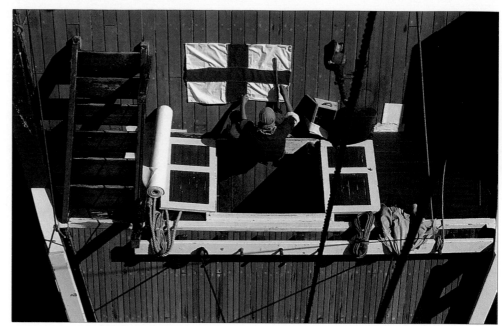

A crewman carefully tends to a flag of St. George—emblem of England—aboard one of the three square-rigged wooden sailing ships on display at Jamestown Settlement. The park also contains a reconstruction of the colony's original fort.

Between the waters of the James River and the York estuary, Virginia's "Historic Triangle" encompasses a unique collection of historic sites relating to the colonial period and to the very birth of the United States. A visit to Colonial National Historical Park begins with Jamestown, the site of the first British colony in America. The 23-mile Colonial Parkway rolls through the Virginia hardwood forests to form a corridor linking Jamestown with Yorktown battlefield, scene of the final engagement of the War of Independence. In between lies the reconstructed colonial capital of Williamsburg.

Jamestown was founded in 1607, when 104 men sailed up the James River in three ships. The expedition was sponsored by the Virginia Company of London, in the hope that the resources of the New World would yield a fortune for the company's investors. The climate of swampy Jamestown Island proved to be unhealthy, and disease and starvation killed a fearsome number of the settlers. However, the colonists persevered, and gradually the settlement prospered, mainly through the cultivation of tobacco.

In historic "James Cittie," the original colony has long since vanished, but trails and paths mark its boundaries. Plaques, oil paintings, statues and monuments throughout the area provide visitors with information about the history of the settlement. Bricks have been placed on the ground to sketch outlines of the shapes of some of the buildings that once stood here. Two loop drives—three and five miles in length—wind through the marshes and pine forests of the island. Jamestown was the first capital city of Virginia, and held

this distinction for 92 years. By the end of the 17th century, it had fallen into decline, following two disastrous fires and a fall in the price of tobacco. In 1699, the nearby town of Williamsburg became the new capital city. Williamsburg prospered with this new honor. Since the 1920's, Williamsburg has been the object of one of the country's most ambitious reconstruction programs. Today, its 173 acres contain 100 restored original structures, and another 400 have been painstakingly reconstructed. Although it is not officially part of Colonial National Historical Park, Williamsburg is certainly an essential link in following the course of history through the area.

WASHINGTON'S VICTORY
The Colonial Parkway winds from Jamestown and Williamsburg to the York River, and then to Yorktown. Here, in 1781, the climactic battle of the Revolutionary War took place.

In September, George Washington assembled his troops near Yorktown, where the British commander Lord Cornwallis had set up fortified positions. Washington's army was considerably strengthened by the arrival of French forces under Admiral Comte de Grasse. On October 9th, Allied forces began a nine-day bombardment of the British positions. On October 19th, Cornwallis surrendered to Washington, effectively ending the war. The actual surrender took place in a field about 2 miles

from Yorktown. (Lord Cornwallis did not attend.) Washington's victory solidified freedom and independence for the newly formed United States of America.

Yorktown is a thriving community, and includes several houses from the colonial period. At the site of the battle, rows of cannon, reconstructed earthworks and commemorative plaques tell the story of the conflict. The events of the siege and the story of the battle are also set forth in a film at the visitor center. On display are tents used by Washington during the siege, a partially reconstructed British frigate and dioramas depicting stages of the battle.

Also nearby is Jamestown Settlement, which contains replicas of the ships that brought the settlers and recreations of the palisaded fort and an Indian village.

In recognition of the area's rich history and great natural beauty, President Herbert Hoover in December 1930 proclaimed it Colonial National Historical Park, and 9,833 acres were set aside to create the park. Each year eight million visitors come here to get a glimpse of where the colonial period began, and where it ended.

FOR MORE INFORMATION:
Superintendent, Colonial National Historical Park, P.O. Box 210, Yorktown, VA 23690. (804) 898-3400.

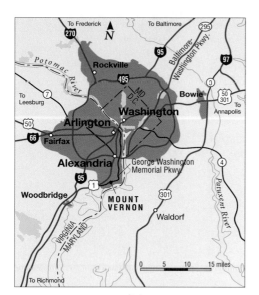

The former home of America's most exalted hero, General George Washington, is an architectural symbol of American strength and virtue as well as a graceful family residence.

The 11-room farmhouse that George Washington lovingly expanded into a 20-room colonial mansion, overlooks the Potomac River 16 miles south of the capital city that bears his name. From the famous eight-columned piazza at the rear of the building spreads the lovely river view that has remained unchanged since America's first president proclaimed the rights and freedoms of his countrymen.

George Washington owned Mount Vernon from 1754 until his death in 1799. He resided there continuously as a gentle-man farmer, apart from two celebrated absences, each of eight years' duration. In the first, from 1775-1783, he was commander-in-chief of the army which won the Revolutionary War. In the second, from 1789-1797, he toiled as the infant nation's first president.

Whether Washington was in residence or not, Mount Vernon, with its 8,000 acres of farms, was never far from his thoughts. To oversee his agricultural estate was his passion. Even when fighting far from home, he wrote weekly letters to his managers demanding detailed reports of work and progress. He delighted in getting his hands as dirty as those of his slaves. Visiting Mount Vernon in 1785, two years after Washington returned from the war, a traveler named Robert Hunter, Jr., wrote of the great man: "Indeed, his greatest pride is to be thought the first farmer in America."

In 1858, a somewhat shabby Mount Vernon was rescued for posterity through the efforts of the Mount Vernon Ladies' Association. It now bears a close resemblance to Mount Vernon as it appeared at the time of Washington's death. Today, roughly a million people flock to Mount Vernon each year, making it the most visited historic house in America after the White House.

RESTORED FOR POSTERITY

Laden with family possessions, the house is open to public inspection along with restored outbuildings, slaves' quarters and a museum of Washington memorabilia. Of special interest is the General's pine-paneled study, where Washington installed himself before five o'clock each morning.

Outside the house, some 30 acres of walks and gardens are laid out in orderly fashion, including several trees planted by George Washington himself. Halfway down the hill leading to the Potomac River, Washington and his wife Martha are buried, as he wished, "in the shadow of my own vine and my own fig tree."

The Mount Vernon Trail winds for 16 miles along the Potomac, from the mansion to the Lincoln Memorial in Washington, D.C. Visitors may bike, jog, or hike along the trail, which passes the Jones Point Lighthouse, the Navy-Marine Memorial, the Dyke Marsh wildlife habitat, Old Town Alexandria, and the Lyndon Baines Johnson Memorial Grove.

A weathervane depicting the Dove of Peace tops Mount Vernon's cupola. The cupola is one of the many additions Washington made.

FOR MORE INFORMATION:

Mount Vernon Ladies' Association, Mount Vernon, VA 22121. (703) 780-2000. Telephone Device for the Deaf (780) 799-8697.

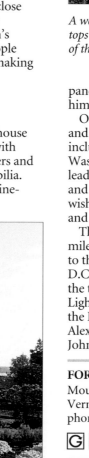

Mount Vernon's extensive formal gardens were laid out by George Washington. In one garden, Washington experimented with growing rare plants and shrubs.

INDEX

PICTURE CREDITS

Front Cover Photograph:
©Brian Payne/Woodfin Camp & Associates.

2 ©Catherine Karnow/Woodfin Camp
  & Associates
5 ©Nathan Benn/Woodfin Camp & Associates

OLD ST. AUGUSTINE

8,9 ©Ken Laffal
10 ©R.L. Zentmaier/Photo Researchers
12 ©Ken Laffal
13 ©Karen Kasmauski/Woodfin
  Camp & Associates
14 (left) ©Karen Kasmauski/Woodfin
  Camp &Associates
14,15 ©Ken Laffal
15 ©Porterfield-Chickering/
  Photo Researchers
16 ©Ken Laffal
17 (left) ©Ken Laffal
17 (right)©Jerry Lee Gingerich/
  Natural Selection

PILGRIMS OF PLIMOTH

18,19 ©Erik Leigh Simmons/The Image Bank
20 (left) ©M.P. Manheim/First Light
20 (right) ©G.V. Faint/The Image Bank
22 (left) ©Brownie Harris/The Stock Market
22,23 ©Francois Gohier/Photo Researchers
23 (right) ©Brownie Harris/The Stock Market
24 ©Brownie Harris/The Stock Market
25 ©Brownie Harris/The Stock Market
26 ©Tom Pollack/Natural Selection
27 (upper) ©Paul Rocheleau
27 (lower) Courtesy New Bedford
  Whaling Museum

STRAITS OF MACKINAC

28,29 ©Raymond J. Malace
30 ©Ron Levine
32 ©Balthazar Korab
33 (left) ©Balthazar Korab
33 (right) ©Balthazar Korab
34 (upper) ©Balthazar Korab
34 (lower) ©Balthazar Korab
34,35 ©Balthazar Korab
36 ©Balthazar Korab
37 (upper) ©Balthazar Korab
37 (lower) ©J.A. Kraulis/Masterfile

COLONIAL WILLIAMSBURG

38,39 ©John Lewis Stage/The Image Bank

40 Courtesy The Colonial
  Williamsburg Foundation
42 (left) ©Andy Levin/Photo Researchers
42,43 ©Henley & Savage/The Stock Market
44 (upper) ©Henley & Savage/The
  Stock Market
44 (lower) ©Olivier Martel/Black Star
44,45 ©John Lewis Stage/The Image Bank
46,47 ©Mary Hemphill/Photo Researchers
47 Courtesy The Colonial
  Williamsburg Foundation
48 Courtesy The Mariners' Museum
49 (upper) Peter Aaron Esto, courtesy The
  Chrysler Museum
49 (lower) ©Paul Rocheleau

REVOLUTION IN BOSTON

50,51 ©R. Kord/AllStock
52 ©Bill Brooks/Masterfile
54 The Bostonian Society
55 (left) ©Stuart Cohen/Comstock
55 (right) ©Akos Szilvasi/Stock Boston
56 ©Kerry Hayes/Masterfile
57 ©Michael Dwyer/Stock Boston
58 (left) ©Stuart Cohen/Comstock
58 (right) ©Paul Hurd/AllStock
59 (upper) ©Stuart Cohen/Comstock
59 (lower) ©Bruce Hands/Comstock

FEDERAL PHILADELPHIA

60,61 ©Doris DeWitt/Tony Stone
  Worldwide
62 ©Ed Wheeler/The Stock Market
64 (left) ©Ed Bohon/The Stock Market
64 (right) ©Kunio Owaki/The Stock Market
65 ©Comstock
66 Courtesy National Park Service
66,67 ©Susan McCartney/Photo Researchers
67 Yale University Art Gallery
68 Courtesy U.S. National Archives
69 ©Robert Kristofik/The Image Bank
70 ©Bullaty/Lomeo
71 (upper) ©A. Wilkinson/Masterfile
71 (lower) Courtesy Brandywine
  River Museum

CALIFORNIA MISSIONS

72,73 ©Kim Newton/Woodfin
  Camp & Associates
74 ©Kim Newton/Woodfin
  Camp & Associates
76 (upper) Santa Barbara Mission Archives

76 (lower) ©Alexander Lowry/
  Photo Researchers
77 ©Chuck Place
78 (left) ©Robert Landau/First Light
78,79 ©Chuck Place
80 (left) ©Robert Landau/First Light
80 (right) ©Chuck Place
81 ©Alon Reininger/Woodfin
  Camp &Associates
82 ©Dale Sanders/Masterfile
83 (upper) ©Craig Aurness/Woodfin
  Camp & Associates
83 (lower) ©J.A. Kraulis/Masterfile

FRONTIER SPIRIT

84,85 David P. Blanchette, courtesy Illinois
  Historic Preservation Agency
86 (upper) ©Alan Briere
86 (lower) Courtesy University of Nebraska
88 Chris Harbison, courtesy Illinois Historic
  Preservation Agency
89 (left) ©Fred J. Maroon/Photo Researchers
89 (right) Chicago Historical Society
90,91 Courtesy Illinois Historic
  Preservation Agency
91 (right) ©Alan Briere
92 ©Fred J. Maroon/Photo Researchers
93 (upper) ©Wilhelm Schmidt/Masterfile
93 (lower) Courtesy Illinois Historic
  Preservation Agency

CONFEDERATE CHARLESTON

94,95 ©Gary Benson/Comstock
96 ©Ken Laffal
98 ©Bruce Roberts/Photo Researchers
98,99 ©Patti McConville/The Image Bank
99 ©George Disario/The Stock Market
100 Courtesy South Caroliniana Library
100,101 ©Bruce Roberts/Photo Researchers
102 ©Tom Cogill
103 ©Jonathan Wallen
104 ©Nathan Benn/Woodfin
  Camp &Associates
105 (upper) ©Gary Randall/Masterfile
105 (lower) ©Mark E. Gibson/The
  Stock Market

GOLD RUSH COUNTRY

106,107 ©Steve Slocomb
108 ©Wayne Scherr
110 (left) ©Michael J. Gordon
110-111 ©Michael J. Gordon

111 ©Michael J. Gordon
112-113 ©Michael J. Gordon
113 ©Michael J. Gordon
114 Bruce Selyem/Museum of the Rockies
115 (left) ©Daniel J. Cox/Natural Selection
115 (right) ©J.A. Kraulis/Masterfile

GAZETTEER

116 ©Chuck Place
117 (upper) ©Harvey Lloyd/Masterfile
117 (lower) ©Kim Heacox
118 (upper) ©Kim Heacox
118 (lower) ©Nancy Simmerman/AllStock
119 ©Al Harvey/Masterfile
120 (both) ©Chuck Place
121 (upper) ©Mike Dobel/Masterfile
121 (lower) ©FPG/Masterfile
122 (upper) ©Stuart Westmorland/AllStock
122 (lower) ©Greg Vaughn/AllStock
123 (both) ©Rita Ariyoshi
124 (both) ©Dale Van Donselaar
125 (upper) John Guillet
125 (lower) Courtesy Louisiana State Parks
126 (both) ©Courtesy Hancock
  Shaker Village
127 ©Leonard Harris/Stock Boston
128 (both) ©Paul Rocheleau
129 (both) ©Robert Frerck/Woodfin
  Camp & Associates
130 (both) ©Paul Rocheleau
131 (both) ©Paul Rocheleau
132 ©Michael Melford
133 ©Chuck Place
134 (upper) ©Derek Caron/Masterfile
134 (lower) ©Mark Tomalty/Masterfile
135 ©Michael Melford
136 ©Michal Heron/Woodfin
  Camp & Associates
137 (upper) ©Leo Touchet/Woodfin
  Camp & Associates
137 (lower) ©Al Harvey/Masterfile
138 (left) ©Ron Levine
138 (right) ©M.L. Deruaz
139 (both) ©Robert Frerck/Woodfin
  Camp & Associates
140 ©Paul Rocheleau
141 (upper) ©Catherine Karnow/Woodfin
  Camp & Associates
141 (lower) ©William Strode/Woodfin
  Camp & Associates

Back Cover Photograph: ©Alan Briere

ACKNOWLEDGMENTS

Teri Bell; Dave Blanchette, Illinois Historic Preservation Agency; Carol City, Plimoth Plantation; Dave Dutcher and Coxey Foogood, Independence NHP; John Ellingsen; Catherine Grosfils and Scott M. Spence, Colonial Williamsburg Foundation; Kirk Hansen, Bovey Restorations; Dave Hedrick; John Middlebrook; Brenda Roth; Sue Wagner, Michigan Travel Bureau; Msgr. Francis J. Weber; Charleston Historical Society; National Park Service; St. Augustine Historical Society

Cartography: Map resource bases compliments of the National Park Service and individual sites; maps produced by Hatra Inc.

The editors would like to thank the following: Tracey Arial, Lorraine Doré, Irene Huang, Geneviève Monette, Brian Parsons, Maryo Proulx, Vicky Ross, Judy Yelon